£1

PUFFIN BOOKS

CW01637122

Letter to a Fr

That's the 65th person
In my gallery
Of friends I've fallen out with
And friends who have fallen out with me.

Friendship is often a very complicated thing, and in this original collection of poems by talented young writers we can see all the ups and downs of friendship, as well as the special qualities that define a real friend. Chosen from top entries and award winners in *The Observer* National Children's Poetry Competition, this is a warm and special collection.

The Observer National Children's Poetry Competition was sponsored by the Water Authorities Association and the judges were Ted Hughes, Roger McGough, Wendy Cope, Sue Townsend, Jannie Howker and Blake Morrison. Royalties from the book go to the charity Water Aid and to sponsor poetry workshops for children organized by the Poetry Society.

Selected Poems from *The Observer*
National Children's Poetry Competition,
sponsored by the Water Authorities Association

Letter to a Friend

Illustrated by Russell Ayto

PUFFIN BOOKS

PUFFIN BOOKS

Published by the Penguin Group
27 Wrights Lane, London W8 5TZ, England
Viking Penguin Inc., 40 West 23rd Street, New York, New York 10010, USA
Penguin Books Australia Ltd, Ringwood, Victoria, Australia
Penguin Books Canada Ltd, 2801 John Street, Markham, Ontario, Canada L3R 1B4
Penguin Books (NZ) Ltd, 182–190 Wairau Road, Auckland 10, New Zealand

Penguin Books Ltd, Registered Offices: Harmondsworth, Middlesex, England

First published 1989
10 9 8 7 6 5 4 3 2 1

This collection copyright © *The Observer* and Penguin Books Ltd, 1989
The copyright in the individual poems is held by the authors
Illustrations copyright © Russell Ayto, 1989
All rights reserved

Made and printed in Great Britain by
Cox and Wyman Ltd, Reading, Berks
Filmset in 11/13pt Linotron Galliard by
Rowland Phototypesetting Ltd, Bury St Edmunds, Suffolk

Except in the United States of America, this book is sold subject
to the condition that it shall not, by way of trade or otherwise, be lent,
re-sold, hired out, or otherwise circulated without the
publisher's prior consent in any form of binding or cover other than
that in which it is published and without a similar condition
including this condition being imposed on the subsequent purchaser

Contents

Ups – and Downs

Friends Lost and Longed For

Introduction

There are people who are said to have 'the gift of friendship'. It is a precious gift and should be valued above all other personal qualities.

When we need to talk about our problems or our small triumphs in life, we don't automatically turn to the cleverest people we know, or the wittiest or the wealthiest, we turn to our best friend – who is unlikely to be a comical, intellectual millionaire.

There is a Kampuchean proverb, 'hardship singles out your true friend.' The truth of this proverb is borne out by the poems in this delightful book: not all of the poems are in celebration of friendship; some of them are about the loss of or separation from a friend and are among the saddest things I have ever read.

When I was a child finding a friend was easy; we children played together in the streets and wandered the countryside in large gangs, playing and exploring and not returning home until dusk. Now, with heavy traffic and a restricted countryside, children are denied such freedoms, and consequently are more restricted in their choice of friends. Many children wrote that their only friend was a pet: a cat or dog and, one, a rabbit. Others chose a grandparent or another elderly person. The most moving poems came from very young children who had left their friends behind when they moved to this country – these children remembered their friends through a dream-like mist of memory.

More passionate were the poems about best friends of the same age and sex – these innocent love affairs describe the torments and the joys of love between two young people.

Once again it was a true pleasure to be able to read what is in the hearts and imaginations of our children. I admire their skill in writing their poems almost as much as I respect the generous sensibilities that their poems reveal.

My fellow judges Wendy Cope, Jannie Howker, Ted Hughes, Roger McGough, Blake Morrison and myself would like to thank *all* of the thousands of children who entered this competition.

Sue Townsend, 1989

Note

Poems marked in the text with an asterisk were all awarded prizes or highly commended in *The Observer* Poetry Competition. A full list of award-winners is given at the back of the book.

Something to Share

The Two Friends

With the exact length and pace of his best friend's
 strides,
The boy walked.
Whatever his friend had earlier said,
Could be heard when he talked.

Once, when the two friends were young,
They walked in the wood.
He imitated his friend's kind smile,
He stood the way he stood.

He still had someone he could trust,
He still had a friend of his own choice.
He smiled with his best friend's smile,
And spoke with his voice.

Vincent Lynskey, 13

Brian

Real comradeship shows in your eyes
As you shake my clenched hand.
Yours are silver-fingered.
They send shivers up the spine
Of your clarinet.
The music hungers for hearing.
I will measure out a tune
For you with my folded fists.

*Davoren Hanna, 13**

'Haiku' Friendship Poem

Two boys by firelight,
One black face the other white,
Friends in the cold night.

James Stevens, 11

Nazrul

Nazrul is my friend,
Nazrul plays with me.
We play racing games
And I always win.

Fawad Hassan, 6

Friends

We sit on the bank of a ditch.
Two lazy fishermen
In our own lazy way
Throwing stones,
Arms swinging back and forth.

Our boots
Camouflaged in mud,
We are bored.
Minds like blank bullets.
Nothing to talk about.

I kick the water.
It sprays up like a sparkler,
Feasting the banks.
Then something leaps into our minds.
We both start to speak . . .
'Let's go down the pit,' he says.

Off we go.
A couple of troopers going into battle.
Up on the cliffs –
Last one down does it again!
I jump,
Flinging myself off
Like a stone from a catapult.
He does it again.

We stagger to the lake,
Wounded soldiers
Suffering from the jump.

Half-way over . . .
'Let's go home.'
Back we march.
'See ya, Jay.'
'See ya.'

Bryan Hall, 13

norwich
Liverpool
man. utd
Sout
everton
arsen

Singing High-Tide Town

Me and Ben
go combing
on the Long Shore
picking through
seaweed heaps and
plastic junk
for sea-coal
wood for the wagons
rope for the marquees.

We pass by
the workshops
where Rob works on the skiff
and the cats play with woodshavings
beneath the trestles.
He asks
if we want one of Vanity's kittens.
He says
he'll only keep them
to the end of the week.

On the sands
Ben picks up
a cormorant feather
for his hat.
Near the pillbox
we find a football
printed with the names
of every team in the First Division.
First kick
Ben slices it into the sea.

We watch it bobbing
for a while.

We stop at Low's caravan –
Low makes tea
in a saucepan
and I ask him
about my poem.
He sits himself down
on a piece of carpet
tenor banjo in his lap
(just like the time
we sat with electric storm
crashing flashing
on the granite brow
of Tater-Du Man).

He starts slow
then picks with wilder fingers
slapping that banjo
like polythene flapping
on the fence singing
in a whisper sort of
growing foaming up
from the back of his throat
singing out
High-Tide Town.

After that
we talk for a while
about fixing the van
getting to Exeter and
seeing John and the Whistlers
before they go to London.

We go away
singing High-Tide Town.

Ben
stoops to wash out shells
in a pool
that's deep enough
for diving.
In another pool
a compass jellyfish
floats like
the head
of a drowned Empress.

I get water in my shoe
jumping across a stream
Ben
opens mussels
with a knife.

Over the town
I see a cloud
that looks just like the Taj Mahal.

*Tim Stone, 18**

Dad's Friend, Jim

My dad has a friend
called Jim.

He comes to my house
and he asks my dad
does he want to go to the pub.

My dad says yes.

If I had friends
when I was bigger,
I would go to the pub
with them.

And have some laughs.

I would like a friend
like my dad's friend,
Jim.

Thomas Egan, 6

Emmanuel Taiwo Jegede

Emmanuel is a musician.
His music is enchanting
Yet that's not all.
When he plays
With clay
He's wicked.

When he writes a poem
Every word turns into
A picture
Or a musical note.

Ketan Amlani, 10

Friend!

He'd brought me
Through the kitchen
And up the stairs
To show me his friend.

I imagined
Another person like him –
Shy and slightly embarrassed.
But that's not what I found.
I didn't find anything.
Well – nothing that fitted the description 'friend'.

The bedroom
Wasn't what you could call tidy.
I glanced round the room
And looked at Albert.
Smiling he went
To a white cupboard set into the wall,
Out of it he took
. . . A stuffed squirrel!

I looked at Albert again.
He was looking at it
With an affectionate look on his face.

I turned green.
How could his friend be a stuffed squirrel?
A thing that doesn't move –
Just stares.
If that's a friend,
I don't want one.

Rachel Brown, 14

The Meeting

On my bike
Round the bend,
Going to meet
My very best friend.

Whizzing past
Adam Day,
Perched on the fence
Like a bird of prey.

Zooming by
The railway line,
Hope I make it
In good time.

Passing Old Man
Conner's shop,
No time today
To stop for pop.

Flashing into
Johnnie's street,
Nearly time
For us to meet.

Spinning sparks
Off silver spokes,
No time to stop
And listen to jokes.

Going down the road
So fast,
Phew! I'm nearly
There at last.

Skid at the door
Of his back yard,
Then start to knock it
Really hard.

No one answers, so
On my bike,
Off I go
To look for Mike!

Kelly Simin, 9 and
Kathryn Chinnock, 9

Augusta

Once, as I lay on a *chaise-longue*
With my shoes on
And with a headache,
My friend brought me water and rubbed
Olive-oil
Into my temples
With warm, slow fingers.

When her grandmother died we draped
Ourselves in black
And walked the hills
For hours until our feet were wet
And tired.
Then we came home
And looked at her.

Grandmother's empty room and her
Thin cat and old slippers,
And we both cried together
And sang a hymn, because it felt right.
She once picked me
A bunch of tulips
From someone's garden

And came to my house by taxi,
And we ate
Belgian chocolates and
Drank as much orange juice as we could hold.
And then we went upstairs
And talked in different accents
About nothing.

For Christmas, she gave me
Boxes of pencils
And paper, and I
Gave her a picture in a frame.
She has fed me
Chocolate mousse, and red wine
And sent me postcards from Paris.

And once, she cried by herself
Without tears and
Without telling me why,
And although I knew she was sad,
We never spoke
About it.
We just left it,
Like a tree that refuses
To blossom.

*Kate Beckinsale, 14**

Mobile Friends

I am comitting suicide
Because I haven't got any friends.
There I am getting run over
By a Suzuki DR 125X
With mono shock suspension,
Fresco exhaust
(Front and back),
Disc brakes, twin cylinders
And wheels.

Wait up – there's a friend.
I'm on the back of his Gamma
With full floater suspension,
Liquid-cooled engine,
Drop handlebars,
Double (front and back)
Disc brakes, and
A seat for two.

*Hakim Bakrim, 12**

As the Universe Infinitely Re-invents Itself

As the universe infinitely re-invents itself
And dead quasars flash
Oblivious to not existing,
It's hard to say it's actually important.
Constantly on infinite evenings people like you
Give infinite lifts to people like me,
And although in some great God-given scheme
(Or more likely not)
One less would hardly matter,
Let the one less be somewhere else.
Let the quasars and me agree, we're each irrelevant,
Infinitely occurring unreasonably often,
But, yes, I'd rather sit in traffic with you and talk
Than face that uphill walk.

William Luscombe, 17

Boyfriend

My vanilla-skinned baby.
All popcorn hair and spearmint breath.

With lips like a wound
And eyes crazy-paved with colour.

I squeeze his plasticine hand
And clear his wispy brow.

His laughter crackles
And his leather creaks.

There is a confession of musk.
A facelift grin.

A casual feeling of intensity.

Samantha Dyche, 17

Sat on the Wall

They spent hour after hour,
Day after day,
Year after year
Sat on the wall.
One,
Thin and frail-looking.
Long chicken neck
Sprouting up from the faded collar
Of his whipped-up shirt.
His eyes,
Short-sighted slits
Swollen round the edges like pink puff-balls,
Lost in the stubby bristle of his face.

The other,
Plump, like a puffed-out cockerel.
His face,
Wrinkled like apple peel
On a compost heap.
Torn nets of burst veins
Knotted in reds and blues
Round his cheek bones,
Overcast by the shadow
Of his flat cap.

They sat on the wall,
Staring in bewilderment at me playing swingball.
Remembering
How once they amused themselves
Throwing pebbles at tin cans.
They sat,

Pondering over the differences
Between their childhood
And mine.

The frail one held tight
To the lead of an old dog,
Which nosed between his legs,
Pining for attention.
The other
Shuffled the dust
With the toe of his boot
And leaned with clasped fingers
On his walking-stick . . .
For year after year,
Sat on the wall.

Then,
The frail one died.
And I never saw the other again.
The plump one never
Sat on the wall.
It wasn't the same
Without his friend . . .

Lara Mair, 12

We Became Friends

I sat,
staring,
at those twig-like legs.
I was embarrassed.
Looking further down, I saw ankles,
the veins on them sticking out
like wrinkles on a rug.

An old lady screamed.
The nurse came in
and started talking to her.
I plucked up courage.
I asked this old lady
with those twig legs and wrinkled ankles,
if she had any brothers or sisters.
'Oh yes, my mother was a good one,' she replied.
I tried again,
'Do you like music?'
'Oh yes, so did mother.'
'Do you enjoy gardening?'
'No, my George was the one for that.'

I smiled.
She must have seen my smile.
She started giggling,
then laughing.
I joined in.
She pointed her finger at me.
I carried on laughing . . .
So did she.
We were friends.

Ruth Sparkes, 12

My Friend, Grandad

My grandad is my best friend,
He lets me drive his car.
Problem is
He can only drive with his left hand,
So I go in the front
Just in case anything happens.
I will not say
What is wrong with him –
It is private
No one must know
(But my gran knows).

We go for rambles,
He gives me a helping hand
(Only one hand),
So here we go
Troromp
Tromp
Tromp
In the mud,
Puff pant puff
Up the steep hill
To the top,
Right to the top.
Now I have to help my granny get up the hill,
But when we got up
It started raining
Very heavily.
I'd got my raincoat on,
My gran had got her raincoat on,
My sister had her raincoat on,

But Grandad insisted
It wasn't going to rain.
Grandad walks so slowly –
He's such a fuddy-duddy
(Even though when he was young
He set a Shetland record
For running).
The rain splashed
It poured and poured
It bucketed down.
Then my grandad
Got soaked,
He got drenched
He coughed
He spluttered
His mouth was full of water.
He had to dry off in the car –
It was such a funny sight!
I laughed so much
Grandad thought
I was a little imp,
'A king-sized pest,' he said
I didn't think I was a king-sized pest.

Michael O'Neill, 10

Just Good Friends

1. War time

Two girls
Huddling in the Underground
While bombs cracked all around like eggs
And searchlights filled the sky.
Just good friends.

2. Work time

Two women
Talking in a dingy factory yard like a prison,
Sharing sandwiches,
Sharing problems.
Just good friends.

3. Winter time

Two old ladies
Sitting on a park bench that was white with sharp frost
Like a box of wrinkled prunes in a freezer.
Just good friends.

Katy Allum, 10

Lines in Time of Great Happiness

Ploughman, you can never know
the pleasure of seafaring,
straddled as you are
across the earth's brown back.
Were I to sail upon the crest
of happiness surging in my heart,
clay thoughts would crumble
and my harrowed tongue be freed.

Davoren Hanna, 13

Garlic

A slow bellowing noise came from the bottom of our
  bellies like a bubble rising to the surface,
Then the groaning and whining stops.
The nod from one another is the signal.
We burst into action against the clock.
The knife ice-skates across the bread leaving a yellow
  march of marg.
The cheese is sliced as thin as a skeleton leaf,
As the juicy tomato squirts its blood.
The garlic is carefully placed in the crusher like a jewel
  from the deepest dungeons
Which we spent our lives looking for.
Then everything's piled into the toaster at a
  tremendous speed.
But the garlic, oh, the garlic is delicately squeezed.
Transforming the mess into a plate of wonders.
We sit back and wait for the tangy, nose-tickling,
  tantalizing smell to fill the room.
I try by myself, but it's nothing without my friend.

*Jonty J. R. Leff, 11**

The Whiskery Confidant

The Call of St Francis

Come to me –
And bring me your truths.

Fish,
Swim to me;
Let your fins
Like softened sea shells
Hear my call and bring
A lock of my hair,
Turned green by algae,
Sealed in your memory
Of plants and stones,
Forward to the sea of my making.

Bird,
Fly to me;
Let your wings
Feel my call and bring
The snap of your beak,
As sharp as the sound that you heard
When you broke into my world,
Forward to the tree of my making.

Animal,
Run to me.
Rabbit,
Let the spring uncoil and
Leap to me
With bent-back ears
Like ballerina's feet.
Snake,

Crawl to me
On your chess-board stomach
and tell me the secrets of the ground.
Lion,
Run to me
With your mane of arrogance
And paws like clover leaves
And share your jungle with me.
Hear my call and bring to me
The space of your desert
Like the palm of my hand;
My sweat,
Your feverish heat.

Walk by my side
Or fly at my shoulder;
Swim at my feet
And give me your souls;
Make me whole with your stories of life
And make yourselves whole with mine.

Leonora Dack, 13

Androcles and the Lion – the Meeting

The dark, dank smell
Barricades the entrance of the cave.
I break through.

A smell so familiar I almost recognize it
Tickles my nose,
Playing with me,
Whispering deep into unknown passages of my brain,
Calling, 'Remember me? Remember me?'

My paw aches.
The pain bangs at my head,
Begging to be let in,
Knocking out any trace of memory
So it is woven into the cobweb of time.
Just another segment to help it grow.

This smell from an unknown figure.
Maybe a friend. Maybe an enemy.
He pulls out a long shining blade.
He lunges. The blade pierces my flesh,
Driving deep into the soft pulp.
I gaze as the dark blood
Dribbles down the coarse fur,
Tinting the ends with an ugly brown.

It's gone – the pain –
The ghost that haunted my stricken body,
That lurked in forgotten corners.
He helped me. My friend.

Emma Clayton, 13

Friends

Sam, my friend,
Who reads the book of my secrets,
Locked up in my mind.
My whiskery confidant,
Who stretches out, before the fire,
And purrs, softly.
Two bright eyes like coal,
Gaze up with trust,
Encouraging me to trust him.

A DIY cat,
Clumsily constructed,
Awkward in his gait.
He jumps, in an attempt to catch a moth,
A simple prey,
He fails, and tumbles through a cobweb –
Nothing more than a family cat,
Off a toy-shop shelf.

My furry, frivolous playmate,
Who chases his tail,
And rolls over in the warm earth,
Tangling and knotting his Falstaff figure.
A wicked habit,
Who coaxes old ladies,
Into feeding him titbits,
And attention.

Sam abandons me,
To hunt,
A sleek malevolent figure,

Among trees and bushes.
A devil among birch and helpless mice.
He leaps, balletic, to seize and destroy a butterfly,
His primitive scream and growl fill the air,
The prey is caught and eaten.
Alone in his independent world,
No longer mine, for love and affection.

But, on his own terms,
Sam – the hunter, hooligan and house-cat –
Is for ever my friend.

Sali-Wyn Ryan, 10

My Friend

My friend is my hamster,
He is called Fluff.
Every night I go to see him
And give him food to stuff
Into his pouches.

Stephen Bartlett, 6

Abi

She filled the field with bleats,
that brown, furry suitcase
with a cement-dense brain
and ears of bendy spaniel noses
twitching in the soft-bitten breeze.
And her lips
which dribbled threads of spit on your lap.
And her tongue,
a goose-pimpled pig's ear
which licked your soft palm
in a friendly manner,
even though she nibbled your fingers.

The squeaking tin bucket
was wedged in a molehill beneath her;
she kicked it
and stepped aside.
I tried again and again
but it didn't work,
so in the end I put Abi over the bucket.
I pulled one teat.
It was like a fat sausage.
Milk dribbled through
in a long thin line
and tapped on the tin
like rain splashes on a glass window.

After one hour's work,
I had a tall tin bucket
full of glossy milk,

but she kicked it over
and stepped aside.

Then . . . one day,
I returned from school
to find Abi had gone.

It was never the same without her.

Helen Ward, 12

Tortoise Friend

I feed it with a wrinkled tomato
left over from breakfast.
It takes a bite
and delicately
rolls it in its mouth
like an old-age pensioner
without his false teeth.
I talk to it in a high but quiet voice
so as not to scare it.
I put my hand on its shell.
The shell is divided into little squares
like a knitted blanket my nana once made.
These squares have a spiral patterned texture.
I put my hand under its body
and as I pick it up
its head slowly slides into the shell;
it's trapped in its own slow-motion life.

Kelly Smith, 11

Friend

Mountain men's policy I have seen
To flurry their bird before shooting
Send it reeling into the sky
– target to be mastered –
Long have I lain here in the summer
Preparing a bed for the quiet assumption
That someone is ready to shoot me down.

That was the summer they stopped at the top
Pitched their voices on rushes as far as
Donegal and woke me to you
– sent me reeling into the sky –
A warning shot circling my leg
The lead to parachute me down
On to whatever nest you'd hope to have found.

*Imelda Cargan, 17**

The Goldfish . . .

is a splinter of mineral,
mined by Neptune.
Nothing stirs
in its own narrow world of undisturbed peace.

Its comfort . . .
reflection.
The duel begins –
a quick bolt from watching eyes
from above,
a challenge with no end.

The goldfish is a sort of . . .
delicate feather
made from tiny mirrors,
reflecting everything beautiful.
Its eyes look like frog-spawn
with minute tadpoles in the middle.

I feed it. I clean it. And talk to it.
But I get nothing in return . . .
As if its body is here,
yet its mind is in a coma far, far away.
I wonder if it can hear me.
I get nothing in return
from this delicate splinter of a fish.

*Adam Hughes, 12**

Ups – and Downs

Most of Them Smoke

Most of them smoke; that is to say
Until a teacher turns the corner,
Or Mum decides to look in coat pockets,
And finds the crumpled remnants of the lunch break.

They go to parties, where dubious things
Happen in the half light, which inevitably
Cause laughter and embarrassment at school,
Red-faced 'couples' avoiding each other.

I don't smoke – fags or hash – and parties
Tend to make me feel depressed;
But we sit at break, and talk,
About nothing, and everything, and both.

Popularity took me by surprise –
By that, I don't mean that I was loathed –
I'd spent years as an acquaintance:
I talked and smiled and was expendable.

And so, I join in and chat,
While Amber's temperamental stereo blares out,
Spasmodically, the Cure and the Cult,
We shout the choruses and laugh a lot.

I look around and see them all,
And consider being 'in a group'.
I am in this unrecognized club,
Part of the 4th year Supermensch.

The scene is idyllic: and so fixed,
That it is hard, impossible, to think
That three short years will bring new 4th years here,
Sitting in our seats among the dust.

I will take English: Abby, Psychology,
Adam, a science, and 'Class of '91'
Will subdivide, like an amoeba,
Until I have forgotten them all.

But, for now, I will stay in the sun
Of the playground, knowing well
That my friends are a temporary beauty, a finite joy,
Like the world in which they live.

*Jonathan Taylor, 14**

Friends

My friend borrowed 20p off me yesterday,
He said, 'Oh, I'll give it back at Junior Club
  tomorrow.'
Well, here I am at Junior Club and he still isn't here,
It ends at 8. It's quarter to now, he's got off.
Next day at school he says, 'Oh, I didn't get back from
  swimming till 8.30.'
A likely story.
Anyway, I'll get me own back on him –
He won't be able to play with my walkie-talkies today.

Christopher Sachn, 9

PHYSICS
$C=\frac{\epsilon_0 A}{d}$
$F(x_1, x_2 \ldots)=0$
$Eit=i^2Rt$
$Eit=i^2Rt$
$C=\frac{\epsilon_0 A}{d}$
$Eit=$
$C=\frac{\epsilon_0 A}{d}$

Friends

This guy, he was my friend,
But he was a bit of a bore.
He talked about Physics
And Quantum Mechanics
And he's not my friend any more.

Graham Foster, 15

Friends

That's the 65th person
In my gallery
Of friends I've fallen out with
And friends who have fallen out with me.

They come and go like flash bulbs –
Friends for only an hour,
Squabbling over stupid things,
Fighting in the shower.

The last friend I had was Jim.
We got on really well,
We thought we'd never break up
Until he caught the spell.

He punched me very hard
In the upper chest,
He also badly ripped
My brand-new thermal vest.

That's the 65th person
In my gallery
Of friends I've fallen out with
And friends who have fallen out with me.

*James Ryder, 10**

Copying

Today me and Natasha done the same thing.

When I took my coat
Natasha took her coat

When I played in the Home Corner
Natasha played in it too.

We both done number work
We both drew a flower
We both played with spinners.

She copies me
Because she is my friend.

I don't copy her
Because I am clever.

Daniella Layne, 5

I Had a Friend

I once had a friend;
he ran the fastest,
swam the furthest,
hit the hardest,
jumped the highest
and even lifted the heaviest.
Then I beat him.

*Jeremy Watson, 15**

For Leanne

You were the first and I would watch you,
shining over the skipping-rope white
like an angel I wrote and wanted
you in no obscene way but
it was filthy to you. Ever
watchful of mother we would smoke
another cigarette and talk of you,
life, endless cups of tea and cycling
in the rain until, carried away
by experiences that remain out
of my reach, you touched your
horizon. I'm older now and a little
wiser and yes I drink and weep
too much and yes you despise
such explosions but
I have fumbled and ached and
perfected myself around so
many people and never found love
like we had, a couple of days when
I came before my brother, before
all those others when your
mother's head was turned.

Lucy

We have changed together you
and I, always remained apart.
Fought for what we call
love but know to be
something more precious,
fought on the playing field,

in the streets, on the dance floor
and you always win, always will,
but your pain lies deeper
still than the daily victory
you swallow with your pill.
We hate and escape but always
return, running with affection
to hit head on. We will look
back on these days, giggling,
charging into the torrent as we do,
and dance on to that ancient
battlefield, still with hope
in our eyes.

And Zoe

You look at me and smile, knowing me
as you do, to wipe the tear from my
eye. You bring me kisses at
dusk and with only ourselves and each
other to blame, we begin on the cruelty
of youth and the infinity of the sky,
the faint murmurs of childhood and
we live in fear, you, and I.

*Rhiannon Wakeman, 17**

Letter to a Friend, February

You would have me bleeding blood, senseless and on
my knees, would have me crawling on your floor,
you would open me up and make people pay at
the door and through the nose to see
structure in my bones and patterns
in vein and artery, weakness in my
watery cells, delicate purple,
violent red of my sinews
and deep pulse of the
heart, strong inspite,
in spite we join up
strings of words
tight enough to
strangle each
other with,
till the
blood
hits
red.
PS: Richard says Saturday would be fine. Bring a
bottle.

Rhiannon Wakeman, 17

A Day Without You

after talking all night
till blackbird strikes
the morning comes out
pale and crumpled

I am not exactly tired
circumstances fuel me
my eyelashes stand like stokers
sooty with silent effort

but if by mistake
the stiff lids are let fall
down I drop too into
the deepest rabbit hole

past shelves of memory
and scurrying faces
I topple through a paper circle
into your white country.

Anon.

Who?

In my house
I got just my sister

Sahima

We are twins

I sleep in a little bed.
Sahima don't sleep there.
She sleep in a big bed
because she's scared of
monsters in little bed.

I say she not my friend.
She say she are.

Summairs Jamil, 6

The Treasure

The lion is as golden as the sun on the waves,
And his eyes are like the jungle,
With every step he takes he is as proud as a king but as
shameful as a beggar,
His mind is upon things that are good and bad,
He has been plotting and planning to get his revenge
on man,
His roar is like the thunder that has just hit a tree,
And his teeth are like daggers that have been
sharpened and polished,
He has only one friend for he prefers to be on his own,
He is England's king, that is the lion.

The bear is as black as coal or as brown as wood
That is ready to be burned,
And when it is burning the bear is in the flame dancing
and leaping,
In his eyes are vicious sparks, for you know he is just
about to pounce on his prey,
His long sharp claws are like cats' but far more powerful,
Every time he runs he leaps in the sky higher than birds,
He looks after his kingdom well,
His kingdom is Russia, that is the bear.

Next the panda who is not like the bear or lion,
But has a heart like a dove that has fallen in love,
Her most guarded treasure is that of bamboo,
She is as shy as a deer but also tough and strong,
Her colour is black as night and white as snow,
Her eyes would show kindness for a wounded animal
or plant,

She is quiet and private,
Her country is China, that is the panda.

Last is the eagle, her eyes tell you when she is hungry,
Her flight is like a tiger jumping from valleys to hills,
She is like one star in the sky,
She is like a surfer surfing on the waves,
She's a stone dropping off a cliff,
The eagle is powerful but at the same time weak,
She cannot be trusted at all, but works hard in her
country and it is the USA,
That is the eagle.

Turquoise blue, were the white waves,
As they splashed upon the sand,
Sapphires, diamonds and emeralds were floating in the
sea,
The lion thought, 'A mermaid's jewels,'
The eagle flew down: 'The sky king dropped them,'
The bear thought of bright berries,
And the panda thought 'eyes'.

Deep in the sea they found a treasure box, full of rings,
bracelets and crowns,
'It's mine,' cried the lion,
The eagle flew down and dug her long sharp claws in
the lion's flesh,
With a loud roar the bear landed on the panda's back,
The panda hid and cried,
There was blood all around,
Then the panda said, 'Please fight no more
Treasure is love and love is friendship,
Share this treasure together.'

*Lily Maler, 10**

Friends Lost and Longed For

I Didn't Write a Poem

I didn't have a friend
Who wove flying Casablancan carpets
And swooped in on the Sultan of Samarkand

I never had a chum
Who nestled inside an armchair
And got flumped on every day

Nor did I have a pal
Who was a mer-boy with a slithering tail
That slapped blue and green in the sunlight

I didn't have a buddy
Who could bloom into a clump of daffodils
All vivid and yellow

I can't say I ever had a sidekick
Who tamed the jungle
And capered about like a whooping monkey

I don't think I had a mate
Who was shanghaied as a cabin boy on a pirate
  schooner
And sported a spotty hanky round his head

I can't recall having a friend
Who twizzled the planets round the searing sun
And got ninety-three blobby blisters

I would've liked an ally
Who could penetrate other people's minds
And disclose sinister schemes festering in their souls

But my friends and I
Have been all these people
In our jauntings, musings and day-dreams . . .

*Christopher Trinnaman, 10**

New Friends

At my last school
I played in the Lego
with Sumwa.

Now I am
in a different school
playing with Nathan and Dwayne.

They are my friends now.

In my old school,
do they think I am on holiday?

But I told Mrs Jessingham.
I told it loud
so Sumwa might know
where I am.

Sumwa will be playing in the Lego
with Iqubal now.

Damian Gordon, 6

I WISH I 'AD A FREND

I wish I 'ad a friend,
Speshly vose littel boy wuns,
I try an' try, I really doo,
Ev-ry day wen they kum owt ov skool,
Kikking borls an' eeting sweets.
I getts owt me own littel treets,
A littel wun kums strate past me,
I givs a littel chukel ov glee.
But wen I offers him a treet
He takes wun look an' givs a shreek!

Diddent he like my worty fase?
Wy diddee fink Im a diskrase?
Diddent hee like my ek-stra tows?
Diddent hee like my snotty nose?
Hee mustuv liked my pointed hat-
And my furee big blak kat-
AND my broomstik tall and thin-
Shorly I carnt look orl vat grim.

WITCH
AGE 123

Francis Moon, 11

Three Months

You were my friend
That cheek-soft hand
Insistent oasis in an undemanding world
Unkilned burden of joy.

I took your grubby grasp
To swing you if you stumbled
But slept
When you clambered in at the hollow of my ear
And sat at the porthole watching
The storm pass
Knees tucked to chin
Dry fingers screening fear

I dreamt I heard you scream
And woke to see the dyke burst in a crumpled face
The torrent which
Flushed out your eyes, while
Slack skin flapped and gaped
Jellyless
And I heard my arms splinter as they fell

Once I thought I saw you
Squatting in the refuse
Gazing dully at me.
I watched the iron jaws
Close
And the dribble of red

You were my friend.

Harriet Castor, 17

I Remember the Day

I remember the day my friend had to go.
A big blue removal van pulled up outside his house.
There was a lot of confusion,
Shouting, talking.
His mum was directing a man
Carrying their best table,
A well-built, tattooed man.
He was whistling to a man at an upstairs window
And shouting something about a bed.

But my friend was nowhere to be seen.

I was standing by the gate,
Leaning up against the lamp-post,
Seeing how far I could kick pieces of stone.
I looked up
And saw one of the removal men
Bolting the back of the truck.
The truck started up,
Leaving a cloud of dust as it sped off.

Through the dust, I saw
The go-kart we had built together,
Left against their fence.
I slowly walked home,
Pulling it behind me.

*Jon Allen, 13**

Thoughts of a Nineteenth-Century Child Worker

Light is my best friend!
I only see it once a day
And that is only for a minute,
As I step from the colliery gate
To my house in the court.

Down in the coal mine
The dark is terrifying,
Wrapping round me
Like a smothering blanket
Until I find the sweetness
Of that glimmer of daylight,
Light is my best friend!

The light reveals
My bruises and scratches
From the whip and coal,
But light is my best friend!

I day-dream that I am playing in the light,
That the light is following me,
Then I hear my name being called
And I'm back . . .

Swinging the axe for coal.
An aching back.
I do wish
That my friend was here now.

Samantha Hughes, 11

Friends

Leaving these green, rain-washed villages
For the wild yellow scrubland,
I am told I shall find new friends.

But I know it won't be the same.
Leaving the cows lying in the fields all lazy and quiet
For the coiled, muscular snakes

Leaving the broad shade
Of the sheltering oak
For the dry, scarred bark of the eucalyptus

Leaving the rusty squirrels
For the dull grey of the koalas
Will not bring me close to home

Leaving the wet damp fields
Where the flowers bloom so slow and quiet
For the dry desert

Where the colour blasts up
At the first touch
Of a spring shower

Where the kangaroo bounds
With a strange grace
Across the dry sands

Leaving the liveliness of our street
For the howling winds and cold nights
Of the desert lands

Leaving happy memories,
Will my heart win the friendship of
This strange mysterious land?

*Nina Gwilliam, 14**

My Friend Sister

In our school
in Africa
the teachers beat us
on the bottom
because we won't sleep

My friend Sister
she told me
to pretend to sleep
then my teacher never smack me

Then I fell asleep
when I was pretending.

So my friend had to wake me
up for dinner.

I forgot the rest
because I came here a long time ago.

But I remember my friend Sister
and I dream about her
in the country
in our school
in Africa.

Joanna Akusuah Usser, 6

A Letter to a Friend (Not to Be Opened for 50 Years)

Do you remember . . .
The time when we collected snails
And had snail races?
They left a silvery thread behind them.
Then we would stamp on them, shattering them.

Do you remember . . .
We used to collect up the grass
After it had been freshly cut,
Throwing it at each other
So that it fell down like confetti?

Do you remember . . .
When we used to make sandcastles,
Piling the sand in the buckets,
Tipping it out, forming the perfect mould,
A perfect pyramid of sand?

Do you remember . . .
When we used to do painting at play school?
We would both fight for the red paint;
I would always paint a red sun
Like a fat-faced farmer smiling down.

I hope you will read this . . .
And remember the last threads of our childhood.

Samantha Bedser, 13

No Friends

I have got no friends –
I can't ask anyone if they
Will lend me felt-tip pens,
There is a girl across the
Table who has got a horse
And stable,
I know all these things
Because I hear her talking.
I am all alone on my table.

Every day when I watch them play,
I don't understand what they say,
They won't let me join in,
I stay in locked away,
My mum and dad say go out,
It is a nice day,
But if I haven't got
Any friends
I can't.

Alethia Walker, 10

Sarah

It has become a tiny scene of thoughts
When I remember Sarah, so much so:
The insurmountable shades of hills,
Steep and silent and clothed in shadow;
The tortuous stream that twists and spills
Out of the stones and the coppery seams
Into the chill of lakes below;
The turning moment of my dreams
And the memories of a girl of sorts.

For, thinking of old friends, Sarah came to me,
With damp black hair, and deep brown eyes
Inquisitively searching frog-spawn in the ponds,
Whilst flowers of weed and mud cover and disguise
The tiny, white, jellied eggs with fronds
Of waving green strands. Beneath the bridge of stone
A huge horrific toad in hiding lies –
I saw it once bounce out, belching, fully grown,
Incomparable in size, incomparably ugly.

Then I distinctly remember that final summer
We were together, little children in the sun,
And under the blazing heat distilled from petals
The red rose humour till sweet aroma was done,
And jars of flowers were filled with water hot from
  kettles,
Till rows of our perfume stood, weakly smelling,
And we two stood abandoned and alone,
To spread the murky water on our fingers, telling
Our favourite mixtures to each other.

How then autumn spread, blaze of gold across town,
Tinted with orange and with scarlet leaf.
We spent an afternoon hunting the four-pronged
clover.
And though I had entertained a strange belief
That this innocence could last for ever,
My family moved that Christmas down from Beeston,
Down to the city, to a different life.
I could not think of her: I dared not
And did not wish to understand the separation
Until the sadness in my heart died down.
Now I do not wear love as a badge for my lapel,
But wear it inside.

*Jonathan Catherall, 17**

The Tree and Uncle George

The tree stands,
Charred as a used match.
Lightning destroyed the mighty oak,
But still there stands a four foot stump
Fifteen years after its fiery fall.

The death of Uncle George
Is woven into the tree's departure.
The way he used to limp
Through Henham Woods
As the rain slowly seeped
Through his battered raincoat.
His half bald head
Covered in a film of water
That shimmered in the sun
Like an over-glazed pot.

At times the sun
Shone down on his wrinkled face,
Lighting the creases
Like furrows on a field.
And his worn shoes
Were the cut-off roots of the stricken tree,
Wedging him firmly
To the living earth.

Matthew Booley, 13

Last Respects

When Duggan's came to
take him away there
was no room for me and
so I sat on the
floor where all I could
see were black legs in

black trousers under tweedy
overcoats and black
stockings with best shoes
that didn't fit properly
because they were kept for
times like this which

are always expected but
never anticipated. All the
people he used to
know had come to see
him, reminiscing, and
he had missed Them.

Then They all went out to see him to
pay their last
respects but I don't think it
was him in there because it didn't
look like him. He was
fatter and I was alone

until They all flooded back
in and I knew that it was time because
there was nowhere else to go.

I was all in knots and my body
ached because there was
no room, and because the last time
I saw my grandad he was
confined to a
coffin.

*Joanne Holroyd, 17**

ANGEL INN

A Friend Gone

He sat,
Comforted by his old chair.
It was part of him.
He was a page in a book,
Everything
Held by the binder
Of his life.
The pictures,
Echoes of his past
As he relaxed
To the sparkle of the waves,
The bow bobbing
Through the water,
Splitting the moonlit
Smoothness.
The plastic cups
Stained as he sipped and dreamed.
The window,
Rotten,
Stained with looking through it
So many times.
The same picture
In a book.
Ashes on the fire –
With his chair.
But I still remember him
As he lies on a hill
Among the domino graves.
A friend,
Gone for ever,

Walking down
An everlasting path,
Up to the pub.

Simon Honeywood, 12

Lists of prize-winners

Age group: 10 years and under

1st prize	*The Treasure* Lily Maler
2nd prize	*Friends* James Ryder
3rd prize	*I Didn't Write a Poem* Christopher Trinnaman

Age group: 11–14 years

1st prize	*I Remember the Day* Jon Allen
2nd prize	*Brian* Davoren Hanna
3rd prize	*Garlic* Jonty J. R. Leff
Commended	*Augusta* Kate Beckinsale
	Mobile Friends Hakim Bakrim
	Friends Nina Gwilliam
	The Goldfish . . . Adam Hughes
	Most of Them Smoke Jonathan Taylor

Age group: 15–18 years

1st prize	*Singing High-Tide Town* Tim Stone
2nd prize	*For Leanne* Rhiannon Wakeman
3rd prize	*Friend* Imelda Cargan
Commended	*Last Respects* Joanne Holroyd
	I Had a Friend Jeremy Watson
	Sarah Jonathan Catherall

School prize

Halesworth Middle School
Suffolk

Teacher: Jill Pirrie

Poems submitted by the school included:

Friends Bryan Hall
We Became Friends Ruth Sparkes
Sat on the Wall Lara Mair
The Call of St Francis Leonora Dack
Androcles and the Lion – the Meeting Emma Clayton
Abi Helen Ward
Tortoise Friend Kelly Smith
The Goldfish . . . Adam Hughes
A Letter to a Friend (Not to Be Opened for 50 Years) Samantha Bedser
The Tree and Uncle George Matthew Booley
A Friend Gone Simon Honeywood

Runner-up school prize

Richard Atkins Primary School
London

Teacher: Muriel Greig

Poems submitted by the school included:

Nazrul Fawad Hassan
Copying Daniella Layne
Who? Summairs Jamil
New Friends Damian Gordon
My Friend Sister Joanna Akusuah Usser

Certificates of Merit

Age group: 10 years and under

Shereen Aiken, Katy Allum, Ketan Amlani, Stephen Bartlett, Eleanor Boase, Kelly Simin and Kathryn Chinnock, Richard Day, Jenny Doherty, Clare Dover, Constance Emerson, Damian Gordon, Camilla Crogor, Sylvia Cyom Boatong, Stephanie Hobday, Emel Kocbayindiran, Emma Linacre, Kirin Nazim, Michael O'Neill, Manish Parmar, Julia Riley, Daniel Ritchie, Sali-Wyn Ryan, Toby Rogers, Christopher Sachn, Matthew Seden, Sangeeta Shah, Sebastian Sutherland, Alethia Walker.

Age group: 11–14 years

Rachel Brown, Joanna Compton, Davoren Hanna, Samantha Hughes, James Jennings, Sung-Jin Kang, Vincent Lynskey, Francis Moon, Ashwin Sathyamoorthy, James Stevens, Rachel Stout, David Tickler.

Age group: 15–18 years

Caroline Bowring, Imelda Cargan, Harriet Castor, Elaine Cusack, Emma Donoghue, Samantha Dyche, Bronagh Finnegan, Graham Foster, Paul Hodges, Philip Jones, William Luscombe, Helen Pike, Claire Usiskin, Rhiannon Wakeman.

FOR THE BEST IN PAPERBACKS, LOOK FOR THE

In every corner of the world, on every subject under the sun, Penguin represents quality and variety – the very best in publishing today.

For complete information about books available from Penguin – including Pelicans, Puffins, Peregrines and Penguin Classics – and how to order them, write to us at the appropriate address below. Please note that for copyright reasons the selection of books varies from country to country.

In the United Kingdom: Please write to *Dept E.P., Penguin Books Ltd, Harmondsworth, Middlesex, UB7 0DA*

If you have any difficulty in obtaining a title, please send your order with the correct money, plus ten per cent for postage and packaging, to *PO Box No 11, West Drayton, Middlesex*

In the United States: Please write to *Dept BA, Penguin, 299 Murray Hill Parkway, East Rutherford, New Jersey 07073*

In Canada: Please write to *Penguin Books Canada Ltd, 2801 John Street, Markham, Ontario L3R 1B4*

In Australia: Please write to the *Marketing Department, Penguin Books Australia Ltd, P.O. Box 257, Ringwood, Victoria 3134*

In New Zealand: Please write to the *Marketing Department, Penguin Books (NZ) Ltd, Private Bag, Takapuna, Auckland 9*

In India: Please write to *Penguin Overseas Ltd, 706 Eros Apartments, 56 Nehru Place, New Delhi, 110019*

In Holland: Please write to *Penguin Books Nederland B.V., Postbus 195, NL–1380AD Weesp, Netherlands*

In Germany: Please write to *Penguin Books Ltd, Friedrichstrasse 10–12, D–6000 Frankfurt Main 1, Federal Republic of Germany*

In Spain: Please write to *Longman Penguin España, Calle San Nicolas 15, E–28013 Madrid, Spain*

In France: Please write to *Penguin Books Ltd, 39 Rue de Montmorency, F-75003, Paris, France*

In Japan: Please write to *Longman Penguin Japan Co Ltd, Yamaguchi Building, 2–12–9 Kanda Jimbocho, Chiyoda-Ku, Tokyo 101, Japan*

COL FRE

This book is due for return on or b

Daniel Stewart's and Melville College

00011862

Eoin Colfer

ARTEMIS FOWL

Traduit de l'anglais
par Jean-François Ménard

FOLIO JUNIOR/GALLIMARD JEUNESSE

Titre original : *Artemis Fowl*
Édition originale publiée par The Penguin Group, 2001
© Eoin Colfer, 2001, pour le texte
© Éditions Gallimard Jeunesse, 2001, pour la traduction française

Pour Jackie

PROLOGUE

Comment pourrait-on décrire Artemis Fowl ? Les nombreux psychiatres qui s'y sont essayés ont dû confesser leur échec. La principale difficulté de l'entreprise réside dans l'intelligence d'Artemis. Celui-ci parvient en effet à déjouer tous les tests auxquels on le soumet. Face à lui, les plus grands esprits du monde médical se sont trouvés plongés dans une infinie perplexité et nombre d'entre eux, balbutiants et hagards, sont retournés dans leurs propres hôpitaux, à titre de patients cette fois.

Artemis est sans nul doute un enfant prodige. Mais pourquoi un être aussi brillant a-t-il décidé de consacrer sa vie à des activités délictueuses ? Voilà une question à laquelle une seule personne serait en mesure de répondre. Or, il prend un malin plaisir à ne jamais parler de lui-même.

La meilleure façon de tracer un portrait fidèle

d'Artemis consiste à faire le compte rendu détaillé de la première entreprise scélérate qui l'a rendu célèbre. Il m'a été possible de procéder à cette reconstitution grâce aux interviews de première main qu'ont bien voulu m'accorder ses victimes.

A mesure que se déroule le récit, chacun pourra constater à quel point la tâche était malaisée.

Toute l'histoire a commencé il y a plusieurs années, à l'aube du XXIe siècle.

Artemis avait alors conçu un plan destiné à rétablir la fortune de sa famille. Un plan qui aurait pu entraîner l'effondrement de deux civilisations et précipiter la planète dans une guerre interespèces.

A cette époque, Artemis Fowl était âgé de douze ans.

CHAPITRE I

LE LIVRE

Hô Chi Minh-Ville en été. Une chaleur étouffante, tout le monde s'accorde à le reconnaître. Inutile de préciser qu'Artemis Fowl n'aurait jamais accepté de subir un tel inconfort si l'enjeu n'avait été aussi important. Important pour son plan.

Le soleil ne convenait pas à Artemis. Il ne lui allait pas au teint. Les longues heures passées enfermé devant un écran d'ordinateur lui avaient décoloré la peau.

Il était aussi pâle qu'un vampire et presque aussi irritable lorsqu'il se trouvait à la lumière du jour.

– J'espère qu'il ne s'agit pas encore d'une fausse piste, Butler, dit-il, d'une voix basse et coupante. Surtout après ce qui s'est passé au Caire.

C'était un aimable reproche. Ils s'étaient en effet rendus en Égypte sur les indications d'un informateur de Butler.

– Non, monsieur. Cette fois-ci, je suis sûr de moi. Nguyen est un homme de confiance.

– Humm, marmonna Artemis, sans conviction.

Les passants auraient été stupéfaits d'entendre l'Eurasien à la carrure d'athlète appeler le jeune garçon « monsieur ». On était quand même au troisième millénaire ! Mais la relation qui existait entre eux n'avait rien d'ordinaire et, d'ailleurs, il ne s'agissait pas de touristes ordinaires.

Ils étaient assis à la terrasse d'un café de la rue Dong Khai et regardaient les jeunes gens du quartier faire le tour de la place sur leurs vélomoteurs.

Nguyen était en retard et la malheureuse tache d'ombre que projetait leur parapluie n'avait guère de chance d'améliorer l'humeur d'Artemis. Mais ce n'était là que la manifestation de son pessimisme quotidien. Derrière la mine renfrognée se cachait une étincelle d'espoir.

Ce voyage donnerait-il véritablement des résultats ? Allaient-ils trouver le Livre ? C'était sans doute trop demander...

Un serveur s'avança vers leur table d'un pas précipité.

– Encore un peu de thé, messieurs ? demanda-t-il, en saluant frénétiquement de la tête.

Artemis poussa un soupir.

– Épargnez-moi votre petit spectacle et asseyez-vous.

Le serveur se tourna instinctivement vers Butler qui était l'adulte, après tout.

– Mais monsieur, je suis le serveur.

Artemis tapota sur la table pour attirer son attention.

– Vous portez des mocassins faits sur mesure, une chemise en soie et trois chevalières en or. Vous avez une pointe d'accent d'Oxford et l'éclat discret de vos ongles montre qu'ils ont été manucurés il y a peu de temps. Vous n'êtes pas serveur. Vous êtes Nguyen Xuan, notre contact, et vous avez adopté ce petit déguisement ridicule pour vérifier discrètement si nous ne sommes pas armés.

Les épaules de Nguyen s'affaissèrent.

– C'est vrai. Stupéfiant.

– Pas vraiment. Il ne suffit pas d'un vieux tablier effiloché pour avoir l'air d'un serveur.

Nguyen s'assit et versa un peu de thé à la menthe dans une minuscule tasse de porcelaine.

– Je vais vous renseigner moi-même en ce qui concerne les armes, poursuivit Artemis. Personnellement, je n'en ai pas. Mais Butler – c'est son nom : Butler, comme le mot qui signifie « majordome » en anglais, ce qui tombe très bien puisque c'est... mon majordome. Butler, donc, possède un pistolet Sig Sauer dans le holster qu'il porte sous l'aisselle, deux poignards à lame mince dans ses bottes, un minuscule derringer à deux coups dans sa manche, un fil de fer dans sa montre pour d'éventuels étranglements et trois grenades à main dans diverses poches. Je n'ai rien oublié, Butler ?

– La matraque, monsieur.

– Ah oui. Une bonne vieille matraque à billes d'acier qu'il cache dans sa chemise.

D'une main tremblante, Nguyen porta la tasse à ses lèvres.

– Ne vous inquiétez pas, Mr. Xuan, dit Artemis avec un sourire. Ces armes ne seront pas utilisées contre vous.

Nguyen ne sembla guère rassuré.

– Non, continua Artemis, ce serait inutile. Butler est capable de vous tuer de cent manières différentes sans avoir besoin de recourir à cette artillerie. Mais inutile d'aller jusqu'à cent, une seule suffirait largement.

Nguyen était terrorisé, à présent. C'était généralement l'effet que produisait Artemis sur ses interlocuteurs. Un adolescent au teint pâle, parlant avec l'autorité et le vocabulaire d'un adulte sûr de son pouvoir. Nguyen avait déjà entendu le nom de Fowl auparavant – qui pouvait l'ignorer dans la pègre internationale ? – mais il pensait qu'il aurait affaire à Artemis senior, pas à ce garçon. Quoique le mot « garçon » ne fût pas le mieux choisi pour définir ce personnage émacié. Quant au géant, Butler... il était évident qu'avec ses mains herculéennes, il serait capable de briser comme une simple brindille la colonne vertébrale de n'importe qui. Nguyen commençait à se dire qu'aucune somme d'argent ne valait la peine de passer une minute de plus en cette étrange compagnie.

– Et maintenant, parlons affaires, dit Artemis en posant un minimagnétophone sur la table. Vous avez répondu à notre annonce Internet.

Nguyen acquiesça d'un signe de tête, priant soudain que son information soit exacte.

– Oui, heu... monsieur Fowl. Ce que vous cherchez... Je sais où le trouver.

– Vraiment ? Et je suis censé vous croire sur parole ? Vous pourriez très bien m'amener tout droit dans un piège. Ma famille n'est pas exempte d'ennemis.

Butler attrapa en plein vol un moustique qui s'était aventuré près de l'oreille de son employeur.

– Non, non, il n'y a pas de piège, répondit Nguyen en sortant son portefeuille. Regardez.

Artemis examina le Polaroid. Il s'efforça de maîtriser son rythme cardiaque. La photo semblait prometteuse mais, de nos jours, on pouvait faire tous les trucages possibles avec un ordinateur et un scanner. L'image montrait une main émergeant de l'ombre. Une main verte et tachetée.

– Mmmm, murmura Artemis. Expliquez-moi ça.

– Cette femme. C'est une guérisseuse, du côté de la

rue Tu Do. Elle se fait payer en alcool de riz. Elle est tout le temps ivre.

Artemis hocha la tête d'un air approbateur. La boisson. L'un des quelques rares faits indiscutables que ses recherches avaient permis de découvrir. Il se leva, lissant les plis de son polo blanc.

– Très bien. Conduisez-nous là-bas, Mr. Nguyen.

Nguyen essuya la sueur qu'on voyait perler parmi les poils de sa moustache filandreuse.

– Il s'agit d'un simple renseignement. Nous étions bien d'accord là-dessus. Je ne veux pas prendre un mauvais sort sur la tête.

D'un geste expert, Butler saisit l'informateur par la nuque.

– Je suis navré, Mr. Nguyen, mais l'époque où vous aviez une certaine liberté de choix est depuis longtemps révolue.

Butler entraîna le Vietnamien qui essayait de protester jusqu'à un 4x4 de location. Ce n'était pas le genre de véhicule absolument indispensable dans les rues plates de Hô Chi Minh-Ville, ou de Saigon comme ses habitants continuaient de l'appeler, mais Artemis aimait mieux s'isoler le plus possible des civils.

La Jeep avança peu à peu à une allure douloureusement traînante, d'autant plus insupportable que l'impatience d'Artemis ne cessait de croître. Il lui était impossible de la dominer plus longtemps. Allaient-ils enfin arriver au terme de leur quête ? Après six fausses alertes qui les avaient amenés sur trois continents, cette guérisseuse imbibée d'alcool serait-elle le trésor au pied de l'arc-en-ciel ? Artemis faillit glousser de rire Le trésor au pied de l'arc-en-ciel. Il venait de faire une sorte de plaisanterie. C'était quelque chose qui n'arrivait pas tous les jours.

Les vélomoteurs s'écartèrent comme s'ils pénétraient dans un immense banc de poissons. La foule, ici, semblait sans fin. La moindre ruelle débordait de colporteurs et de vendeurs à la sauvette. Dans un crépitement d'huile bouillante, des cuisiniers jetaient des têtes de poisson dans leurs woks et des gamins des rues se faufilaient dans les jambes de tout le monde, à la recherche d'objets de valeur mal surveillés. D'autres, assis à l'ombre, s'usaient les pouces sur leur Gameboy.

Nguyen transpirait dans sa chemise kaki. L'humidité n'y était pour rien, il y était habitué. C'était plutôt à cause de cette maudite situation dans laquelle il s'était fourré. Il aurait dû savoir qu'on ne doit jamais mélanger magie et filouterie. Il se fit la promesse silencieuse que, s'il parvenait à se sortir de là, il changerait de conduite. Il cesserait de répondre aux annonces louches diffusées sur Internet et n'irait certainement plus se compromettre avec les rejetons des grandes familles de la pègre européenne.

La Jeep ne pouvait passer partout. Les petites rues

qu'ils empruntaient devenaient trop étroites pour le 4x4. Artemis se tourna vers Nguyen.

– Il semblerait que nous devions continuer à pied, Mr. Nguyen. Si vous avez envie de vous enfuir en courant, ne vous gênez surtout pas, mais il faudra vous attendre à éprouver une douleur cuisante et fatale entre les omoplates.

L'homme regarda brièvement Butler dans les yeux. Ils étaient bleu foncé, presque noirs. Des yeux dépourvus de toute pitié.

– Ne vous inquiétez pas, dit-il, je ne chercherai pas à m'enfuir.

Ils descendirent de voiture et un bon millier de regards les suivirent tandis qu'ils s'enfonçaient dans la ruelle suffocante. Un malheureux pickpocket essaya de voler le portefeuille de Butler. Le serviteur brisa les doigts du voleur sans même lui accorder un regard.

Aussitôt, tout le monde s'écarta largement sur leur passage.

La ruelle se rétrécit encore pour devenir une allée creusée d'ornières. Des canalisations et des tuyaux d'égout se déversaient directement sur le sol boueux. Des infirmes et des mendiants se serraient les uns contre les autres sur des tapis en paille de riz qui formaient comme des îlots dans la fange. Les résidents de l'allée étaient décidés à n'épargner personne, à part ces trois-là.

– Alors ? demanda Artemis d'un ton impérieux. Où est-elle ?

Nguyen pointa l'index en direction d'un triangle noir, sous un escalier d'incendie rouillé.

– Là. Là-dessous. Elle n'en sort jamais. Même pour acheter de l'alcool, elle envoie quelqu'un. Je peux m'en aller, maintenant ?

Artemis ne prit pas la peine de répondre. Il s'avança dans l'allée boueuse et s'approcha de l'escalier d'incendie. Il distinguait des mouvements furtifs parmi les ombres.

– Butler, pourriez-vous me donner les lunettes ?

Butler prit une paire de lunettes à vision nocturne accrochée à sa ceinture et la déposa dans la main tendue d'Artemis.

Le moteur de mise au point automatique bourdonna pour adapter les lunettes à la lumière ambiante.

Artemis les fixa devant ses yeux. Le décor se colora aussitôt d'un vert radioactif. Prenant une profonde inspiration, il tourna son regard vers l'ombre qui gigotait. Quelque chose était accroupi sur un tapis de raphia, s'agitant avec nervosité dans une très faible lueur. Artemis régla la mise au point de ses lunettes. La silhouette était d'une taille anormalement petite, enveloppée dans un châle crasseux. Autour d'elle, des cruchons d'alcool vides étaient à moitié enfoncés dans la boue. Un bras pointait sous l'étoffe. Il paraissait verdâtre. Mais tout le reste l'était aussi.

– Madame, dit Artemis, j'ai une proposition à vous faire.

La tête de la silhouette vacilla d'un air ensommeillé.

– De l'alcool, du vin, dit-elle d'une voix grinçante, comme des ongles sur un tableau noir. Du vin. Anglais ?

Artemis sourit.

Le don pour les langues, l'aversion pour la lumière. Parfait, parfait.

– Irlandais, précisément. Alors, ma proposition ?

D'un geste avisé, la guérisseuse agita un doigt osseux.

– L'alcool d'abord, on parlera après.

– Butler ?

Le garde du corps plongea la main dans une poche et en retira une flasque d'un whiskey irlandais de la meilleure qualité. Artemis brandit la bouteille d'un air tentateur devant la tache d'ombre. A peine avait-il eu le temps d'enlever ses lunettes qu'une main griffue jaillit de l'obscurité pour se saisir du whiskey. Une main verte et tachetée. Il n'y avait plus aucun doute.

Artemis réprima un sourire triomphant.

– Payez notre ami, Butler. La somme totale. Et souvenez-vous, Mr. Nguyen, tout cela doit rester entre nous. Vous n'auriez pas envie que Butler revienne vous voir, n'est-ce pas ?

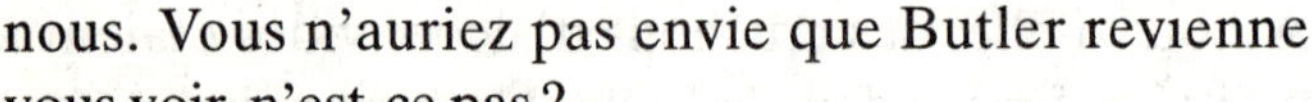

– Non, non, monsieur Fowl. Mes lèvres resteront cousues.

– Cela vaut mieux. Sinon, c'est Butler qui se chargera de les coudre à tout jamais.

Nguyen fila le long de l'allée, si soulagé d'être encore en vie qu'il ne se donna même pas la peine de compter la liasse de billets verts qu'on venait de lui remettre. Ce qui ne lui ressemblait pas. De toute façon, tout était bien là. Vingt mille dollars. Pas mal pour une demi-heure de travail.

Artemis se tourna à nouveau vers la guérisseuse.

– Et maintenant, madame, il se trouve que j'ai besoin de quelque chose que vous seule pouvez me donner.

La langue de la guérisseuse lécha une goutte d'alcool au coin de sa bouche.

– Oui, l'Irlandais. Mal de tête, mal de dents, je guéris.

Artemis remit ses lunettes à vision nocturne et s'accroupit auprès d'elle pour être à son niveau.

– Je suis en parfaite santé, madame, à part une légère allergie à certains acariens dont je ne pense pas que quiconque puisse me guérir, même vous. Non, ce qui m'intéresse, c'est votre Livre.

La harpie se figea. Des yeux étincelants flamboyèrent sous le châle.

– Livre ? répéta-t-elle avec prudence. Je ne connais

pas de livre. Je suis guérisseuse. Tu veux un livre, tu vas à la bibliothèque.

Artemis soupira avec une patience exagérée.

– Vous n'êtes pas guérisseuse. Vous êtes un lutin, une fée, un farfadet, un korrigan, appelez ça comme vous voudrez dans la langue que vous voudrez. Et je veux votre Livre.

Pendant un long moment, la créature resta silencieuse puis elle rejeta le châle qui lui couvrait le front.

Dans la lumière verte des lunettes, ses traits surgirent devant Artemis comme un masque de Halloween. La fée avait un long nez busqué et deux yeux bridés couleur d'or. Ses oreilles étaient pointues et l'alcool avait ramolli sa peau jusqu'à la rendre semblable à du mastic.

– Si tu connais l'existence du Livre, humain, dit-elle lentement en combattant l'engourdissement dû au whiskey, tu dois également savoir de quelle magie je dispose dans ma main. Je pourrais te tuer en claquant des doigts !

Artemis haussa les épaules.

– Je ne pense pas. Regardez-vous. Vous êtes presque morte. L'alcool de riz a émoussé vos sens. Vous en êtes réduite à guérir les verrues. Consternant. Je suis venu ici pour vous sauver, en échange du Livre.

– Qu'est-ce qu'un humain pourrait faire avec notre Livre ?

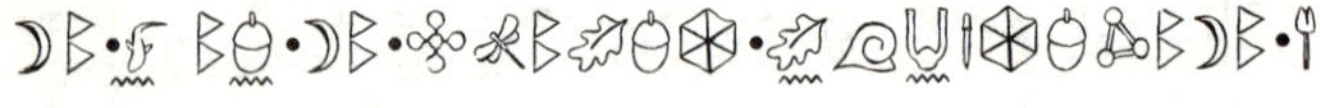

– Cela ne vous regarde pas. Tout ce que vous devez savoir, c'est le choix qui vous reste.

Les oreilles pointues de la créature frémirent.

– Le choix ?

– Ou bien vous refusez de nous donner ce Livre et nous rentrons chez nous en vous laissant pourrir dans cet égout.

– En effet, c'est ce que je choisis, dit la fée.

– Ne soyez pas si pressée. Si nous repartons sans le Livre vous serez morte dans un jour ou deux.

– Un jour ou deux !

La guérisseuse éclata de rire.

– Je vivrai encore un siècle après ta mort. Même les fées attachées au royaume des hommes peuvent survivre une éternité.

– Pas avec une demi-pinte d'eau bénite à l'intérieur du corps, répliqua Artemis en tapotant la bouteille de whiskey vide.

La fée devint livide, puis elle poussa un hurlement, une longue plainte suraiguë, horrible.

– De l'eau bénite ! Tu m'as assassinée, humain !

– Exact, admit Artemis. Vous devriez commencer à ressentir les premières brûlures incessamment.

La fée se tâta le ventre d'un geste prudent.

– Qu'est-ce que je peux choisir d'autre ?

– On m'écoute, maintenant, n'est-ce pas ? Très bien. Alors, deuxième possibilité : vous me donnez le Livre pendant une demi-heure seulement. Ensuite, je vous rends votre pouvoir magique.

La fée resta bouche bée.

– Me rendre mon pouvoir magique ? Impossible.

– Oh, mais si. J'ai en ma possession deux ampoules. L'une contient de l'eau de source qui provient du puits des Fées, à soixante mètres sous l'anneau de Tara – l'endroit peut-être le plus magique au monde. Elle annulera les effets de l'eau bénite.

– Et l'autre ?

– Dans l'autre, il y a de quoi faire une petite piqûre de magie humaine. Un virus qui se nourrit d'alcool, mélangé à un agent de croissance. Ce liquide va débarrasser votre corps de la moindre goutte d'alcool de riz, vous délivrer de votre dépendance et même régénérer votre foie défaillant. Ce sera terriblement répugnant, mais dans vingt-quatre heures, vous sauterez partout comme si vous aviez retrouvé la vigueur de vos mille ans.

La fée passa à nouveau la langue sur ses lèvres. Pouvoir rejoindre le Peuple ? C'était tentant.

– Comment savoir si je puis te croire, humain ? Tu m'as déjà joué un mauvais tour.

– C'est vrai. Voici le marché. Je vous donne l'eau de source en toute confiance. Ensuite, quand j'aurai consulté le Livre, vous aurez le remontant. A prendre ou à laisser.

La fée réfléchit. La douleur s'insinuait déjà dans son ventre. Elle tendit la main.

– Je prends.

– Je m'y attendais. Butler ?

Le gigantesque serviteur ouvrit le rabat d'une trousse qui contenait une seringue et deux ampoules. Il prit d'abord celle qui était remplie d'un liquide clair et l'injecta dans le bras moite de la fée. La créature se raidit un instant puis se détendit.

– Puissante magie, dit-elle d'une voix haletante.

– Oui, mais pas aussi puissante que la vôtre lorsque vous aurez eu la deuxième injection. Et maintenant, le Livre.

La fée plongea la main dans les plis de sa robe crasseuse et y fouilla pendant une éternité. Artemis retint son souffle. Enfin ! Bientôt, les Fowl auraient retrouvé toute leur gloire. Un nouvel empire allait naître avec, à sa tête, Artemis Fowl II.

La fée montra son poing serré.

– Ça ne te servira à rien, c'est écrit dans l'ancienne langue.

Artemis hocha la tête, préférant ne pas prendre le risque de parler.

Elle ouvrit ses doigts noueux. Au creux de sa main reposait un minuscule volume à la reliure d'or, de la taille d'une boîte d'allumettes.

– Voilà. Tu peux le regarder pendant trente de tes minutes d'humain. Pas plus.

Butler prit le minuscule ouvrage avec révérence. Il

actionna un appareil photo numérique et entreprit de photographier l'intégralité du Livre dont les pages étaient aussi minces que du papier à cigarette. L'opération dura plusieurs minutes. Lorsqu'il eut terminé, le volume tout entier était contenu dans la puce de l'appareil photo. Artemis préférait ne courir aucun risque en matière d'information.

On avait souvent vu des disques d'une importance vitale effacés par les équipements de sécurité d'un aéroport.

Il ordonna donc à son majordome de transférer le fichier sur son téléphone portable puis, par courrier électronique, au manoir familial, à Dublin. Avant que les trente minutes se soient écoulées, le fichier contenant jusqu'au dernier symbole du *Livre des fées* se trouva ainsi enregistré en toute sécurité sur le serveur des Fowl.

Artemis rendit le minuscule ouvrage à sa propriétaire.

– J'ai été content de faire affaire avec vous.

La fée se redressa sur les genoux en vacillant.

– Et l'autre potion, humain ?

Artemis sourit.

– Ah oui, le remontant. Je crois bien vous l'avoir promis

– Oui, humain, tu me l'as promis.

– Très bien. Mais avant de vous l'administrer, je dois

vous avertir que cette purge n'a rien de plaisant. Vous n'allez pas passer un très bon moment.

La fée montra la saleté sordide qui s'étalait autour d'elle.

– Et ici, tu crois que je passe de bons moments ? Je veux m'envoler à nouveau.

Butler fixa la deuxième ampoule à la seringue et fit cette fois la piqûre directement dans la carotide.

La fée s'effondra aussitôt sur son tapis, sa carcasse tout entière secouée de tremblements violents.

– Il est temps de prendre congé, commenta Artemis. Un siècle d'alcool sortant d'un corps par tous les moyens possibles n'offre pas un spectacle très attirant.

Les Butler étaient au service des Fowl depuis des siècles. Il en avait toujours été ainsi. Il se trouvait même quelques linguistes éminents pour affirmer que c'était le nom de la famille Butler qui avait donné à la langue anglaise le mot signifiant « majordome ». D'après les archives, l'origine de cet arrangement inhabituel remontait à l'époque où Virgil Butler avait été engagé comme valet, garde du corps et cuisinier par Lord Hugo de Fole lors d'une des premières grandes croisades des Normands.

A l'âge de dix ans, les enfants Butler étaient envoyés dans un centre de formation privé en Israël où on leur prodiguait l'enseignement spécialisé nécessaire pour assurer le service du dernier Fowl de la lignée. Cet enseignement comportait des cours de haute cuisine, une formation de tireur d'élite, la pratique d'un mélange d'arts martiaux conçu sur mesure, ainsi qu'une éducation poussée en matière de médecine d'urgence et de technologies de l'information. Si, à la fin de leur entraînement, il ne se trouvait aucun Fowl pour les prendre à son service, les Butler étaient immédiatement engagés comme gardes du corps par diverses personnalités appartenant à des familles royales, généralement à Monaco ou en Arabie Saoudite.

Une fois qu'un Fowl et un Butler se trouvaient associés, c'était pour la vie. Il s'agissait d'un travail exigeant et solitaire, mais dont la rétribution était coquette si l'on arrivait à survivre suffisamment longtemps pour en profiter. Dans le cas contraire, la famille recevait à titre de dédommagement une somme d'argent à sept chiffres à laquelle venait s'ajouter une pension mensuelle.

L'actuel Butler avait passé douze ans au service de son jeune maître, depuis le jour de sa naissance. Et tout en sacrifiant aux exigences du formalisme traditionnel, ils étaient bien davantage qu'un maître et son serviteur. Artemis était pour Butler ce qui pouvait le plus ressembler à un ami et Butler était pour Artemis ce qui s'approchait le plus d'un père, bien qu'il soit celui des deux qui obéissait aux ordres.

Butler tint sa langue jusqu'à leur décollage de l'aéroport de Bangkok, où ils avaient changé d'avion pour embarquer à bord d'un vol à destination de Heathrow. Il ne put alors s'empêcher de poser la question :

– Artemis ?

Artemis leva les yeux de l'écran de son PowerBook. Il avait commencé à travailler sur la traduction.

– Oui ?

– La fée. Pourquoi n'avons-nous pas simplement gardé le Livre en la laissant mourir ?

– Un cadavre est une preuve, Butler. En procédant à ma manière, il n'y a aucune raison pour que le Peuple ait des soupçons.

– Mais la fée ?

– Je serais très étonné qu'elle avoue avoir montré le Livre à des humains. De toute façon, j'ai mélangé un léger amnésique à la deuxième injection. Lorsqu'elle se réveillera, tous les événements de la semaine écoulée lui paraîtront très flous.

Butler hocha la tête d'un air appréciateur. Toujours deux coups d'avance, tel était maître Artemis. Les gens disaient qu'il avait de qui tenir, qu'on reconnaissait en lui le sang de ses ancêtres. Ils avaient tort. Maître Artemis était un sang neuf à lui tout seul, et ce sang-là n'avait jamais coulé dans les veines de quiconque d'autre.

Ses doutes dissipés, Butler se replongea dans la lecture de son livre intitulé *Armes et munitions*, laissant son employeur démêler seul les secrets de l'univers.

CHAPITRE II

TRADUCTION

Sans doute aura-t-on deviné à présent jusqu'où Artemis Fowl était prêt à aller pour atteindre son objectif. Mais quel était exactement cet objectif ? Quel étrange projet pouvait bien nécessiter un chantage exercé sur une fée alcoolique ? La réponse était simple : l'or.

Les recherches d'Artemis avaient commencé deux ans auparavant lorsqu'il était devenu un adepte de l'Internet. Il n'avait pas tardé à explorer les arcanes des sites les plus mystérieux : enlèvements par des extraterrestres, observations d'OVNI et phénomènes surnaturels.

Mais il s'était intéressé plus spécifiquement à l'existence du Peuple.

Naviguant parmi des gigabits de données, il avait découvert des centaines d'informations sur les fées dans presque tous les pays du monde. Chaque civilisation avait son propre vocabulaire pour désigner les êtres qui constituent le Peuple, mais il ne faisait aucun doute que tous étaient membres d'une même famille secrète. Divers récits mentionnaient un livre que les fées portaient toujours sur elles. C'était comme une bible contenant, disait-on, toute l'histoire de l'espèce et les divers commandements qui régissaient leur très longue existence. Bien entendu, ce livre était écrit en gnomique, la langue des fées, et ne pouvait être d'aucune utilité aux humains.

Artemis était convaincu qu'avec les outils de la technologie moderne, il était possible de traduire le Livre Et grâce à cette traduction, on pouvait envisager d'exploiter tout un ensemble de créatures encore inconnues.

« Connais ton ennemi », telle était la devise d'Artemis, et c'est ainsi qu'il s'était immergé dans les traditions du Peuple pour rassembler une gigantesque base de données sur ses principales caractéristiques.

Mais ce n'était pas suffisant. Aussi avait-il fait passer une annonce sur le Web : « Homme d'affaires irlandais prêt à payer somme importante en dollars américains pour rencontrer fée, lutin, farfadet ou autres. »

La plupart des réponses s'étaient révélées des escroqueries, mais celle de Hô Chi Minh-Ville avait fini par être la bonne.

Artemis était sans doute la seule personne vivante qui pût tirer pleinement avantage de sa récente acquisition. Il conservait en la magie une croyance d'enfant que tempérait une détermination d'adulte à en tirer profit. S'il existait quelqu'un capable de soulager les fées d'un peu de leur or magique, c'était bien Artemis Fowl II.

Ils rejoignirent le manoir des Fowl dans les premières heures de la matinée. Artemis avait hâte d'ouvrir son fichier sur l'ordinateur mais il décida d'aller d'abord voir sa mère.

Angeline Fowl ne quittait pas son lit. Elle n'en avait plus bougé depuis la disparition de son mari. Tension nerveuse, disaient les médecins. On ne pouvait rien faire d'autre que prescrire du repos et des pilules pour dormir. Il y avait presque un an de cela, à présent.

Juliet, la petite sœur de Butler, était assise au pied de l'escalier. On aurait dit qu'elle essayait de creuser un trou dans le mur avec son seul regard. Même son mascara étincelant ne parvenait pas à adoucir l'expression de son visage. Artemis lui avait déjà vu ce regard ; c'était juste avant qu'elle n'inflige ce qu'elle appelait un « suplix » à un livreur de pizza particulièrement insolent. Artemis en avait déduit que le suplix était une prise de lutte. Un sport pour lequel elle éprouvait une passion inhabituelle chez une jeune fille. Mais, après tout, c'était une Butler.

– Des ennuis, Juliet ?

Elle se releva précipitamment.

– C’est ma faute, Artemis. Apparemment, j’ai laissé les rideaux entrebâillés. Mrs. Fowl n’a pas pu dormir.

– Mmmm, marmonna-t-il en montant lentement les marches du vieil escalier de chêne.

Il s’inquiétait de la santé de sa mère. Depuis longtemps maintenant, elle n’avait même plus revu la lumière du jour. D’un autre côté, si elle guérissait miraculeusement, si, animée d’une énergie nouvelle, elle sortait soudain de sa chambre, ce serait l’annonce que l’extraordinaire liberté dont bénéficiait Artemis toucherait à sa fin. Cela voudrait dire le retour à l’école et : « Fini les entreprises délictueuses, mon garçon. »

Il frappa doucement à l’un des battants de la double porte en arcade.

– Mère ? Vous êtes réveillée ?

Quelque chose s’écrasa contre la porte, de l’autre côté du panneau. Quelque chose qui devait coûter assez cher, à en juger par le son.

– Bien sûr que je suis réveillée ! Comment pourrais-je dormir dans cette clarté aveuglante ?

Artemis s’aventura à l’intérieur. Un antique lit à baldaquin jetait dans l’obscurité des ombres pointues, et un rai de lumière pâle transperçait l’entrebâillement des rideaux de velours. Angeline Fowl était assise dans son lit, les épaules voûtées, ses membres blafards brillant d’une lueur blanchâtre dans la pénombre.

– Artemis, mon chéri, où étais-tu passé ?

Il soupira. Elle le reconnaissait. C'était bon signe.

– J'étais parti en voyage avec l'école, mère Une classe de neige en Autriche.

– Ah, la neige, le ski, chantonna Angeline. Comme ça me manque ! Peut-être quand ton père sera revenu.

Artemis sentit sa gorge se serrer. Une réaction très inhabituelle.

– Oui. Peut-être quand père sera revenu.

– Mon chéri, pourrais-tu fermer ces abominables rideaux ? La lumière est insupportable.

– Bien sûr, mère.

Artemis traversa la pièce à tâtons, prenant garde aux coffres à vêtements qui parsemaient le sol à hauteur de tibia.

Ses doigts se refermèrent enfin sur les draperies de velours.

Pendant un instant, il eut la tentation de les ouvrir en grand puis il soupira et les ferma étroitement.

– Merci, mon chéri. Ah, au fait, il faudrait renvoyer cette bonne. Elle n'est vraiment bonne à rien.

Artemis retint sa langue. Depuis trois ans, Juliet travaillait avec courage et loyauté au service de la maison Fowl. Le moment était venu d'utiliser à son avantage la distraction de sa mère.

– Vous avez raison, mère, bien sûr. Il y a déjà un certain temps que je voulais le faire. Butler a une sœur qui pourrait parfaitement la remplacer. Je crois que je vous ai déjà parlé d'elle. Elle s'appelle Juliet.

Angeline fronça les sourcils.

– Juliet ? Oui, le nom me dit quelque chose. De toute façon n'importe qui conviendra mieux que la petite idiote que nous avons en ce moment. Quand pourrait-elle commencer ?

– Tout de suite. Je vais dire à Butler d'aller la chercher dans la maison des gardiens.

– Tu es un très gentil garçon, Artemis. Et maintenant, viens embrasser ta maman.

Il s'avança vers les plis obscurs de la robe de chambre que portait sa mère. Elle avait une odeur de parfum, comme des pétales de fleur dans l'eau. Mais ses bras étaient froids et graciles.

– Oh, mon chéri, murmura-t-elle, et sa voix donna la chair de poule à Artemis. J'entends des choses. La nuit. Je les entends ramper sur les oreillers et puis ils me rentrent dans les oreilles.

Artemis sentit à nouveau sa gorge se serrer.

- Nous devrions peut-être ouvrir les rideaux, mère.

– Non, sanglota-t-elle en desserrant son étreinte. Non, parce que dans ce cas, je les verrais.

– Mère, s'il vous plaît.

Mais c'était inutile. Angeline était partie. Elle se glissa à l'autre bout du lit, ramenant la couette sous son menton.

– Envoie-moi la nouvelle bonne.

– Oui, mère.

– Dis-lui d'apporter des tranches de concombre et de l'eau.

– Oui, mère.

Angeline lui jeta un regard insidieux.

– Et arrêtez de m'appeler mère. Je ne sais pas qui vous êtes, mais vous n'êtes certainement pas mon petit Arty.

Artemis refoula quelques larmes rebelles.

– Bien sûr. Désolé, mè... désolé.

– Mmmm. Et ne remettez plus les pieds ici ou je demanderai à mon mari de s'occuper de vous. C'est un homme très important, vous savez.

– Très bien, Mrs. Fowl. Vous ne me reverrez plus.

– Ça vaudrait mieux pour vous.

Angeline se figea brusquement.

– Vous les entendez ?

Artemis hocha la tête en signe de dénégation.

– Non, je n'entends pas de...

– Ils viennent me chercher. Ils sont partout.

Angeline se réfugia sous les couvertures. Artemis entendait encore ses sanglots terrifiés lorsqu'il descendit l'escalier.

Le Livre se révéla beaucoup plus récalcitrant que ne l'avait prévu Artemis. C'était comme s'il lui avait opposé une résistance active. Il avait beau le faire passer par tous les programmes possibles, l'ordinateur restait muet.

Artemis avait fait une copie papier de chaque page et les avait toutes punaisées aux murs de son bureau. Parfois, il était utile de mettre les choses sur papier. L'écriture ne ressemblait à rien de ce qu'il connaissait et pourtant, elle lui paraissait étrangement familière. Constitué d'un mélange de symboles et de caractères, le texte paraissait onduler tout autour de la page sans ordre apparent.

Il fallait créer un programme à partir d'un cadre de références, un point central sur lequel construire un ensemble. Il sépara les caractères les uns des autres et les compara à des textes écrits en anglais, chinois, grec, arabe, cyrillique et même en ogham, l'écriture des anciens Irlandais. Rien.

L'humeur assombrie par ses échecs, Artemis envoya promener Juliet lorsqu'elle l'interrompit pour lui apporter des sandwichs et se replongea dans ses symboles. Le pictogramme qui revenait le plus fréquemment représentait une petite silhouette masculine. C'était en tout cas ce qu'il supposait mais, étant donné sa connaissance limitée de l'anatomie des fées, elle aurait pu tout aussi bien être féminine. Une idée lui vint alors en tête. Artemis ouvrit le fichier de son Power Translator consacré aux langues anciennes et sélectionna les hiéroglyphes égyptiens.

Enfin. Il avait marqué un point. La silhouette masculine ressemblait de manière frappante à la représentation du dieu Anubis qui figurait sur les inscriptions de la chambre de Toutânkhamon. Voilà qui recoupait ses autres découvertes. Les premières histoires écrites par les hommes parlaient de créatures féeriques, laissant entendre que leur civilisation avait précédé celle de l'homme lui-même. Il semblait que les Égyptiens avaient simplement adapté à leurs propres besoins une écriture qui existait déjà.

Il y avait d'autres ressemblances. Mais les caractères présentaient juste assez de différences pour échapper aux filets de l'ordinateur. Il faudrait procéder manuellement. Chaque graphisme gnomique devrait être agrandi, imprimé, puis comparé aux hiéroglyphes.

Artemis sentit l'excitation du succès accélérer son rythme cardiaque. Presque chaque pictogramme ou caractère avait un équivalent égyptien. La plupart possédaient un sens universel, tels le soleil ou les oiseaux. Mais d'autres semblaient appartenir exclusivement au monde surnaturel et devraient être adaptés pour trouver leur correspondance. La silhouette d'Anubis, par exemple, n'avait aucune signification en tant que dieu à tête de chien, et Artemis dut l'interpréter comme représentation du roi des fées.

Vers minuit, il avait entré avec succès ses découvertes dans le Macintosh. La seule chose qui lui restait

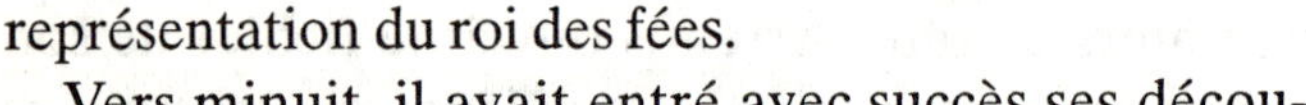

à accomplir à présent, c'était d'activer la fonction « décoder ». Ce qu'il fit. Il en émergea alors un long charabia alambiqué et incompréhensible.

Un enfant normal aurait depuis longtemps renoncé à la tâche. Un adulte moyen en aurait sans doute été réduit à donner un coup de poing rageur sur le clavier. Mais pas Artemis. Ce livre le narguait et il n'allait pas lui abandonner la victoire.

Les lettres étaient élucidées, il en était sûr. C'était l'ordre dans lequel elles étaient disposées qui présentait une difficulté. Frottant ses yeux ensommeillés, Artemis examina à nouveau ses pages d'écriture. Chaque fragment était bordé d'une ligne continue qui délimitait peut-être des paragraphes ou des chapitres. En tout cas, il ne servait à rien de les lire à la manière habituelle, de gauche à droite et de haut en bas.

Il fit diverses expériences. Il essaya de les lire de droite à gauche, à la manière des Arabes, ou en colonnes comme les Chinois. Rien ne marchait. Il remarqua alors que toutes les pages avaient quelque chose en commun : une partie centrale. Les autres pictogrammes étaient disposés autour de cet axe. Peut-être fallait-il partir de là ? Mais dans quelle direction ? Artemis étudia les pages une par une pour essayer de découvrir un autre trait commun. Au bout d'un certain temps, il le trouva enfin. Sur chaque page, il y avait un minuscule signe en forme de pointe dans un coin du texte. S'agissait-il d'une flèche ? D'une direction à suivre ? Il faudrait alors commencer la lecture au milieu puis suivre la flèche et lire en spirale.

Le logiciel de l'ordinateur n'était pas conçu pour un tel exercice et Artemis dut improviser. Avec un cutter et une règle, il disséqua la première page du Livre et réunit les lettres dans l'ordre traditionnel des langues européennes – de gauche à droite en rangées parallèles.

Puis il scanna à nouveau la page ainsi obtenue et la soumit au logiciel de traduction en langue égyptienne modifiée.

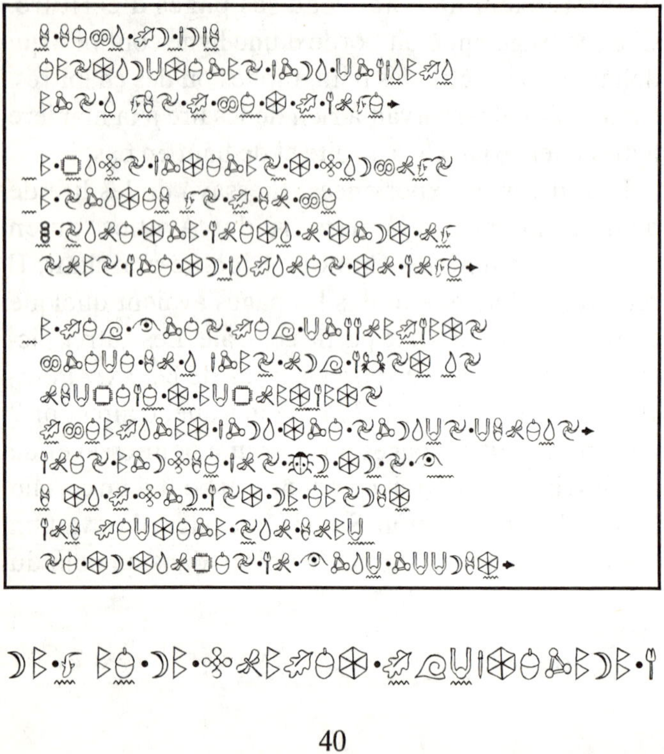

L'ordinateur bourdonna, ronronna, tandis qu'il convertissait les nouvelles données en langage binaire. A plusieurs reprises, il s'interrompit pour demander confirmation d'un caractère ou d'un symbole. Il le fit d'ailleurs de moins en moins à mesure qu'il assimilait le nouveau langage. Enfin, deux mots scintillèrent sur l'écran : « Fichier converti ».

Les mains tremblantes d'épuisement et d'excitation, Artemis cliqua sur « Imprimer ». Une unique page sortit de l'imprimante laser. Le texte était en anglais, à présent. Certes, il y avait des erreurs, quelques mises au point s'imposaient, mais tout était parfaitement lisible et, plus important encore, parfaitement compréhensible.

Avec la pleine conscience qu'il était sans doute le premier être humain depuis des milliers d'années à avoir réussi à décoder les mots magiques, Artemis alluma sa lampe de bureau et commença à lire.

LE LIVRE DU PEUPLE

INSTRUCTIONS POUR COMPRENDRE NOS RÈGLES DE VIE ET DE MAGIE

En herbes, potions et breuvages
En sortilèges de la vie
Je serai ton maître à tout âge
Sans moi, tu perdrais ta magie.

En dix fois dix commandements
Voici la réponse aux mystères,
Alchimie et enchantements
Deviendront pour toi sources claires.

Mais n'oublie pas que tu es fée,
L'Être de Boue m'est une insulte
Malédiction sera lancée
Si tu trahis ma force occulte.

Artemis entendait le sang battre à ses oreilles. Il les tenait. Ils allaient être comme des fourmis sous ses pieds.

Leur moindre secret serait percé grâce à la technologie.

Soudain, l'épuisement le submergea et il s'abandonna contre le dossier de son fauteuil. Il y avait encore tant de choses à faire. Quarante-trois pages à traduire, pour commencer.

Il appuya sur le bouton de l'interphone relié à des haut-parleurs disséminés dans toute la maison.

– Butler, allez chercher Juliet et venez me rejoindre ici. Il va falloir m'aider à reconstituer un puzzle.

A cet endroit du récit, il ne serait peut-être pas inutile de donner quelques indications sur l'histoire de la famille.

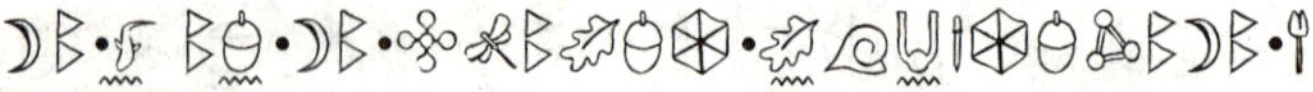

En vérité, les Fowl étaient des malfaiteurs légendaires.

Pendant des siècles, ils avaient ferraillé du mauvais côté de la loi et avaient fini par rassembler suffisamment d'argent pour acquérir une certaine respectabilité. Comme on pouvait s'y attendre, cette respectabilité n'était pas de leur goût et ils avaient presque immédiatement replongé dans l'illégalité.

C'était Artemis Ier, le père de notre protagoniste, qui avait mis en péril la fortune de la famille. Lorsque la Russie communiste s'était effondrée, Artemis senior avait estimé judicieux d'investir une grande partie du capital des Fowl dans l'acheminement de marchandises diverses à destination de ce vaste continent. Tous ces nouveaux consommateurs, s'était-il dit, allaient avoir besoin de nouveaux biens de consommation.

Mais la mafia russe n'avait guère apprécié qu'un Occidental se mêle de s'installer sur son marché et avait donc décidé de lui envoyer un message.

Le message avait pris la forme d'un missile Stinger volé qui avait été lancé sur le *Fowl Star* au moment où le cargo passait devant Mourmansk. Artemis senior se trouvait à bord du navire, en compagnie de l'oncle de Butler et de deux cent cinquante mille boîtes de soda à la noix de cola. L'explosion avait été des plus spectaculaires.

Les Fowl n'étaient pas tombés dans la misère pour

autant, loin de là. Mais ils avaient cessé d'être milliardaires. Une situation à laquelle Artemis II comptait bien remédier. Il était fermement décidé à rétablir la fortune familiale. Et il allait le faire à sa façon, qui était unique en son genre.

Une fois le Livre traduit, Artemis pouvait commencer à se mettre sérieusement au travail.

Il connaissait déjà son objectif ultime, il convenait à présent de trouver les moyens de l'atteindre.

L'objectif, bien sûr, c'était l'or. L'acquisition d'une grande quantité d'or. Il semblait que le Peuple éprouvait la même attirance que les humains pour le précieux métal. Chaque fée avait sa propre cachette, mais plus pour très longtemps si Artemis parvenait à réaliser son projet.

Lorsqu'il en aurait terminé, le peuple des fées compterait au moins un individu qui se promènerait désormais les poches vides.

Après dix-huit heures d'un sommeil profond et un petit déjeuner léger, Artemis monta dans le bureau qu'il avait hérité de son père. C'était une pièce d'apparence traditionnelle – chêne sombre un peu partout, murs tapissés de rayonnages du sol au plafond – mais Artemis avait pris soin de la remplir d'un matériel informatique dernier cri. Une série d'AppleMac en réseau ronronnaient dans divers coins de la pièce. L'un d'eux était branché en permanence sur le site Internet de CNN et relié à un projecteur numérique qui déployait sur le mur du fond les images agrandies de l'actualité.

Butler était déjà là, occupé à mettre les programmes en route.

– Fermez-les tous, à part celui du Livre, j'ai besoin de tranquillité.

Le serviteur eut une réaction de surprise. Le site CNN était branché en permanence depuis près d'un an. Artemis était convaincu que la nouvelle du sauvetage de son père lui viendrait par ce canal. Le fermer signifiait qu'il avait fini par abandonner tout espoir.

– Tous ?

Artemis regarda le mur du fond pendant quelques instants.

– Oui, dit-il enfin. Tous.

Butler prit la liberté de donner une unique petite tape sur l'épaule de son employeur, en guise de réconfort, avant de retourner à son travail. Artemis fit craquer ses jointures. Le moment était venu de faire ce pour quoi il était le plus doué : manigancer d'inavouables agissements.

CHAPITRE III
HOLLY

Étendue sur son lit, Holly Short bouillait d'une rage silencieuse. Ce qui n'avait rien d'inhabituel. D'une manière générale, les farfadets n'étaient pas réputés pour leur cordialité. Mais Holly était d'une humeur particulièrement détestable, même pour une fée. En langage plus technique, c'était une elfe, le mot « fée » étant un terme général. Elle était aussi farfadet, mais uniquement à titre professionnel.

Une description sera sans doute plus utile qu'un cours magistral sur la classification des fées. Holly Short avait une peau couleur noisette, des cheveux auburn coupés ras et des yeux de la même couleur que sa peau. Son nez était busqué et ses lèvres charnues comme celles d'un chérubin, ce qui n'avait rien de surprenant puisque Cupidon était son arrière-grand-père. Sa mère était une elfe d'Europe, dotée d'un caractère irascible et d'une silhouette élancée. Holly aussi avait un corps mince avec de longs doigts effilés, parfaits pour s'enrouler autour d'une électrotrique, la matraque réglementaire. Bien entendu, elle avait les oreilles pointues. Avec une taille d'un mètre exactement, Holly n'avait qu'un centimètre de moins que la moyenne des fées, mais un unique centimètre peut faire une terrible différence quand on en a si peu à sa disposition.

Le commandant Root était la cause de l'affliction de Holly. Root n'avait cessé de s'en prendre à elle depuis le jour où elle avait commencé à travailler avec lui. Le commandant s'offusquait du fait que le premier officier féminin dans l'histoire du service de Détection avait été affecté à son unité. Le service de Détection était connu pour être particulièrement dangereux, avec un taux de pertes élevé, et Root pensait qu'une fille n'y avait pas sa place. Pourtant, il faudrait bien qu'il s'y fasse, car Holly Short n'avait aucune intention de démissionner, ni pour lui ni pour quiconque d'autre.

Même si elle n'était pas du tout disposée à le reconnaître, l'irascibilité de Holly avait peut-être une autre cause : le Rituel. Depuis plusieurs lunes, elle s'était promis de l'accomplir, mais il lui semblait qu'elle n'en avait jamais le temps. Et si Root découvrait que ses réserves de magie étaient au plus bas, nul doute qu'elle serait aussitôt mutée à la circulation.

Holly roula sur elle-même, se leva de son futon et se

dirigea vers la douche d'un pas incertain. C'était l'un des avantages d'habiter près du centre de la terre – l'eau était toujours chaude. Bien sûr, il n'y avait pas de lumière naturelle, mais c'était un prix modeste à payer en échange de la tranquillité. Sous terre. Le dernier espace dépourvu d'êtres humains. Il n'y avait rien de plus agréable que de rentrer chez soi après une longue journée de travail, d'éteindre son bouclier et de se plonger dans un bain de vase bouillonnante. Une véritable félicité.

La fée s'habilla, remontant jusqu'au menton la fermeture de sa combinaison vert foncé et fixant son casque sur sa tête. Les uniformes des FARfadet étaient assez élégants, de nos jours. Pas comme les costumes genre « petit matin radieux » que ses membres avaient dû porter dans le temps. Des chaussures à boucle et des pantalons de golf ! Non mais vraiment ! Pas étonnant que les farfadets soient devenus des êtres aussi ridicules dans le folklore humain. Mais finalement, c'était sans doute mieux ainsi. Si le Peuple de la Boue savait que le mot « farfadet » venait en fait des FARfadet, un sigle qui désignait les Forces Armées de Régulation auxquelles étaient rattachées les Fées Aériennes de Détection, il prendrait sans doute des mesures pour les exterminer. Mieux valait rester invisibles et laisser les humains garder leurs idées toutes faites.

La lune se levait déjà en surface, il ne restait donc pas assez de temps pour prendre un petit déjeuner convenable. Holly attrapa dans le réfrigérateur un reste de nectar d'ortie et le but en parcourant les tunnels. Comme d'habitude, un véritable chaos régnait sur l'axe central. Les lutins volants qui encombraient l'avenue provoquaient un terrible embouteillage. Les gnomes n'arrangeaient rien avec leurs gros derrières qui se balançaient négligemment en bloquant deux voies d'un coup. Des crapauds jureurs infestaient le moindre coin d'humidité en lançant des gros mots à faire rougir un pirate. Cette espèce un peu particulière était née d'une simple plaisanterie mais s'était répandue comme une épidémie. Celui qui avait créé cette engeance aurait mieux fait d'oublier sa baguette magique ce jour-là.

Holly se fraya un chemin à travers la foule en direction du poste de police. Il y avait déjà une véritable émeute devant les grands magasins Pelle-Mêle.

Le caporal Newt, des FAR, essayait de mettre un peu d'ordre. Holly lui souhaita bien du plaisir. Un vrai cauchemar. Elle, au moins, avait la chance de travailler en surface.

L'entrée du poste des FAR était bondée de mécontents. La guerre des gangs entre nains et gobelins avait à nouveau éclaté et, chaque matin, des hordes de parents furieux se précipitaient pour exiger qu'on libère leur progéniture innocente.

Holly Short renifla d'un air dédaigneux. S'il existait vraiment un gobelin innocent, elle ne l'avait encore jamais rencontré. Entassés dans les cellules, ils hurlaient à présent des slogans à la gloire de leurs gangs et se lançaient des boules de feu à la tête.

Holly s'avança en écartant la foule à coups d'épaules.

– Laissez passer, grogna-t-elle. Police.

Ils se précipitèrent sur elle comme des mouches sur un ver gluant.

– Mon petit Grumpo est innocent !

– Ce sont des brutalités policières !

– Officier, pourriez-vous apporter sa petite couverture à mon bébé chéri ? Il n'arrive pas à dormir sans elle.

Holly mit sa visière en position réfléchissante et ne leur prêta aucune attention. Il y avait eu une époque où l'uniforme imposait un certain respect. Ce n'était plus le cas. Aujourd'hui, il représentait plutôt une cible. « Excusez-moi, officier, mais je n'arrive plus à mettre la main sur mon bocal de verrues. » Ou : « Excusez-moi, jeune elfe, mais mon chat est monté à une stalagmite et il est resté coincé tout en haut. » Ou encore : « Si vous avez une minute, capitaine, vous pourriez peut-être m'indiquer le chemin de la fontaine de Jouvence ? » Holly fut parcourue d'un frisson. Les touristes. Elle avait suffisamment d'ennuis comme ça.

Et plus encore qu'elle ne croyait, comme elle n'allait pas tarder à s'en rendre compte.

Dans le couloir, un nain kleptomane était occupé à voler dans les poches de tout le monde, le long de la file d'attente des délinquants, y compris dans celles de l'officier auquel il était menotté.

Holly lui passa son électrotrique dans le dos. La décharge brûla légèrement le fond de son pantalon de cuir.

– Qu'est-ce que tu fiches là, Mulch ?

Le nain sursauta, laissant tomber de ses manches divers objets dérobés.

– Capitaine Short, gémit-il, l'air contrit. Je n'y peux rien. C'est dans ma nature.

– Je sais, Mulch. Et notre nature à nous, c'est de te jeter au fond d'une cellule pendant un siècle ou deux.

Elle lança un regard à l'officier qui avait arrêté le nain.

– Ça fait plaisir de voir que vous êtes toujours aussi vif.

L'elfe rougit et s'agenouilla pour ramasser son portefeuille et son insigne tombés des manches de Mulch.

Holly passa précipitamment devant la porte du bureau de Root, espérant atteindre son box avant que...

– SHORT ! VENEZ ICI TOUT DE SUITE !

Holly soupira. Allons bon. Ça recommençait.

Calant son casque sous son bras, Holly lissa les plis de son uniforme et entra dans le bureau du commandant Root.

Le visage de son chef était violet de rage. C'était, dans son cas, un état plus ou moins permanent qui lui avait valu le surnom de commandant Rouge. Les paris étaient ouverts dans le service pour savoir combien de temps il tiendrait avant que son cœur n'explose. On pouvait raisonnablement miser sur un demi-siècle, tout au plus.

Le commandant Root tapotait le lunomètre attaché à son poignet.

– Alors ? dit-il d'un ton impérieux. Vous appelez ça une heure pour venir travailler ?

Holly sentit son propre visage se colorer. Elle avait à peine une minute de retard. Il devait y avoir au moins une douzaine d'officiers qui n'étaient même pas encore arrivés. Mais c'était toujours elle que Root choisissait pour exercer son goût de la persécution.

– Les embouteillages, marmonna-t-elle maladroitement. Il y avait quatre files bloquées sur l'avenue.

– N'essayez pas de me faire avaler des excuses pareilles, c'est insultant ! rugit le commandant. Vous savez bien que le centre-ville est encombré ! Vous n'avez qu'à vous lever quelques minutes plus tôt !

C'était vrai, elle savait très bien comment on circulait à Haven. Short était une elfe des villes, née citadine et élevée comme telle. Depuis que les humains avaient commencé à faire des forages pour chercher des minerais et des combustibles, un nombre croissant de fées, chassées des forts situés à proximité de la surface, avaient dû se réfugier dans les profondeurs plus sûres de Haven-Ville. La métropole était surpeuplée et sous-équipée. Il y avait même à présent un lobby qui cherchait à obtenir l'autorisation pour les automobiles de circuler dans le centre piétonnier. Comme si l'endroit n'était pas déjà suffisamment odorant avec tous ces gnomes de la campagne qui traînaient là-bas.

Root avait raison. Elle devrait se lever un peu plus tôt. Mais elle ne le ferait pas. Pas tant que les autres n'y seraient pas forcés, eux aussi.

– Je sais à quoi vous pensez, dit le commandant. Pourquoi est-ce que je m'en prends toujours à vous ? Pourquoi est-ce que je ne dis jamais rien aux autres fainéants ?

Holly resta silencieuse mais l'approbation se lisait clairement sur son visage.

– Vous voulez que je vous dise pourquoi ?

Holly se risqua à acquiescer d'un signe de tête.

– C'est parce que vous êtes une fille.

Holly sentit ses doigts se replier en un poing serré. Elle le savait !

– Mais ce n'est pas pour les raisons auxquelles vous songez, poursuivit Root. Vous êtes le premier élément féminin qui ait jamais été affecté aux FARfadet. Le premier. Vous êtes un test pour la suite. Vous avez un flambeau à porter. Des millions de fées observent le moindre de vos gestes. De nombreux espoirs reposent sur vos épaules. Mais vous devez également faire face à beaucoup de préjugés. L'avenir de l'ordre public est entre vos mains. Et, pour le moment, je dirais qu'il a pesé un peu lourd.

Holly cilla. Root ne lui avait jamais parlé de cette façon. D'habitude, c'était simplement : « Attachez votre casque », « Tenez-vous droite », et bla-bla-bla.

– Vous devez toujours donner le meilleur de vous-même, Short, ce qui signifie être meilleure que tous les autres.

Root soupira, s'enfonçant dans son fauteuil pivotant.

– Mais franchement, Holly, je ne sais pas quoi vous dire. Depuis l'affaire de Hambourg.

Holly fit une grimace. L'affaire de Hambourg s'était soldée par un véritable désastre. Un délinquant qu'elle avait arrêté s'était évadé en surface et avait tenté de demander asile au Peuple de la Boue. Root avait été obligé d'organiser une suspension temporelle, d'envoyer un commando de Récupération et de procéder à quatre effacements de mémoire. La police avait perdu beaucoup de temps. Tout ça par sa faute.

Le commandant prit un formulaire sur son bureau.

– Ça ne servirait à rien d'insister. J'ai pris une décision. Je vous mute à la circulation et je vous remplace par le caporal Frond.

– Frond ! explosa Holly. Mais c'est une poupée ! Elle n'a rien dans la tête. Vous ne pouvez quand même pas en faire un test !

Le teint de Root devint d'un violet encore plus foncé.

– Si, je le peux, et c'est ce qui va se passer. Qui m'en empêcherait ? Vous ne m'avez jamais donné le meilleur de vous-même... Ou alors, le meilleur de vous-même est insuffisant. Désolé, Short, vous avez eu votre chance...

Le commandant reporta son attention sur ses papiers. L'entretien était terminé. Holly resta là, atterrée. Elle avait raté son coup. La plus belle occasion qu'elle aurait jamais dans sa carrière, elle l'avait gâchée. Une seule erreur avait suffi à transformer son avenir en passé. C'était injuste. Holly sentit une colère inhabituelle s'emparer d'elle, mais elle la réprima. Ce n'était pas le moment de perdre son sang-froid.

– Commandant Root, je crois que je mérite une nouvelle chance.

Root ne prit même pas la peine de lever les yeux de ses papiers.

– Et en quel honneur ?

Holly prit une profonde inspiration.

– A cause de mes états de service. Ils parlent d'eux-mêmes, en dehors de l'histoire de Hambourg. Dix missions de détection réussies. Pas un seul effacement de mémoire, pas une seule suspension temporelle, à part...

– A part l'histoire de Hambourg, acheva Root.

Holly courut le risque :

– Si j'étais un mâle, dit-elle, un de vos précieux lutins, nous n'aurions même pas eu cette conversation.

Root leva brusquement les yeux.

– Bon, écoutez-moi bien, capitaine Short...

Il fut interrompu par la sonnerie d'un des téléphones posés sur son bureau. Un autre téléphone sonna, puis un troisième. Au même moment, un écran géant s'anima sur le mur, derrière lui.

Root enfonça le bouton du haut-parleur, mettant tous ses interlocuteurs en mode conférence.

– Oui ?

– Nous avons une évasion.

Root hocha la tête.

– Il y a quelque chose sur les scopes ?

Les scopes étaient le nom technique des instruments d'observation dissimulés dans les satellites de communication américains.

– Ouais, dit le deuxième correspondant. Un signal bien net en provenance d'Europe. Du sud de l'Italie, exactement. Aucun bouclier.

Root poussa un juron. Une fée sans bouclier

pouvait être facilement vue par des mortels. Ce ne serait pas trop grave si le fuyard avait une apparence humanoïde.

– Classification ?

– Mauvaise nouvelle, commandant, répondit le troisième correspondant. Il s'agit d'un troll en vadrouille.

Root se frotta les yeux. Pourquoi ces choses-là arrivaient-elles toujours lorsqu'il était de service ? Holly comprenait qu'il soit irrité. Les trolls étaient les créatures les plus malfaisantes des profondeurs. Ils erraient dans le labyrinthe de tunnels et s'en prenaient à quiconque avait la malchance de croiser leur chemin. Leurs cerveaux minuscules ne laissaient place à aucune retenue, aucun respect des lois.

De temps à autre, l'un d'eux arrivait à se faufiler dans un puits à pression. Le plus souvent, il était carbonisé par le courant d'air brûlant mais, parfois, il survivait et se trouvait propulsé à la surface.

Rendu fou par la douleur et la lumière, si faible qu'elle fût, il s'employait généralement à tout détruire sur son passage.

Root secoua rapidement la tête pour reprendre contenance.

– O.K., capitaine Short. La voilà, votre nouvelle chance, on dirait. J'imagine que vous êtes chauffée au rouge, question magie ?

– Oui, commandant, mentit Holly, sachant bien que

Root la suspendrait immédiatement de ses fonctions s'il savait qu'elle avait négligé le Rituel.

– Très bien. Alors, allez prendre une arme et transportez-vous sur l'objectif.

Holly jeta un coup d'œil à l'écran. Les scopes transmettaient des images à haute résolution d'une ville fortifiée italienne. Un point rouge se déplaçait rapidement dans la campagne en direction de la population humaine.

– Procédez à une reconnaissance détaillée et revenez faire votre rapport. Ne tentez aucune manœuvre de récupération. Vous m'avez bien compris ?

– Oui, commandant.

– Nous avons perdu six membres des FAR lors d'attaques de trolls, ces trois derniers mois. Six morts, et c'était sous terre, en territoire connu.

– Je comprends, commandant.

Root pinça les lèvres d'un air sceptique.

– Vous comprenez vraiment, Short ? Pour de bon ?

– Je crois, commandant.

– Avez-vous déjà eu l'occasion de voir ce qu'un troll est capable de faire à un être de chair et de sang ?

– Non, commandant. Pas de près.

– Très bien. Alors arrangez-vous pour qu'aujourd'hui ne soit pas la première fois.

– Compris.

Root lui lança un regard noir.

– Je ne sais pas comment ça se fait, capitaine, mais chaque fois que vous approuvez ce que je dis, je ne me sens pas du tout tranquille.

Root avait raison de ne pas se sentir tranquille. S'il avait su comment cette simple mission de détection allait tourner, il aurait sans doute choisi de prendre immédiatement sa retraite. Ce soir-là, une page d'histoire était sur le point de s'écrire. Et ce ne serait pas un événement heureux du genre découverte du radium ou premiers pas de l'homme sur la lune. Ce serait plutôt un grand malheur, style Inquisition espagnole ou voyage du *Hindenburg*. Un malheur pour les humains et pour les fées. Un malheur pour tout le monde.

Holly se rendit directement dans la zone des puits. Habituellement bavarde, elle serrait les lèvres et sa bouche n'était plus qu'un trait sombre qui exprimait sa détermination. Sa nouvelle chance était là.

Elle allait se concentrer sur sa tâche et ne se laisserait distraire par rien.

L'habituelle queue des amateurs de vacances qui espéraient obtenir un visa de sortie s'étendait jusqu'au coin de la place des Ascensions, mais Holly contourna la file d'attente en brandissant son insigne. Un gnome querelleur refusa de s'écarter.

– Vous autres, les gens des FAR, vous voulez toujours passer avant tout le monde. Pour qui vous vous prenez ?

Holly inspira profondément par le nez. Courtoisie en toutes circonstances.

– Mission de police, monsieur. Et maintenant, si vous voulez bien m'excuser.

Le gnome gratta son dos massif.

– J'ai entendu dire que vous autres, les gens des FAR, vous vous inventez des missions pour aller admirer le clair de lune. C'est ce qu'on m'a dit.

Holly s'efforça d'esquisser un sourire amusé. Mais le rictus qui se forma sur ses lèvres aurait plutôt laissé penser qu'elle venait de sucer un citron.

– Celui qui vous a dit ça est un imbécile... monsieur. Les membres des FAR ne s'aventurent en surface qu'en cas de nécessité absolue.

Le gnome fronça les sourcils. De toute évidence, il avait inventé la rumeur lui-même et soupçonnait Holly de l'avoir traité d'imbécile en toute connaissance de cause. Mais, avant qu'il ait pu tirer une conclusion définitive, elle s'était déjà faufilée de l'autre côté de la porte à double battant.

Foaly l'attendait dans la salle des opérations. Foaly était un centaure paranoïaque convaincu que les services secrets humains surveillaient son réseau de transport et d'observation.

Pour les empêcher de lire dans ses pensées, il portait en permanence un chapeau en papier d'aluminium.

Il leva vivement les yeux lorsque Holly franchit la double porte pneumatique.

– Quelqu'un vous a vue entrer ?

Elle réfléchit un instant.

– Le FBI, la CIA, la NSA, la DEA, le MI6 et le TLMDI.

Foaly fronça les sourcils.

– Le TLMDI ?

– Tout Le Monde Dans l'Immeuble, répondit Holly avec un sourire goguenard.

Foaly se leva de son fauteuil pivotant et s'approcha d'elle dans un bruit de sabots.

– C'est très drôle, Short. Absolument désopilant. Je pensais que l'affaire de Hambourg vous aurait un peu rabattu le caquet. Si j'étais vous, je me concentrerais sur le travail à faire.

Holly reprit son sérieux. Il avait raison.

– O.K., Foaly. Expliquez-moi tout ça.

Le centaure lui montra des images retransmises en direct par le satellite Eurosat sur un grand écran à plasma.

– Ce point rouge représente le troll. Il se dirige vers Martina Franca, une ville fortifiée proche de Brindisi, au sud de l'Italie. D'après ce que nous savons, il a réussi à entrer dans le conduit E7 qui était en phase de refroidissement après un tir en surface.

C'est pour ça que le troll n'avait pas fini sous forme de steak carbonisé.

Holly fit une grimace. « Charmant », pensa-t-elle.

– Nous avons eu la chance que notre cible trouve de la nourriture sur son chemin. Il a attrapé deux vaches sur lesquelles il a pu se faire les dents pendant une heure ou deux, ça nous a fait gagner un peu de temps.

– Deux vaches ? s'exclama Holly. Il est gros comment, ce troll ?

Foaly rajusta son bonnet d'aluminium.

– C'est un mâle adulte. Pleinement développé. Cent quatre-vingts kilos avec des défenses de sanglier sauvage. Vraiment très sauvage.

Holly déglutit difficilement. Soudain, il lui sembla nettement préférable de travailler au service de Détection plutôt que dans les commandos de Récupération.

– Bien. Et qu'est-ce que vous avez pour moi ?

Foaly s'approcha au petit trot de la table des accessoires sur laquelle il prit ce qui ressemblait à une montre-bracelet rectangulaire.

– C'est un localisateur. Vous trouvez le troll et nous on vous retrouve grâce à cet appareil. Travail de routine.

– La vidéo ?

Le centaure logea un petit cylindre dans une rainure prévue à cet effet sur le casque de Holly.

– Retransmission directe. Batterie nucléaire. Pas de limite de temps. Le micro est activé par le son de la voix.

– Très bien, approuva-t-elle. Root a dit que je devrais emporter une arme sur ce coup-là. Au cas où.

– J'ai toujours une bonne longueur d'avance, répondit Foaly.

Il prit sur sa table un pistolet en platine.

– C'est un Neutrino 2000, expliqua-t-il. Le dernier modèle. Même les gangs des tunnels n'en ont pas. Avec trois positions, s'il vous plaît. Légèrement grillé, bien cuit, réduit en cendres. Énergie nucléaire également, alors vous pouvez y aller. Ce bébé-là vous survivra pendant environ mille ans.

L'arme était légère et Holly la cala facilement dans le holster qu'elle portait sous l'aisselle.

– Je suis prête... je crois.

Foaly gloussa de rire.

– J'en doute. Personne ne peut se vanter d'être vraiment prêt quand il s'agit d'un troll.

– Merci pour les encouragements, ça donne confiance.

– La confiance, c'est de l'ignorance, déclara le centaure d'un ton docte. Quand on se sent sûr de soi, c'est qu'il y a quelque chose qu'on ignore.

Holly songea à discuter mais elle y renonça. Peut-être parce qu'elle avait la vague impression que Foaly disait vrai.

Les puits à pression étaient activés par des colonnes gazeuses qui s'échappaient du cœur de la terre.

Sur les indications de Foaly, les techniciens des FAR avaient réalisé des capsules de titane en forme d'œuf qui pouvaient être propulsées par les courants souterrains.

Les capsules étaient équipées de moteurs indépendants mais rien ne valait une bonne explosion d'énergie venue du centre de la terre pour atteindre la surface en un temps record.

Foaly emmena Holly jusqu'au conduit E7 en passant devant la longue rangée de portes d'embarquement qui donnaient accès aux autres puits. La capsule posée sur son socle paraissait bien fragile pour être lancée par un flux de magma. Sa partie inférieure était noircie par le feu et criblée de bosses dues à des projections de roches.

Le centaure tapota affectueusement une aile de l'engin.

– Ça fait cinquante ans que ce bébé-là est en service. Le plus vieux modèle qu'on puisse encore voir dans les conduits.

Holly déglutit avec difficulté. Les puits à pression l'inquiétaient suffisamment sans avoir besoin de surcroît de voyager dans une antiquité.

– Quand est-ce qu'on va la retirer de la circulation ?

Foaly gratta son poitrail velu.

– Avec les crédits qu'on nous donne, il faudra attendre qu'il y ait un mort.

Holly actionna la manivelle qui ouvrait la lourde porte dont la garniture de caoutchouc céda dans un sifflement. La capsule n'avait pas été conçue pour offrir un grand confort à son passager. Elle était tout juste assez grande pour contenir un siège à harnais au milieu de tout un fatras électronique.

– Qu'est-ce que c'est que ça ? demanda-t-elle en montrant du doigt une tache grisâtre sur l'appuie-tête du siège.

Foaly parut un peu gêné.

– Heu... des sécrétions cérébrales, je crois. Nous avons eu une fuite dans la pressurisation lors de la dernière mission. Mais c'est réparé maintenant. Et l'officier a survécu. Il a perdu quelques points de Q.I., mais il est vivant, et il arrive encore à se nourrir d'aliments liquides.

– Ah bon, dans ce cas, ça va, lança Holly d'un ton narquois en se glissant parmi les câbles entremêlés.

Foaly l'attacha dans son harnais, vérifiant soigneusement chaque sangle.

– Tout va bien ?

Elle acquiesça d'un signe de tête.

Foaly tapota le micro du casque.

– On garde le contact, dit-il, avant de verrouiller la porte de la capsule.

« N'y pense pas, se dit Holly. Ne pense pas au flot de magma chauffé à blanc qui va engloutir ton minuscule vaisseau. Ne pense pas que tu vas être propulsée vers la surface à une vitesse de Mach 2 par une force qui essayera de te retourner comme un gant. Et ne pense surtout pas à ce troll assoiffé de sang, prêt à t'arracher les entrailles avec ses défenses de sanglier sauvage. Non. Ne pense à rien de tout ça... D'ailleurs, il est trop tard. »

La voix de Foaly retentit dans son écouteur :

– T moins vingt secondes, dit-il. Nous sommes branchés sur un canal de sécurité, au cas où le Peuple de la Boue aurait commencé à surveiller nos communications souterraines. On ne sait jamais. Un jour, un pétrolier du Moyen-Orient a intercepté une de nos transmissions. Ça a provoqué une jolie pagaille !

Holly ajusta le micro de son casque.

– Concentrez-vous, Foaly. Ma vie est entre vos mains.

– Hein ? Ah, oui, excusez-moi. On va vous mettre sur les rails pour vous envoyer dans le puits principal du conduit E7. Il y aura une éruption d'une minute à l'autre. Elle devrait vous faire passer les cent premiers kilomètres, ensuite, il faudra vous débrouiller seule.

Holly hocha la tête, refermant les doigts sur les deux poignées du manche à balai.

– *Check-list* terminée. Vous pouvez y aller.

Les moteurs de la capsule s'allumèrent dans un bruit de bourrasque. Le minuscule engin se mit à trépider dans son conduit en secouant Holly comme une bille dans un hochet. Elle avait du mal à entendre Foaly qui lui parlait dans son écouteur.

– Vous êtes maintenant dans le puits secondaire. Préparez-vous au décollage, Short.

Holly prit un cylindre de caoutchouc sur le tableau de bord et l'enfonça entre ses dents. Pas la peine d'avoir une radio si on avale sa langue. Elle brancha les caméras externes et activa les écrans.

L'entrée du puits principal E7 glissait lentement vers elle. Une brume de chaleur ondoyait à la lueur des feux d'atterrissage. Des étincelles enflammées voletaient dans le conduit secondaire. Holly n'entendait pas le rugissement qui résonnait tout autour, mais elle l'imaginait. Un vent à arracher la peau soufflait en produisant le même vacarme qu'un million de trolls en train de hurler.

Les doigts de Holly se crispèrent sur les poignées du manche à balai. La capsule s'arrêta tout au bord du conduit. Le puits vertical s'étirait des profondeurs de la terre jusqu'à la surface. Immense. Infini. Holly allait ressembler à une fourmi précipitée dans un tuyau de vidange.

– O.K., crépita la voix de Foaly dans l'écouteur. Accrochez-vous à votre petit déjeuner. Les montagnes russes, c'est une promenade de santé à côté de ça.

Holly hocha la tête. Il lui était impossible de parler

avec le morceau de caoutchouc dans la bouche. Mais le centaure pouvait la voir grâce à la caméra de bord.

– *Sayonara*, ma jolie, dit Foaly et il appuya sur le bouton.

Le socle de la capsule bascula, projetant Holly dans les abysses. Son estomac se contracta tandis que la force d'accélération l'entraînait vers le centre de la terre. Le service de sismologie avait installé un million de capteurs tout au fond et pouvait prédire avec un taux de succès de 99,8 % la fréquence des explosions de magma. Mais il restait toujours les 0,2 %.

La chute sembla durer une éternité. Au moment où Holly se préparait mentalement à finir dans un tas de ferraille, elle la sentit enfin. Une vibration inoubliable. La sensation qu'au-dehors de sa sphère minuscule, le monde était sur le point d'éclater. « Ça y est », pensa-t-elle.

– Ailettes, dit-elle, parvenant à cracher le mot malgré le cylindre de caoutchouc.

Foaly lui avait peut-être répondu mais elle ne pouvait plus l'entendre. Elle n'aurait même pas pu s'entendre elle-même ; elle vit cependant sur son écran de contrôle les ailettes de stabilisation se mettre en place.

Le flux de magma la frappa de plein fouet, comme un ouragan, faisant tournoyer la capsule jusqu'à ce que les ailettes rétablissent l'équilibre. Des roches à moitié fondues criblaient la partie inférieure de l'engin en le projetant contre les parois. Holly rectifiait la trajectoire à coups de manche à balai.

La chaleur était effarante dans cet espace confiné, il y aurait eu de quoi rôtir un être humain. Mais les poumons d'une fée sont d'une tout autre constitution. L'accélération distendait son corps comme avec des mains invisibles, étirant la peau sur ses bras et son visage. Holly battit des paupières pour chasser de ses yeux des gouttes de sueur salée et se concentra sur son écran de contrôle. L'explosion avait complètement englouti la capsule et la poussée était d'une puissance exceptionnelle. Force sept au bas mot. Avec une étendue d'au moins cinq cents mètres. Un magma aux rayures orange tourbillonnait dans un sifflement assourdissant autour de l'engin, cherchant un point faible dans l'enveloppe de métal.

La capsule gémissait, protestait, les rivets de cinquante ans d'âge menaçaient de sauter comme des bouchons. Holly hocha la tête. La première chose qu'elle allait faire à son retour serait de donner un grand coup de pied dans le derrière chevalin de Foaly. Elle avait l'impression d'être une noisette dans sa coquille, prise entre les molaires d'un gnome. Autrement dit, condamnée.

Une plaque métallique à l'avant de l'engin se tordit, s'enfonçant soudain comme si elle avait été frappée par un poing gigantesque. L'indicateur de pression se mit à clignoter. Holly sentit sa tête comme serrée dans un étau. Ses yeux seraient les premiers à céder – jaillissant de leurs orbites comme des fruits mûrs.

Elle vérifia les cadrans. Encore vingt secondes et elle sortirait du flux de magma pour être portée par les forces thermiques de l'écorce terrestre. Elle crut que ces vingt secondes ne finiraient jamais.

Holly abaissa la visière de son casque pour se protéger les yeux, passant enfin la dernière barrière rocheuse.

Et soudain, la capsule sortit du chaos, flottant sur une spirale d'air chaud relativement plus calme. Holly ajouta la force de ses propres moteurs au courant ascendant. Elle n'avait pas de temps à perdre à se promener au gré des vents souterrains.

Au-dessus d'elle, un cercle de lumières au néon indiquait la zone d'atterrissage. Elle fit basculer l'engin en position horizontale et se dirigea à vue vers les points d'ancrage. C'était une manœuvre délicate. De nombreux pilotes des FARfadet, après avoir réussi à arriver jusque-là, avaient perdu un temps précieux en ratant leur amarrage. Mais pas Holly. Elle avait ça dans le sang. Première de sa promotion à l'académie.

Elle appuya encore une fois sur la manette des gaz puis laissa la capsule parcourir les dernières centaines de mètres en planant sur sa lancée. A l'aide du palonnier qu'elle manœuvrait avec les pieds, elle pénétra en douceur dans le cercle de lumière et descendit sur son socle, dans l'aire d'atterrissage. Les bras articulés pivotèrent pour venir se loger dans leurs rainures. Elle était saine et sauve.

Holly détacha le harnais de sécurité en faisant claquer la boucle sur sa poitrine. Une fois la porte étanche ouverte, l'air de la surface inonda de sa douceur l'intérieur de la capsule. Rien n'était plus délicieux que cette première bouffée de fraîcheur après l'ascension d'un puits. Elle respira profondément, vidant ses poumons de l'air confiné de l'engin. Comment était-il possible que le Peuple ait jamais quitté la surface de la terre ? Parfois, elle regrettait que ses ancêtres ne soient pas restés pour affronter le Peuple de la Boue. Mais ils étaient décidément trop nombreux. A la différence des fées, qui ne pouvaient mettre au monde qu'un seul enfant tous les vingt ans, les Êtres de la Boue avaient la faculté de se reproduire comme des rongeurs. La multitude aurait eu raison de la magie elle-même.

Tout en appréciant l'air de la nuit, Holly sentait tous les produits polluants qui y flottaient. Les Êtres de la Boue détruisaient tout ce qu'ils touchaient. Bien sûr, ils avaient cessé de vivre dans la boue. Dans ce pays-là, en tout cas. Oh oui, c'était bien fini. Maintenant, ils avaient de vastes demeures luxueuses avec des pièces différentes pour tout – des pièces pour dormir, des pièces pour manger et même une pièce pour aller aux toilettes ! Dans la maison ! Holly eut un frisson de dégoût. Comment pouvait-on avoir l'idée d'aller aux toilettes à l'intérieur de sa propre maison ? Répugnant ! La seule chose utile dans le fait d'aller aux toilettes, c'était de rendre des substances minérales à la terre, mais même ça, le Peuple de la Boue avait réussi à le gâcher en traitant la... matière... avec des bouteilles remplies de produits chimiques bleuâtres. Si quelqu'un lui avait dit un siècle auparavant que les humains allaient ôter aux fertilisants tout ce qu'ils contenaient d'utile à la fertilité, elle leur aurait conseillé de se faire percer quelques trous dans le crâne pour y laisser passer un peu d'air.

Holly décrocha une paire d'ailes de son support. C'étaient des doubles ovales, avec un vieux moteur essoufflé. Elle poussa un grognement. Des Libellules. Elle détestait ce modèle. Moteur à essence, imaginez-vous ! Et plus lourd qu'un cochon sortant de son bain de boue. Le Colibri Z7, ça c'était du matériel. Silencieux comme un murmure, avec une batterie solaire alimentée par des satellites équipés de réflecteurs qui vous permettaient de faire deux fois le tour de la terre. Mais là encore, on manquait de crédits.

Le localisateur attaché à son poignet émit un bip. Elle avait le contact. Holly sortit de la capsule et descendit sur l'aire d'atterrissage. Elle se trouvait à l'intérieur d'un de ces monticules de terre camouflés, communément désignés sous le nom de « forts de fée ». C'était là que le Peuple vivait jusqu'à ce qu'il soit chassé dans les profondeurs. L'équipement technologique était modeste. Quelques écrans de contrôle pour surveiller l'extérieur et un dispositif d'autodestruction en cas de découverte intempestive par des humains.

Il n'y avait rien sur les écrans. La voie était libre. Les portes pneumatiques avaient été légèrement tordues par le troll quand il les avait forcées pour s'échapper, sinon, tout paraissait en bon état. Holly fixa les ailes sur son dos puis elle sortit dans le monde extérieur.

La nuit italienne était fraîche et vive, imprégnée d'un parfum de vigne et d'olive. Des cigales stridulaient dans l'herbe sauvage et des papillons de nuit voletaient à la lueur des étoiles. Holly ne put s'empêcher de sourire.

Ça, au moins, ça valait la peine de prendre des risques !

En parlant de risques... Elle consulta son localisateur. Le bip était beaucoup plus intense à présent. Le troll avait presque atteint les remparts de la ville ! Elle pourrait apprécier les agréments de la nature lorsque sa mission serait terminée. Pour le moment, il était temps d'agir.

Holly essaya de mettre le moteur en marche en tirant par-dessus son épaule le câble du démarreur

Rien. Elle enragea en silence. Tous les enfants gâtés de Haven-Ville avaient un Colibri lorsqu'ils partaient en vacances dans la nature, mais les membres des FAR, eux, devaient se contenter d'ailes qui, même à l'état neuf, étaient bonnes pour la ferraille. Elle tira à nouveau sur le câble, une fois, deux fois. Au troisième coup, le moteur démarra enfin, crachant dans la nuit un jet de fumée et de vapeurs d'essence.

– Il était temps, grommela Holly en poussant à fond la manette des gaz.

Les ailes se mirent en mouvement puis, dans un battement régulier, emportèrent à grand-peine le capitaine Short dans le ciel nocturne.

Même sans le localisateur, le troll aurait été facile à suivre. Il avait tout détruit sur son passage avec autant d'efficacité qu'un tunnelier. Holly volait à basse altitude, se faufilant entre les arbres et les traînées de brume, suivant les traces du troll.

Le monstre fou avait creusé un chemin en plein milieu d'une vigne, transformé un mur de pierre en décombres et terrorisé un chien de garde qui jappait lamentablement sous une haie. Holly survola alors les deux vaches.

Ce n'était pas un spectacle très réjouissant. Sans entrer dans les détails, disons simplement qu'il ne restait plus grand-chose, à part les cornes et les sabots.

Le bip accompagné d'une lumière rouge retentissait

de plus en plus fort. Plus fort signifiait plus proche. Holly voyait la ville qui s'étendait au-dessous d'elle, nichée au sommet d'une colline basse, entourée de remparts crénelés qui dataient du Moyen Age. La plupart des fenêtres étaient encore allumées. Il était temps de pratiquer un peu de magie.

Bien souvent, la magie qu'on attribue au Peuple relève simplement de la superstition. Certains de ses pouvoirs sont cependant bien réels. Par exemple, le don de guérison, le mesmer et le bouclier. Bouclier n'est d'ailleurs pas le terme qui convient. En réalité, les fées ont la faculté de faire vibrer leur corps à des fréquences si élevées qu'elles ne restent jamais au même endroit assez longtemps pour qu'on ait le temps de les voir. Les humains peuvent parfois percevoir un très léger scintillement dans l'air, lorsqu'ils regardent avec une attention suffisante – ce qui est rarement le cas. Mais quand il leur arrive de remarquer ce scintillement, ils l'attribuent généralement à un processus d'évaporation. Inventer une raison compliquée pour expliquer un phénomène simple est d'ailleurs typique du Peuple de la Boue.

Holly déclencha son bouclier. Il lui fallut un peu plus de temps qu'à l'ordinaire. Les efforts qu'elle dut produire firent apparaître des gouttes de sueur sur son front. « Je devrais véritablement accomplir le Rituel, songea-t-elle. Et le plus tôt serait le mieux. »

Un grand fracas au niveau du sol vint interrompre ses pensées. Quelque chose qui ne collait pas avec les bruits habituels de la nuit.

Holly régla les gouvernes de son engin pour aller voir de plus près. Voir seulement, se répéta-t-elle, car tel était son travail. Les officiers du service de Détection étaient envoyés en surface dans les puits à pression pour aller repérer les cibles, alors que les commandos de Récupération voyageaient dans une belle navette bien confortable.

Le troll était juste au-dessous d'elle, frappant à grands coups la muraille extérieure dont de gros morceaux de pierre se détachaient sous ses mains puissantes. Holly en eut le souffle coupé. C'était un véritable monstre ! Aussi grand qu'un éléphant et dix fois plus méchant. Mais pire encore que méchant, il était affolé.

– Allô, centre de contrôle, dit-elle dans son micro. Fugitif localisé. Situation critique en surface.

Ce fut Root lui-même qui répondit :

– Précisez, capitaine.

Holly dirigea sa caméra vidéo sur le troll.

– Fugitif en train de franchir le mur de la ville. Contact imminent avec les humains. A quelle distance se trouve la Récupération ?

– Temps estimé, cinq minutes minimum. Nous sommes encore dans la navette.

Holly se mordit la lèvre. Root était dans la navette ?

– C'est trop long, commandant. Toute la ville va exploser dans dix secondes... J'y vais.

– Négatif, Holly... capitaine Short. Vous n'y avez pas été invitée. Vous connaissez la loi. Maintenez votre position, c'est tout.

– Mais, commandant...

Root l'interrompit :

– Il n'y a pas de mais, capitaine ! Restez où vous êtes, c'est un ordre !

Holly eut l'impression que son corps tout entier n'était plus qu'un battement de cœur. Les vapeurs d'essence lui brouillaient le cerveau. Que pouvait-elle faire ? Quelle était la bonne décision ? Sauver des vies ou obéir aux ordres ?

Le troll réussit alors à ouvrir une brèche dans la muraille et une voix d'enfant déchira la nuit :

– *Aiuto* ! cria la voix.

Au secours. Une invitation à agir. Sans tarder.

– Désolée, commandant. Le troll est fou furieux et il y a des enfants en face de lui.

Elle imaginait parfaitement le visage de Root, violacé de fureur tandis qu'il crachait dans le micro :

– Je vous arracherai vos galons, Short ! Vous passerez les cent prochaines années au service des égouts !

Mais c'était inutile. Holly avait débranché son propre micro et s'était lancée sur les traces du troll.

Tendant son corps pour améliorer l'aérodynamique, le capitaine Short s'engouffra dans la brèche que le troll avait ouverte dans la muraille. Elle se retrouva dans ce qui paraissait être un restaurant. Et un restaurant bondé. Le troll, momentanément aveuglé par la lumière électrique, gesticulait de tous ses membres au milieu de la salle.

Les clients étaient pétrifiés. Même l'enfant qui avait appelé au secours restait à présent sans voix. Les convives, bouche bée, immobiles sur leurs chaises, semblaient un peu ridicules avec les chapeaux pointus qu'ils avaient coiffés pour faire la fête. Les serveurs s'étaient figés sur place, de grands plateaux de pâtes frémissant entre leurs mains tremblantes. Des bébés italiens joufflus se couvraient les yeux de leurs doigts potelés. C'était toujours comme ça, au début : un silence stupéfait.

Ensuite venaient les hurlements.

Une bouteille de vin se brisa par terre. La fascination fut rompue. Le tohu-bohu se déclencha. Holly fit la grimace. Les trolls détestaient le bruit presque autant que la lumière.

La créature souleva ses épaules massives et velues, ses griffes rétractables jaillirent de ses doigts avec un bruit sinistre. Scrîîîîk ! Comportement classique du prédateur. La bête était sur le point d'attaquer.

Holly sortit son arme et la régla sur la position

numéro deux. Elle n'avait pas le droit de tuer le troll, quelles que soient les circonstances. Pas pour sauver des humains. Mais elle pouvait sans nul doute le mettre hors de combat en attendant l'arrivée du commando de Récupération.

Visant le point faible à la base du crâne, elle infligea au troll une longue décharge de rayons ionisants à haute concentration. La créature vacilla, fit quelques pas en trébuchant, puis fut saisie d'une fureur intense.

« Ce n'est pas grave, pensa Holly, j'ai déclenché mon bouclier. » Elle était invisible. Quiconque regarderait dans sa direction penserait que le rayon bleu de son arme venait de nulle part.

Le troll se tourna vers elle, ses dreadlocks crasseuses oscillant comme des chandelles.

« Pas de panique. Il ne peut pas me voir. »

Le troll s'empara d'une table.

« Invisible. Totalement invisible. »

Il leva son bras hirsute et la lança.

« Juste un léger scintillement dans l'air. »

La table fut projetée droit vers sa tête.

Holly fit un pas de côté. Une seconde trop tard. La table heurta l'engin attaché sur son dos et arracha le réservoir d'essence qui se mit à tournoyer dans les airs en répandant son contenu inflammable.

Comme chacun sait, les restaurants italiens sont pleins de chandelles. Le réservoir passa au-dessus d'un candélabre ornementé qui explosa comme un feu d'artifice meurtrier. La plus grande partie de l'essence se déversa sur le troll. Et Holly tomba sur lui à son tour.

Le troll la voyait. Impossible d'en douter. Il la regardait en plissant les yeux pour se protéger de la lumière haïe, ses sourcils crispés en une grimace de douleur apeurée. Le bouclier de Holly ne fonctionnait plus. Ses réserves de magie étaient épuisées.

Holly se tortillait entre les mains du troll pour essayer de lui échapper. C'était inutile. Les doigts de la créature avaient la taille d'une banane mais ils étaient beaucoup moins tendres. Sauvagement, sans effort, ils lui écrasaient la cage thoracique pour en faire sortir jusqu'au dernier souffle d'air. Des griffes pointues comme des aiguilles s'enfonçaient dans le tissu renforcé de son uniforme. Dans un instant, elles allaient parvenir à le transpercer et ce serait la fin.

Holly n'avait plus les idées claires. Le restaurant était devenu une sorte de manège chaotique. Le troll faisait grincer ses défenses et des molaires graisseuses essayaient de mordre son casque. Holly sentait son haleine fétide à travers ses filtres. Elle sentait aussi une odeur de fourrure brûlée à mesure que le feu se répandait le long du dos de la créature.

La langue verdâtre de la bête passa sur sa visière en laissant une traînée gluante. La visière ! C'était ça, la dernière chance. Holly réussit à glisser sa main libre jusqu'aux commandes de son casque. Les feux de tunnel. Pleins phares.

Elle appuya sur le bouton incurvé et huit cents watts de lumière non filtrée jaillirent aussitôt des deux projecteurs, au-dessus de ses yeux.

Le troll se cabra, un cri perçant jaillit comme une explosion d'entre ses dents monstrueuses. Des dizaines de verres et de bouteilles volèrent en éclats sur les tables et les étagères. C'en était trop pour la malheureuse créature. Frappée par un rayon ionisant, embrasée et maintenant aveuglée. Le choc et la douleur s'insinuèrent jusqu'à son cerveau minuscule en lui ordonnant de se mettre hors service. Le troll obéit, s'abattant sur le sol avec une raideur presque comique. Holly dut rouler sur elle-même pour éviter une de ses défenses qui menaçait de la faucher.

Il y eut un silence total, en dehors des tintements de verre, du crépitement de la fourrure en feu et des soupirs de soulagement soudain exhalés. Holly se releva péniblement. Une multitude de regards s'étaient fixés sur elle – des regards humains. Elle était visible à cent pour cent. Pour l'instant, ces humains paraissaient plutôt satisfaits mais ils ne le resteraient pas très longtemps. Ce n'était pas l'habitude, dans cette espèce. Une manœuvre d'apaisement s'imposait.

Holly leva ses mains vides. Un geste de paix.

– *Scusatemi tutti*, dit-elle, les mots coulant sans effort de sa bouche.

Les Italiens, toujours courtois et élégants, murmurèrent que ce n'était rien du tout.

Holly plongea lentement la main dans sa poche et en sortit une petite sphère qu'elle posa par terre, au milieu de la salle.

– *Guardate*, dit-elle. Regardez.

Les clients du restaurant obéirent, se penchant en avant pour observer la petite boule d'argent. Elle émettait un tic-tac de plus en plus rapide comme un compte à rebours. Elle tourna le dos à la sphère. Trois, deux, un...

Boum ! Flash ! Perte de conscience collective. Rien de grave, de simples maux de tête une quarantaine de minutes plus tard. Holly soupira. Sauvée. Pour le moment. Elle se précipita vers la porte et ferma le loquet. Personne ne pouvait plus ni sortir ni entrer. Sauf par la grande brèche ouverte dans le mur. Elle éteignit ensuite la fourrure fumante du troll à l'aide de l'extincteur du restaurant en espérant que la poudre glacée n'allait pas réveiller le monstre endormi.

Holly contempla le gâchis qu'elle avait provoqué. On pouvait sans nul doute parler de ravages. Pire qu'à Hambourg. Root allait l'écorcher vive. Elle aimerait encore mieux affronter le troll. C'était certainement la fin de sa carrière mais tout cela lui sembla soudain sans importance, car ses côtes étaient devenues douloureuses et un mal de tête fulgurant lui brouillait la vue.

Peut-être devrait-elle se reposer quelques instants pour reprendre ses esprits avant l'arrivée du commando de Récupération.

Holly ne se donna même pas la peine de trouver une chaise. Ses jambes fléchirent et elle se laissa tomber sur le linoléum à damier.

Se réveiller devant le visage aux yeux exorbités du commandant Root avait de quoi nourrir les pires cauchemars. Holly battit des paupières ; pendant un instant, elle aurait juré avoir vu une lueur d'inquiétude dans ces yeux-là. Mais la lueur disparut aussitôt, remplacée par l'habituelle fureur qui gonflait dangereusement ses veines.

– Capitaine Short ! rugit-il, sans se soucier du mal de tête de Holly. Est-ce que vous pouvez m'expliquer ce que signifie toute cette folie ?

Elle se releva, les jambes tremblantes.

– Je... C'est-à-dire... Il y a eu...

Elle était incapable de faire une phrase.

– Vous avez désobéi à un ordre direct. Je vous avais dit de rester où vous étiez ! Vous savez très bien qu'il est interdit d'entrer dans un lieu occupé par des humains sans y avoir été invité.

Holly chassa les ombres qui lui obscurcissaient la vue.

– Justement, j'ai été invitée. Un enfant a appelé au secours.

– Vous êtes sur des sables mouvants, Short.

– Il y a un précédent, commandant. Vous vous souvenez du procès qui a opposé le caporal Rowe à l'État ? Le jury a estimé que les appels au secours de la femme prise au piège pouvaient être considérés comme une invitation à entrer dans le bâtiment. De toute façon, vous êtes là, maintenant. Ce qui signifie que vous aussi, vous avez accepté l'invitation.

– Mmmm, marmonna Root d'un air dubitatif. Je pense que vous avez eu de la chance. Les choses auraient pu être pires.

Holly regarda autour d'elle. Il était difficile d'imaginer que les choses puissent être encore pires. Le restaurant était dévasté et il y avait quarante humains K.O. Les techniciens étaient en train de fixer des électrodes sur les tempes des convives inconscients.

– On a réussi à boucler le secteur, bien que la moitié de la ville soit venue tambouriner à la porte.

– Et la brèche dans le mur ?

Root eut un petit rire.

– Voyez vous-même.

Holly jeta un coup d'œil. En bricolant les prises électriques du restaurant, le commando de Récupération avait réussi à brancher un appareil à hologrammes qui projetait sur la brèche l'image d'un mur intact. Les hologrammes étaient pratiques pour les camouflages rapides mais ne résistaient pas à un examen attentif. Quiconque y aurait regardé d'un peu plus près n'aurait pas manqué de remarquer que le raccord, légèrement transparent, était la réplique exacte du morceau de mur situé juste à côté. On pouvait notamment observer deux fissures en forme de toile d'araignée rigoureusement identiques et deux reproductions du même Rembrandt.

Mais les clients du restaurant n'étaient pas en état d'examiner quoi que ce soit et lorsqu'ils auraient repris connaissance, le mur aurait été réparé par la division Télécinétique et cet épisode surnaturel aurait été entièrement effacé de leur mémoire

Un sous-officier du commando de Récupération surgit soudain des toilettes.

– Commandant !

– Oui, sergent ?

– Il y a un humain là-dedans, mon commandant. L'assommoir ne l'a pas atteint. Il vient par ici. Il arrive !

– Boucliers ! aboya Root. Tout le monde !

Holly essaya. Elle fit ce qu'elle put. Mais elle n'y arriva pas. Son pouvoir magique était complètement épuisé.

Un bambin sortit alors des toilettes, les yeux ensommeillés. Il pointa vers Holly un index potelé.

– *Ciao, folletta*, dit-il, avant de grimper sur les genoux de son père pour continuer son somme.

Root refit son apparition dans le spectre du visible. Il était plus furieux que jamais, si toutefois c'était possible.

– Qu'est-ce qui est arrivé à votre bouclier, Short ?

Holly déglutit avec difficulté.

– Le stress, commandant, répondit-elle en espérant se montrer convaincante.

Mais Root ne voulut rien entendre.

– Vous m'avez menti, capitaine. Vous n'êtes pas du tout chauffée au rouge, question magie.

Elle hocha silencieusement la tête.

– Il y a combien de temps que vous avez accompli le Rituel pour la dernière fois ?

Holly se mordit la lèvre.

– Je dirais... environ... quatre ans, commandant.

Root faillit avoir une attaque.

– Quatre... quatre ans ? C'est un miracle que vous ayez duré aussi longtemps ! Vous allez vous en occuper dès maintenant. Cette nuit ! Je ne veux plus vous voir sous terre sans vos pouvoirs. Vous êtes un danger pour vous-même et pour vos collègues officiers !

– Oui, commandant.

– Demandez à la Récupération de vous donner un Colibri et filez droit vers le Vieux Pays. C'est la pleine lune, ce soir.

– Oui, commandant.

– Et n'imaginez pas que je vais oublier les dégâts que vous avez faits dans ce restaurant. Nous en reparlerons à votre retour.

– Oui, commandant. Bien, commandant.

Holly tourna les talons mais Root s'éclaircit la gorge pour attirer son attention.

– Ah, et aussi, capitaine Short...

– Oui, commandant ?

Le visage de Root avait perdu son teint violacé et il semblait presque gêné.

– Vous avez bien fait de sauver toutes ces vies. Ça aurait pu être pire, bien pire.

Holly rayonna derrière la visière de son casque. Après tout, peut-être qu'elle ne serait pas renvoyée des FARfadet.

– Merci, commandant.

Root grogna et son teint reprit sa couleur écarlate.

– Maintenant, filez d'ici. Et ne vous avisez pas de reparaître devant moi avant d'avoir fait le plein de magie jusqu'au bout des oreilles !

Holly soupira. Fini les félicitations.

– Oui, commandant. Je pars immédiatement, commandant.

CHAPITRE IV
ENLÈVEMENT

La difficulté essentielle à laquelle Artemis se trouvait confronté, c'était la localisation – comment faire pour repérer un farfadet ?

Toutes ces fées étaient décidément très rusées : elles avaient réussi à se promener un peu partout pendant Dieu sait combien de millénaires sans qu'on ait jamais pu en saisir la moindre photo, la moindre image vidéo.

Pas même sous forme d'une mystification genre monstre du Loch Ness. C'était à n'en pas douter une communauté peu sociable, mais d'une grande intelligence. Personne n'avait jamais réussi à mettre la main sur la moindre pépite d'or des fées.

Il faut dire que personne jusqu'à présent n'avait jamais eu accès au Livre.

Et les énigmes devenaient si simples à résoudre lorsqu'on en possédait la clé.

Artemis avait convoqué les Butler dans son bureau

et leur donnait quelques explications, un petit pupitre posé devant lui.

– Il existe certains rituels que chaque fée doit accomplir pour renouveler son pouvoir magique, déclara-t-il.

Butler et Juliet acquiescèrent d'un signe de tête, comme s'il s'agissait d'un exposé de routine.

Artemis feuilleta le Livre qu'il avait imprimé sur papier et en choisit un passage.

De la terre s'écoule ta puissance,
Sache la prendre avec reconnaissance.
Tu dois cueillir la magie en sa graine
Là où se rencontrent la lune pleine,
Une eau sinueuse, ainsi qu'un très vieux chêne.
Loin de ce lieu replante alors la graine
Pour que soit rendu ailleurs à la terre
Le cadeau offert près de la rivière.

Artemis referma le volume.

– Vous comprenez ?

Butler et Juliet firent un nouveau signe de tête affirmatif tout en paraissant totalement déconcertés.

Artemis soupira.

– Les farfadets sont tenus de se soumettre à certains

rituels. Je dirais même des rituels très précis. Nous pourrions nous servir de ça pour repérer une de ces créatures.

Juliet leva la main comme une écolière, bien qu'elle eût quatre ans de plus qu'Artemis.

– Oui ?

– Ce que je voudrais dire, Artemis... commença-t-elle d'un ton hésitant.

Elle tortilla entre ses doigts une mèche de cheveux blonds avec ce geste particulier qui paraissait si séduisant à bon nombre de voyous des environs.

– Ce que je voudrais dire, c'est que cette histoire de farfadets...

Artemis fronça les sourcils. C'était mauvais signe

– Explique-toi, Juliet.

– Eh bien, les farfadets n'existent pas vraiment, tout le monde sait ça.

Butler fit la grimace. En fait, c'était sa faute. Il n'avait jamais pris la peine d'informer sa sœur des paramètres de la mission.

Artemis lui lança un regard réprobateur.

– Butler ne t'a pas encore mise au courant ?

– Non, pourquoi ? Il devait le faire ?

– Sans aucun doute. Il a peut-être cru que tu te moquerais de lui.

Butler se tortilla sur sa chaise.

C'était exactement ce qu'il avait pensé. Juliet était la seule personne au monde qui se permettait de se moquer de lui avec une régularité embarrassante. La plupart de ceux qui se risquaient à cet exercice ne le faisaient qu'une seule fois. Une seule.

Artemis s'éclaircit la gorge.

– Nous allons partir du postulat que le peuple des fées existe bel et bien et que je ne suis pas un crétin délirant.

Butler exprima son approbation d'un faible signe de tête. Juliet ne paraissait pas convaincue.

– Bien. Comme je le disais, les créatures du Peuple doivent accomplir un rituel bien précis pour renouveler leurs pouvoirs. Selon mon interprétation du texte que je vous ai lu, il leur faut ramasser une graine tombée d'un très vieux chêne près d'une rivière qui forme un méandre. Et ce geste doit être accompli par une nuit de pleine lune.

Une lueur s'alluma dans le regard de Butler.

– Donc, tout ce qui nous reste à faire...

– C'est d'établir à l'aide des satellites météo une liste des endroits possibles. Je m'en suis déjà occupé. Croyez-moi si vous voulez, il ne reste pas tellement de très vieux chênes, si on entend par vieux un siècle ou plus. Quand on ajoute un méandre de rivière et une pleine lune bien visible, on obtient exactement cent vingt-neuf sites à observer dans tout le pays.

Butler sourit. Une mission de surveillance. Le maître parlait enfin un langage qu'il comprenait.

– Il va falloir procéder à des aménagements pour

accueillir notre hôte, dit Artemis en tendant à Juliet une feuille de papier A4. La cave devra être modifiée selon ces indications. Tu y veilleras, Juliet. En respectant le plan à la lettre.

- Oui, Arty.

Artemis eut un froncement de sourcils, mais à peine perceptible. Pour des raisons qu'il avait du mal à analyser, il lui était assez indifférent que Juliet l'appelle par le diminutif que sa mère lui avait donné.

Butler se gratta le menton d'un air songeur. Artemis remarqua son geste.

– Une question ?

– Eh bien, voilà, Artemis. La fée de Hô Chi Minh-Ville...

Le garçon hocha la tête.

– Je sais. Pourquoi ne l'avons-nous pas enlevée, tout simplement ?

– C'est ça, monsieur.

– Si l'on en croit l'*Almanach du peuple de Chi Lun*, un manuscrit du VIIe siècle retrouvé dans la cité perdue de Sh'shamo : « Dès lors qu'une fée aura pris des spiritueux avec le Peuple de la Boue » – ça, c'est nous – « elle sera à tout jamais morte pour ses frères et pour ses sœurs. » Nous n'avions donc aucune garantie que la fée d'Hô Chi Minh-Ville puisse valoir la moindre once d'or. Non, mon cher ami, nous avons besoin de sang neuf. C'est clair ?

Butler approuva d'un signe de tête.

– Très bien. A présent, voici divers objets que vous devrez vous procurer pour nos escapades au clair de lune.

Butler lut la liste : équipement de base pour sorties en plein air, quelques petites choses qui pouvaient provoquer un ou deux haussements de sourcils mais, dans l'ensemble, rien de trop déconcertant, à part...

– Des lunettes de soleil ? En pleine nuit ?

Lorsque Artemis souriait, ce qui était le cas en cet instant, on s'attendait presque à voir des dents de vampire jaillir de ses gencives.

– Oui, Butler. Des lunettes de soleil. Faites-moi confiance.

Et Butler lui faisait confiance. Aveuglément.

Holly activa le système de réchauffement de sa combinaison et monta à quatre mille mètres d'altitude. Les ailes du Colibri étaient les meilleures qu'on puisse trouver. L'indicateur de la batterie affichait quatre barres rouges – plus qu'il n'en fallait pour une rapide excursion au-dessus de l'Europe et des îles Britanniques. Bien entendu le règlement exigeait qu'on voyage toujours au-dessus des mers et des océans lorsque c'était possible mais Holly ne pouvait jamais résister au plaisir d'aller taquiner les sommets enneigés des Alpes.

La combinaison la protégeait contre la rigueur des éléments mais elle sentait quand même le froid s'insinuer jusque dans ses os. A cette altitude, la lune paraissait immense, on distinguait nettement ses cratères. Ce soir, elle formait une sphère parfaite. Une pleine lune magique. Les services de l'Immigration ne sauraient plus où donner de la tête lorsque les milliers de fées nostalgiques de la surface suivraient leur envie irrésistible de remonter à l'air libre. Nombre d'entre elles parviendraient à passer et se livreraient à des réjouissances qui provoqueraient sans doute un beau tumulte. Le manteau de la terre était sillonné de tunnels clandestins et il était impossible à la police de les surveiller tous.

Holly suivit la côte italienne jusqu'à Monaco puis mit le cap sur les Alpes françaises. Elle adorait voler, comme toutes les fées. D'après le Livre, elles étaient jadis dotées de leurs propres ailes, mais l'évolution les en avait privées par la suite. Seuls les lutins en avaient encore. Il existait une école de pensée selon laquelle le Peuple descendrait des dinosaures ailés. Peut-être des ptérodactyles. La structure du squelette dans la partie supérieure du corps était très semblable. Cette théorie expliquait la protubérance osseuse présente sur chaque omoplate.

Holly songea à aller visiter Disneyland Paris. Les FAR disposaient d'agents secrets en poste sur place, la plupart employés sur le stand Blanche-Neige. C'était l'un des rares endroits à la surface de la terre où le Peuple pouvait passer inaperçu. Mais si un touriste prenait une photo d'elle, qui finissait sur Internet, Root lui ferait certainement sauter ses galons. Avec un soupir de regret elle passa sans s'arrêter au-dessus de la gerbe des feux d'artifice multicolore qui s'élevait du sol.

Arrivée sur la Manche, Holly vola à basse altitude, sautillant parmi les vagues aux crêtes d'écume. Elle appela les dauphins qui remontèrent à la surface, bondissant dans l'eau pour suivre son allure. Elle voyait sur eux les dégâts causés par la pollution, leur peau décolorée, les plaies rouges sur leur dos. Elle avait beau sourire, elle avait le cœur brisé. Le Peuple de la Boue avait décidément beaucoup de comptes à rendre.

Enfin, la côte se dessina devant elle. Le Vieux Pays. Eire, la terre où commença le temps. L'endroit le plus magique de la planète. C'était ici, dix mille ans plus tôt, que l'ancienne race des fées, les Dé Danann, avait combattu les démoniaques Fomors, traçant la célèbre chaussée des Géants par la puissance de leurs déflagrations magiques. C'était là que se dressait la *Lia Fáil*, la pierre de la Destinée, le centre de l'univers, où les rois des fées et plus tard les *Ard Rí* humains, les grands rois, étaient couronnés. C'était là aussi, malheureusement, que le Peuple de la Boue était le plus réceptif à la magie, et les cas d'observation de fées par des humains y étaient plus nombreux que partout ailleurs sur la planète. Par chance, le reste du monde considérait les Irlandais comme des fous, une opinion que les Irlandais eux-mêmes ne faisaient rien pour démentir. Ils avaient fini par se mettre dans la tête que toutes les fées traînaient une marmite d'or avec elles partout où elles allaient. Il était vrai que les FAR disposaient de fonds secrets destinés à payer une éventuelle rançon, en raison des risques élevés que couraient leurs officiers, mais aucun humain n'avait jamais réussi à en obtenir la moindre parcelle. Ce qui n'empêchait pas la population irlandaise en général de rôder sous les arcs-en-ciel en espérant gagner le gros lot.

Mais, en dépit de tout cela, s'il y avait une catégorie d'êtres humains avec laquelle le Peuple ressentait une affinité, c'étaient bien les Irlandais.

Peut-être était-ce dû à leur excentricité, ou à leur dévotion au *craic*, le mot qu'ils emploient pour désigner la fête – dans les pubs où coule la bière. Et si véritablement le Peuple était apparenté aux humains, comme le prétendait une autre théorie, il y avait de bonnes raisons de croire que tout avait commencé sur l'île d'Émeraude.

Holly fit apparaître une carte sur le localisateur qu'elle portait au poignet et déclencha le système de repérage pour déterminer les lieux chargés de magie. Le meilleur endroit serait évidemment Tara, à proximité de la pierre de la Destinée mais, une nuit comme celle-ci, toutes les fées traditionalistes munies d'un laissez-passer avaient dû venir danser sur le site sacré ; il valait donc mieux y renoncer.

Il existait un autre endroit proche, sur la côte sud-est. Facilement accessible par les airs, mais lointain et désolé pour des humains voyageant par voie terrestre. Holly réduisit les gaz et descendit jusqu'à quatre-vingts mètres. Elle survola une forêt d'arbres aux branches hérissées, puis arriva au-dessus d'une clairière éclairée par la lune. Le fil argenté d'une rivière traversait un pré et là, niché au creux d'un méandre, s'élevait fièrement un vieux chêne.

Holly consulta son localisateur pour détecter les formes de vie alentour. Jugeant que les deux vaches qui dormaient dans un pré voisin ne représentaient aucune menace, elle coupa son moteur et se laissa planer jusqu'au pied de l'arbre au tronc imposant.

Quatre mois à guetter. Même Butler, le professionnel aguerri, commençait à redouter les longues nuits humides, peuplées d'insectes affamés. Par bonheur, la lune n'était pas pleine toutes les nuits.

C'était toujours la même chose. Ils restaient accroupis dans leur abri d'aluminium, sans faire le moindre bruit, Butler consultant ses instruments à intervalles réguliers tandis qu'Artemis observait fixement les lieux à l'aide de son périscope. Dans des moments comme celui-ci, la nature semblait assourdissante, au sein de leur espace confiné. Butler avait envie de siffler, de parler, de faire n'importe quoi pour briser leur silence anormal. Mais la concentration d'Artemis était totale. Il ne tolérait aucune interférence, aucune interruption. Il était là pour affaires.

Cette nuit, ils se trouvaient dans le Sud-Est. Sur le site le plus inaccessible qu'ils aient trouvé jusqu'à présent. Butler avait dû faire trois voyages entre la Jeep et leur lieu d'observation pour transporter l'équipement. Il fallait franchir une clôture, une tourbière et deux prés. Ses bottes et son pantalon étaient fichus. Et maintenant, il devait s'asseoir dans la cachette sur un sol détrempé qui imprégnait d'humidité le fond de son pantalon. Artemis, lui, avait réussi à ne pas avoir la moindre tache sur ses vêtements.

L'abri était d'une conception très ingénieuse et les droits d'exploitation industrielle avaient déjà suscité un certain intérêt – surtout de la part de représentants de l'armée – mais Artemis avait décidé de vendre son brevet à une multinationale spécialisée dans les équipements sportifs.

Il s'agissait d'un polymère d'aluminium élastique

tendu sur une structure en fibre de verre articulée par une multitude de charnières. L'aluminium, semblable à celui utilisé par la NASA, emprisonnait la chaleur à l'intérieur, empêchant ainsi l'enveloppe extérieure de chauffer sous son camouflage. Ce procédé permettait d'éviter que les animaux sensibles à la chaleur détectent sa présence. Grâce aux charnières, l'abri pouvait changer de forme avec presque la même facilité qu'un liquide, s'adaptant à n'importe quel creux dans lequel on le laissait tomber. Cachette immédiate et poste d'observation.

Il suffisait pour l'installer de poser le sac fermé par une bande Velcro dans un trou et de tirer le cordon.

Mais toute l'ingéniosité du monde ne pouvait améliorer l'atmosphère qui régnait dans l'abri. Quelque chose tracassait Artemis. On le voyait nettement aux rides précoces qui dessinaient des pattes-d'oie au coin de ses yeux d'un bleu profond.

Après plusieurs nuits passées en vaine surveillance, Butler rassembla suffisamment de courage pour poser la question...

– Artemis, commença-t-il d'un ton hésitant, je sais que ce n'est pas mon rôle de dire ça, mais je sens bien quand quelque chose ne va pas. Et si je peux faire n'importe quoi pour aider...

Artemis resta silencieux un long moment. Et pendant ce long moment, Butler eut devant lui le visage d'un très jeune garçon. Le jeune garçon qu'Artemis aurait pu être.

– C'est à cause de ma mère, dit-il enfin. Je commence à me demander si elle arrivera jamais à...

A cet instant, le voyant rouge qui signalait une présence proche se mit à clignoter.

Holly accrocha ses ailes à une branche basse et enleva son casque pour donner un peu d'air à ses oreilles. Il fallait faire attention aux oreilles d'elfe – quelques heures sous un casque suffisaient à les faire peler. Elle en massa les extrémités. La peau n'était pas sèche, grâce au régime d'hydratation qu'elle s'imposait quotidiennement, à la différence de certains officiers masculins des FAR. Lorsqu'ils enlevaient leur casque, on avait l'impression qu'il s'était mis à neiger.

Holly prit le temps d'admirer la vue. L'Irlande était décidément très pittoresque. Même le Peuple de la Boue n'avait pas réussi à la détruire. Pas encore, en tout cas... Il faudrait lui donner encore un siècle ou deux. La rivière ondulait doucement devant elle comme un serpent argenté et un murmure s'élevait de l'eau qui ruisselait sur un affleurement de pierres. Le chêne craquait au-dessus de sa tête, ses branches frottant les unes contre les autres dans la brise vivifiante.

Et maintenant, au travail. Elle pourrait jouer les touristes la nuit entière une fois qu'elle en aurait terminé. Une graine. Elle avait besoin d'une graine.

Holly se pencha sur le sol, écartant les feuilles séchées et les brindilles qui couvraient le sol d'argile. Ses doigts se refermèrent sur un gland du chêne. « Ce n'était vraiment pas difficile », songea-t-elle. Tout ce qu'il lui restait à faire, c'était de le planter quelque part, dans un autre endroit et, aussitôt, ses pouvoirs magiques jailliraient à nouveau en elle.

Butler consulta le radar portable en coupant le son pour qu'il ne risque pas de trahir leur présence. Le faisceau rouge balayait l'écran avec une indolence exaspérante, puis soudain... Flash ! Une silhouette verticale à côté de l'arbre. Trop petite pour être celle d'un adulte, avec des proportions qui ne correspondaient pas à celles d'un enfant. Il se tourna vers Artemis en levant le pouce. On y était peut-être.

Artemis approuva d'un signe de tête, fixant sur son front ses lunettes de soleil à verres réfléchissants. Butler l'imita puis enleva le cache du viseur à infrarouge de son arme. Son fusil à fléchettes n'avait rien d'un modèle ordinaire. Il avait été spécialement fabriqué pour un chasseur d'ivoire kenyan et pouvait tirer des rafales avec la rapidité et la portée d'une kalachnikov.

Butler l'avait acheté pour une bouchée de pain à un fonctionnaire de l'administration après l'exécution du braconnier.

Ils s'avancèrent au cœur de la nuit dans un silence qui témoignait d'une longue pratique. La petite silhouette qui se tenait devant eux ôta un appareil attaché à ses épaules et souleva son casque intégral, révélant un visage qui, de toute évidence, n'était pas celui d'un humain. Butler passa la lanière du fusil deux fois autour de son poignet, appuyant la crosse contre son épaule. Il activa le viseur et un point rouge apparut au milieu du dos de la silhouette.

Artemis fit un signe de tête et son serviteur pressa la détente.

Bien qu'une telle coïncidence n'eût pas plus d'une chance sur un million de se produire, ce fut à ce moment précis que la silhouette se pencha vers le sol.

Quelque chose siffla au-dessus de la tête de Holly, quelque chose qui étincela à la lueur des étoiles. La fée avait suffisamment d'expérience de terrain pour comprendre qu'on lui tirait dessus et elle se roula aussitôt en boule pour réduire la surface de la cible.

Elle dégaina son arme, roulant à nouveau sur elle-même pour se mettre à l'abri de l'arbre. Dans sa tête défilèrent toutes sortes d'hypothèses. Qui pouvait bien lui tirer dessus et pourquoi ?

Quelque chose attendait à côté de l'arbre. Quelque chose qui avait à peu près la taille d'une montagne, en beaucoup plus mobile.

– Jolie petite pétoire, dit la silhouette avec un sourire, en faisant disparaître la main et l'arme de Holly dans un poing de la taille d'un melon.

La fée parvint à dégager ses doigts une nano seconde avant qu'ils ne se brisent comme des spaghetti.

– J'imagine que vous n'envisagez pas de vous rendre pacifiquement ? dit une voix glaciale derrière elle.

Holly fit volte-face, les coudes levés, prête au combat.

– Non, bien sûr, soupira le garçon. Je m'y attendais.

La fée s'efforça d'arborer une expression héroïque.

– Arrière, humain. Tu ne sais pas à qui tu as affaire.

Le garçon éclata de rire.

– Je crois plutôt, madame la fée, que c'est vous qui ne comprenez pas très bien la situation.

Madame la fée ? Il savait donc qu'elle était une fée.

– J'ai des pouvoirs magiques, monsieur le ver de vase. Suffisants pour transformer votre gorille en crotte de cochon.

Le garçon s'avança d'un pas.

– Courageux discours, madame. Malheureusement pour vous, ce sont des mensonges. Si vous aviez, comme vous le dites, des pouvoirs magiques, nul doute que vous en auriez déjà fait usage. Non, en réalité, je vous soupçonne d'être restée trop longtemps sans accomplir le Rituel et d'être venue ici pour refaire le plein de magie.

Holly était stupéfaite. Elle avait face à elle un humain qui dissertait avec désinvolture sur les secrets les plus sacrés. C'était un désastre. Une catastrophe. Voilà qui pouvait signifier la fin de siècles de paix. Si les humains apprenaient l'existence d'une sous-culture féerique, il ne se passerait pas longtemps avant qu'une guerre éclate entre les deux espèces. Elle devait absolument faire quelque chose et il ne lui restait plus qu'une seule arme dans son arsenal.

Le mesmer est la forme la plus élémentaire de magie et n'exige qu'un très faible pouvoir. Il existe même des humains qui ont un certain don dans ce domaine.

Même une fée vidée de ses facultés magiques peut encore soumettre à son emprise l'esprit de n'importe quel humain.

Holly fit appel aux dernières ressources de magie qui subsistaient à la base de son crâne.

– Monsieur l'humain, dit-elle, sa voix devenant soudain grave, à partir de cet instant, votre volonté sera soumise à la mienne.

Artemis sourit, parfaitement protégé par ses lunettes réfléchissantes.

– J'en doute, dit-il avec un bref signe de tête.

Holly sentit la piqûre de la fléchette qui venait de transpercer le tissu renforcé de sa combinaison, répandant aussitôt dans son épaule un anesthésique à base de curare et de chlorure de succinylcholine. Le monde se décomposa alors en une multitude de bulles colorées et, malgré tous ses efforts, Holly ne put se concentrer que sur une seule pensée. Une pensée qui pouvait se résumer ainsi : comment savaient-ils ? La question tourbillonna dans sa tête tandis qu'elle plongeait dans l'inconscience. Comment savaient-ils ? Comment savaient-ils ? Comment sav...

Artemis vit la douleur dans les yeux de la créature au moment où l'aiguille s'enfonça dans son corps.

Pendant un instant, il éprouva un certain malaise. Une fille, une femme, comme Juliet ou sa mère. Puis l'instant passa et il redevint lui-même.

– Bien visé, dit-il en se penchant pour examiner leur prisonnière.

C'était une fille, impossible d'en douter. Et jolie, en plus. Pour ceux qui aimaient le genre pointu.

– Monsieur ?

– Mmm ?

Butler montrait le casque de la créature. Il était à moitié enfoui dans un tas de feuilles mortes, là où la fée l'avait laissé tomber. Un bourdonnement s'en échappait.

Artemis ramassa le casque par sa lanière, cherchant l'origine du bruit.

– Ah, voilà.

Il sortit la caméra vidéo de son logement et prit bien soin de tourner l'objectif dans la direction opposée.

– Technologie de fée. Très impressionnant, marmonna-t-il en faisant sauter la batterie de sa rainure.

La caméra émit un grésillement puis se tut.

– Énergie nucléaire, si je ne me trompe. Nous devrons prendre garde à ne pas sous-estimer nos adversaires.

Butler aquiesça d'un signe de tête et allongea leur captive dans un énorme sac de voyage. Il aurait une charge supplémentaire à porter lorsqu'il traverserait dans l'autre sens les deux prés, la tourbière et la clôture.

CHAPITRE V

PORTÉE DISPARUE

Le commandant Root mâchonnait un cigare au champignon particulièrement pestilentiel. Plusieurs membres du commando de Récupération s'étaient déjà évanouis dans la navette.

Même la puanteur qui s'élevait du troll menotté semblait légère en comparaison. Bien entendu, personne ne faisait la moindre remarque, leur chef étant plus sensible qu'un furoncle infecté au milieu d'une fesse.

Foaly, pour sa part, prenait un malin plaisir à contrarier son supérieur.

– Je ne veux pas de vos cigares nauséabonds ici, commandant ! hennit-il à l'instant où Root fit son retour dans la salle des opérations. Les ordinateurs ne supportent pas la fumée !

Root se renfrogna, convaincu qu'il s'agissait là d'une invention de Foaly. Mais il ne voulait pas prendre le risque de provoquer une panne d'ordinateur au milieu d'une alerte et il éteignit son cigare en le trempant dans la tasse de café d'un gremlin qui passait à portée de main.

– Maintenant, Foaly, parlez-moi un peu de cette prétendue alerte. Et cette fois, j'espère pour vous que c'est vrai !

Le centaure avait une nette tendance à se mettre dans tous ses états pour des vétilles. Un jour, il avait alerté le Defcon 2 à cause d'une interruption dans les transmissions de ses stations satellites humaines.

– Cette fois-ci, c'est pour de bon, assura Foaly. Je devrais plutôt dire pour le pire.

Root sentit son ulcère à l'estomac se réveiller comme un volcan.

– Qu'est-ce que vous entendez par le pire ?

Foaly montra l'Irlande sur l'image d'Eurosat.

– Nous avons perdu le contact avec le capitaine Short.

– On va encore se demander pourquoi ça ne me surprend pas, grogna Root en plongeant son visage dans ses mains.

– On l'a suivie pendant tout son trajet au-dessus des Alpes.

– Les Alpes ? Elle est passée au-dessus des terres ?

Foaly acquiesça d'un signe de tête.

– C'est contraire au règlement, je sais. Mais tout le monde le fait.

Le commandant approuva à contrecœur. Qui pourrait résister à une telle vue ? Lorsqu'il n'était encore qu'un bleu, on avait fait un rapport sur lui pour la même raison.

– O.K. La suite. Quand est-ce qu'on l'a perdue ?

Foaly brancha un lecteur vidéo sur l'écran.

– Voilà les images envoyées par le casque de Holly. Ici, nous survolons Disneyland Paris...

Le centaure appuya sur la touche d'avance rapide.

– Là, les dauphins de la Manche avec le folklore habituel, maintenant, les côtes d'Irlande. Pour l'instant, tout va bien. Regardez, son localisateur entre dans le champ. Le capitaine Short cherche les endroits magiques. Le site 57 apparaît en rouge, elle met donc le cap dans cette direction.

– Pourquoi pas à Tara ?

Foaly s'ébroua.

– Tara ? Tous les hippies que compte le peuple des fées dans l'hémisphère Nord vont danser à Tara au moment de la pleine lune. Il y a tellement de boucliers ces nuits-là que l'endroit semble plongé sous l'eau.

– Allez-y, grogna Root entre ses dents serrées, continuez.

– D'accord. Inutile de vous mettre les oreilles en tire-bouchon.

Foaly fit défiler plusieurs minutes d'enregistrement.

– Voilà, on arrive au passage intéressant... Bel atterrissage en douceur, elle accroche ses ailes à un arbre, enlève son casque.

– Contraire au règlement, intervint Root. Les officiers des FAR ne doivent jamais enlever...

– Les officiers des FAR ne doivent jamais enlever leur casque en surface à moins que le casque en question ne soit défectueux, compléta Foaly. Oui, commandant, nous savons tous ce que dit le manuel. Mais est-ce que vous pouvez prétendre que vous n'avez jamais respiré une bouffée d'air après quelques heures de vol ?

– Non, admit Root. Et alors, à quoi jouez-vous ? Vous avez décidé d'être sa nounou ou quoi ? Venez-en à l'essentiel !

Foaly ricana en se cachant derrière sa main. Faire monter la tension de Root était l'un des avantages de ce métier. Personne d'autre n'oserait s'y risquer. Tout simplement parce que les autres étaient tous remplaçables.

Mais pas Foaly. A lui seul, il avait mis le système en place en partant de zéro, et si quelqu'un d'autre essayait de le lancer, un virus caché détruirait tout devant son nez pointu.

– L'essentiel. Nous y voilà. Regardez. Holly lâche soudain son casque. Il tombe sans doute caméra en avant car nous perdons l'image. Mais nous avons encore le son et je vais vous le faire entendre.

Il amplifia le signal audio, filtrant le bruit de fond.

– La qualité n'est pas très bonne. Le micro est intégré à la caméra. Il était donc contre le sol, lui aussi.

« Jolie petite pétoire, dit une voix. »

Humaine sans aucun doute. Grave également. Ce qui signifiait en général que son propriétaire était de grande taille.

Root leva un sourcil.

– Pétoire ?

– Une arme à feu en argot.

– Ah.

Il fut alors frappé par l'importance de ce simple mot.

– Elle avait donc dégainé son arme.

– Attendez. Ça empire.

« J'imagine que vous n'envisagez pas de vous rendre pacifiquement ? dit une seconde voix. »

En l'entendant, le commandant se sentit parcouru de frissons.

« Non, bien sûr, je m'y attendais, poursuivit la voix. »

– C'est grave, dit Root, le visage exceptionnellement pâle. On dirait un piège. Ces deux malfrats l'attendaient. Comment est-ce possible ?

La voix de Holly résonna alors dans le haut-parleur, impudente face au danger comme on pouvait s'y attendre.

Le commandant soupira. Au moins, elle était vivante.

Mais les choses ne s'arrangeaient pas : il y avait ensuite un échange de menaces et le deuxième humain manifestait une connaissance extraordinaire du monde des fées.

– Il est au courant du Rituel ?

– Le pire arrive maintenant.

Root resta bouche bée.

– Le pire ?

La voix de Holly retentit à nouveau. Déformée cette fois par le mesmer.

– Là, elle les a en son pouvoir, croassa Root.

Mais, apparemment, ce n'était pas le cas. Non seulement le mesmer se révélait inefficace mais les deux mystérieux personnages semblaient bien s'amuser.

– C'est tout ce que nous avons de Holly, expliqua Foaly. L'un des deux autres tripote la caméra pendant un petit moment et ensuite, on perd tout.

Root frotta les plis qui étaient apparus entre ses sourcils.

– Pas grand-chose comme indice. Pas d'image, pas même un nom. On ne peut pas être sûrs à cent pour cent qu'il se soit passé quelque chose d'anormal.

– Vous voulez une preuve ? demanda Foaly en remontant la bande. Je vais vous la donner.

Il remit le magnétoscope en lecture.

– Maintenant, regardez bien, je vais vous le passer au ralenti. Une image par seconde.

Root se pencha tout près de l'écran, si près qu'il parvenait à voir les pixels.

– Le capitaine Short atterrit. Elle enlève son casque, se penche, sans doute pour ramasser un gland, et... là, regardez !

Foaly enfonça la touche « pause », figeant complètement l'image.

– Vous ne voyez rien d'anormal ?

Le commandant sentit son ulcère enclencher le turbo. Quelque chose était apparu dans le coin supérieur droit de l'écran. A première vue, on aurait dit un rayon de lumière, mais une lumière qui venait d'où ou qui se reflétait sur quoi ?

– Vous pouvez me faire un agrandissement ?

– Pas de problème.

Foaly sélectionna la partie de l'image demandée et l'agrandit de quatre cents pour cent. Le rayon de lumière s'étala sur toute la surface de l'écran.

– Oh, non, murmura Root.

Là, sous leurs yeux, suspendue en l'air, se dessinait une seringue hypodermique. Aucun doute possible.

Le capitaine Holly Short devait être officiellement portée disparue. Elle était probablement morte ou, à tout le moins, retenue prisonnière par une force hostile.

– Dites-moi, on a toujours le localisateur ?

– Ouais. Un signal très clair. Il se déplace vers le nord à environ quatre-vingts kilomètres-heure.

Root resta silencieux un moment, réfléchissant à la stratégie qu'il allait décider.

– Déclenchez l'alerte maximale, sortez du lit les gars du commando de Récupération et faites-les venir ici. Préparez-les pour une expédition en surface. Je veux une équipe d'intervention au complet et deux techniciens. Vous venez aussi, Foaly. Nous aurons peut-être besoin d'arrêter le temps, cette fois-ci.

– Bien reçu, commandant. Vous voulez quelqu'un de la Détection ?

Root approuva d'un signe de tête.

– Et comment !

– Je vais appeler le capitaine Vein. C'est notre numéro un.

– Oh non, dit Root, pour une mission comme celle-ci, il nous faut le meilleur. Et le meilleur, c'est moi. Je reprends du service.

Foaly était tellement stupéfait qu'il fut incapable de faire le moindre commentaire.

– Vous... vous… vous...

– Oui, Foaly, n'ayez pas l'air si étonné. J'ai réussi plus de missions de détection que n'importe quel autre officier dans l'histoire. En plus, j'ai suivi ma formation de base en Irlande. Au temps où les habitants de ce pays portaient encore des chapeaux hauts de forme et brandissaient les bâtons traditionnels.

– Oui, mais ça, c'était il y a cinq cents ans et vous

n'étiez déjà plus un débutant à l'époque, sans vouloir vous offenser.

Root eut un sourire menaçant.

– Ne vous inquiétez pas, Foaly. Je suis toujours chauffé au rouge. Et pour compenser mon âge, je prendrai un très gros pistolet. Maintenant, préparez-moi une capsule. Je pars à la prochaine flambée.

Foaly obéit aux ordres sans lancer le moindre quolibet. Lorsque le commandant avait cette lueur dans les yeux, il fallait marcher droit et la fermer.

Mais sa docilité silencieuse avait une autre raison. Il venait de comprendre que Holly avait peut-être de véritables ennuis. D'une manière générale, les centaures ne comptent pas beaucoup d'amis et Foaly se demandait avec inquiétude s'il ne risquait pas de perdre l'une des rares qu'il avait encore.

Artemis s'était attendu à découvrir quelques avancées technologiques, mais rien de semblable au véritable trésor que représentait l'appareillage féerique étalé sur le tableau de bord du 4x4.

- Impressionnant, murmura-t-il. Nous pourrions mettre un terme à cette mission à l'instant même et ramasser quand même une fortune en brevets.

Artemis passa un scanneur à main sur le bracelet de l'elfe évanouie. Puis il entra dans son PowerBook les caractères inscrits en langue des fées.

– C'est une espèce de localisateur. De toute évidence, les amis de ce farfadet sont à nos trousses.

Butler déglutit difficilement.

– Vous voulez dire en ce moment même, monsieur ?

– C'est ce qu'il semble. Ou, en tout cas, ils essayent de retrouver le bracelet...

Artemis s'interrompit soudain et son regard se voila tandis qu'une décharge électrique envoyait dans son cerveau une nouvelle idée de génie.

– Butler ?

Le serviteur sentit son pouls s'accélérer. Il connaissait ce ton. Quelque chose se préparait.

– Le baleinier japonais. Celui que les autorités portuaires ont saisi. Il est toujours amarré dans les docks ?

Butler fit un signe de tête affirmatif.

– Oui, je crois.

Artemis entortilla le bracelet du localisateur autour de son index.

– Très bien. Emmenez-nous là-bas. Je crois qu'il est temps que nos amis lilliputiens sachent exactement à qui ils ont affaire.

Root remplit les papiers qui lui permettaient de reprendre du service actif et les tamponna lui-même à une vitesse remarquable – et très inhabituelle dans la haute administration des FAR. En général, il fallait des mois et plusieurs entretiens d'un ennui à se taper la tête contre les murs pour faire approuver toute candidature au service de Détection. Fort heureusement, Root bénéficiait d'une certaine influence auprès du commandant.

C'était une bonne chose de pouvoir remettre un uniforme de combat et Root parvint même à se convaincre que sa combinaison ne le serrait pas plus qu'avant au niveau de la taille. La bosse de son ventre avait pour seule cause, selon lui, tous les nouveaux équipements qu'on fourrait là-dedans. Personnellement, il n'avait pas de temps à consacrer à ces gadgets. Les seuls accessoires qui l'intéressaient, c'étaient les ailes sur son dos et le pistolet à triple canon multiphase refroidi par eau accroché à sa hanche – l'arme de poing la plus puissante du monde souterrain. L'engin n'était plus tout jeune, bien sûr, mais il avait permis à Root de se sortir à son avantage d'une bonne douzaine de fusillades et, en le sentant à son côté, il avait l'impression d'être redevenu un véritable officier de terrain.

Le puits à pression le plus proche de la position de Holly était le E1 : Tara. Pas vraiment l'endroit idéal pour une mission discrète mais, avec les deux heures de lune qui restaient avant l'aube, il n'y avait plus assez de temps pour une balade en surface.

Si on voulait avoir une chance de régler cette histoire avant le lever du soleil, la rapidité était essentielle. Root réquisitionna la navette du conduit E1 pour son équipe, en annulant les réservations d'un groupe de touristes qui avaient l'air d'avoir fait la queue depuis deux ans.

– Pas de chance, grogna-t-il à l'adresse du guide qui emmenait les vacanciers. En plus, j'annule tous les vols qui ne sont pas indispensables jusqu'à ce que la situation de crise soit terminée.

– Et ça nous mène à quand, ça ? couina la petite créature à tête de gnome d'un air courroucé, en brandissant un carnet comme si elle s'apprêtait à aller se plaindre quelque part.

Root cracha le mégot de son cigare et l'écrasa méticuleusement sous le talon de sa botte. Le symbolisme du geste était évident.

– Madame, les puits rouvriront au moment où je le jugerai opportun, rugit-il. Et si vous ne dégagez pas immédiatement de mon chemin, vous et votre uniforme fluo, je vous fais sauter votre licence d'agent de voyage et je vous expédie au trou pour obstruction à un officier des FAR dans l'exercice de ses fonctions.

La créature se ratatina devant lui et se fondit dans la file d'attente en regrettant que son uniforme soit d'un rose si vif.

Foaly attendait devant la capsule. Malgré la gravité du moment, il ne put s'empêcher de lancer un hennissement amusé en voyant le ventre de Root trembloter légèrement dans sa combinaison moulante.

– Vous êtes sûr que ça va aller, commandant ? En général nous ne laissons monter qu'un seul passager par capsule.

– Qu'est-ce que vous voulez dire ? grogna Root. Il n'y a qu'un seul...

Il remarqua alors le regard éloquent de Foaly, fixé sur son ventre.

– Ah, oui, ha ! ha ! Très drôle. Faites un peu attention, Foaly. Il y a des limites, vous savez !

Mais c'était une menace en l'air et ils le savaient tous les deux. Non seulement Foaly avait bâti leur réseau de communication en partant de zéro, mais c'était également un pionnier en matière de prédiction des explosions de magma. Sans lui, la technologie humaine aurait pu facilement rattraper celle des fées.

Root se sangla dans la capsule. Pas question de donner un de ces vieux engins de cinquante ans d'âge au commandant. Ce bébé-là sortait tout juste de la chaîne d'assemblage. Argenté et flambant neuf, il était équipé des nouveaux stabilisateurs à ailerons crantés, censés rectifier automatiquement la trajectoire dans les flux de magma. Une innovation de Foaly, bien entendu. Pendant environ un siècle, ses capsules avaient eu des lignes futuristes – pleines de néon et de caoutchouc. Mais dernièrement, sa sensibilité était devenue plus rétro et il avait remplacé les gadgets par des tableaux de bord en ronce de noyer et une sellerie en cuir. Root trouvait ce décor à l'ancienne étrangement réconfortant.

Il referma les doigts sur les poignées du manche à balai et se rendit soudain compte de tout le temps qui s'était écoulé depuis la dernière fois qu'il avait *cavalé dans la fournaise*. Foaly remarqua son embarras.

– Ne vous inquiétez pas, chef, dit-il d'un ton dépourvu de son cynisme habituel. C'est comme chevaucher une licorne, ça ne s'oublie pas.

Root poussa un grognement ; il n'était pas convaincu.

– Bon, commençons le spectacle avant que je ne change d'avis, marmonna-t-il.

Foaly rabattit la porte jusqu'à ce que le chuintement pneumatique indique qu'elle était soigneusement verrouillée. Le visage de Root prit une teinte verdâtre à travers le panneau de quartz. Il n'avait plus l'air si redoutable. C'était même tout le contraire.

Artemis procédait à une petite intervention chirurgicale improvisée sur le localisateur de la fée. Ce n'était pas une mince affaire de modifier certains détails sans détruire les mécanismes. Les deux technologies étaient décidément incompatibles. On avait l'impression de tenter une opération à cœur ouvert à l'aide d'un marteau.

La première difficulté consistait à ouvrir le maudit

objet. Les vis défiaient à la fois les tournevis plats et cruciformes. Même dans toute sa panoplie de clés hexagonales, il n'y en avait pas une seule qui s'adaptait à ces creux minuscules. « Il faut penser futuriste, se dit Artemis. Penser technologies de pointe. »

L'idée lui vint après un moment de contemplation silencieuse. Des vis magnétiques. Évident, en fait. Mais comment produire un champ magnétique circulaire à l'arrière d'un 4x4 ? Impossible. La seule solution, c'était d'essayer de faire tourner les vis manuellement en se servant d'un simple aimant.

Artemis délogea le petit aimant rangé dans un casier de la boîte à outils et dirigea les deux pôles vers les vis minuscules. Le pôle négatif les fit légèrement bouger. Ce fut suffisant pour permettre à Artemis de les saisir avec une pince de précision et il eut bientôt sous les yeux le localisateur démonté.

Les circuits étaient microscopiques. Et pas la moindre trace de soudure. Ils devaient utiliser une autre forme de fixation. S'il avait eu du temps, il aurait peut-être pu élucider le fonctionnement de cet appareil mais, dans l'immédiat, il devait improviser. Il faudrait compter sur l'inattention des autres. Si les êtres du Peuple ressemblaient aux humains, probablement ne voyaient-ils, eux aussi, que ce qu'ils voulaient voir.

Artemis leva le localisateur dans la lumière du plafonnier. Il était translucide. Légèrement polarisé, mais on y voyait assez. Il écarta un faisceau de fils brillants et ultrafins et inséra dans l'espace ainsi dégagé une minuscule caméra. Il fixa l'émetteur de la taille d'un petit pois à l'aide d'une touche de silicone. Rudimentaire mais efficace. Il fallait tout au moins l'espérer.

En l'absence d'outil adéquat, les vis magnétiques refusèrent de retourner dans leur logement et Artemis fut contraint de les coller également. Pas très propre mais sans doute suffisant, tant que personne n'aurait l'idée d'examiner le localisateur de trop près. Et si cela se produisait ? Dans ce cas, il perdrait un avantage dont il n'avait de toute façon jamais prévu de disposer.

Lorsqu'ils entrèrent en ville, Butler éteignit les feux de route.

– On approche des docks, Artemis, dit-il par-dessus son épaule. Il y a sûrement une patrouille du service des douanes dans les environs.

Le garçon fit un signe de tête approbateur. Judicieuse remarque. Le port était un centre florissant d'activités illégales. Plus de la moitié des produits de contrebande qui entraient dans le pays arrivaient le long de ces huit cents mètres de côtes.

– Il faudra faire une diversion, Butler. Deux minutes, je n'ai pas besoin de plus.

Le serviteur hocha la tête d'un air songeur.

– Comme d'habitude ?

– Je ne vois pas pourquoi on changerait. Défoncez-vous... Ou plutôt non, pas vous.

Artemis cligna des yeux. C'était sa deuxième plaisanterie ces derniers temps. Et la première à haute voix. Il devrait faire attention. Le moment n'était pas à la frivolité.

Les dockers se roulaient des cigarettes. Ce n'était pas facile avec des doigts de la taille d'une barre de fer, mais ils se débrouillaient. Et si un peu de tabac brun tombait par terre, quelle importance. On pouvait s'en procurer des paquets par caisses entières auprès d'un petit bonhomme qui ne se souciait pas d'ajouter les taxes d'État au prix de la marchandise.

Butler s'approcha du groupe, les yeux cachés sous un bonnet de marin.

– Il fait froid, ce soir, dit-il aux hommes rassemblés.

Personne ne répondit. Les policiers pouvaient apparaître sous toutes les formes possibles.

L'inconnu à la carrure d'athlète insista :

– Il vaudrait encore mieux travailler que de rester dehors par une nuit aussi glaciale.

L'un des dockers, un peu faible d'esprit, ne put s'empêcher d'approuver d'un signe de tête. Un camarade lui donna un coup de coude dans les côtes.

– Mais de toute façon, poursuivit le nouveau venu,

je ne pense pas que vous ayez jamais travaillé un seul jour de votre vie, pas vrai, les filles ?

Il n'y eut pas davantage de réponse. Mais, cette fois, c'était parce que les dockers bouche bée restaient muets de stupéfaction.

– Oui, vous faites vraiment pitié à voir, reprit Butler d'un ton léger. Oh, bien sûr, vous auriez pu vous faire passer pour des hommes au temps de la grande famine mais, aujourd'hui, vous avez l'air d'une bande d'avortons en corsage.

– Arrrrgh ! laissa échapper l'un des dockers.

Il fut incapable d'en dire davantage.

Butler haussa un sourcil.

– Argh ? Pitoyable et même pas articulé. Jolie combinaison. Vos mères doivent être fières de vous.

L'inconnu venait de franchir une frontière sacrée. Il avait mentionné leurs mères. A présent, plus rien ne pouvait le dispenser d'une raclée, même le fait qu'il s'agissait de toute évidence d'un idiot. Mais d'un idiot qui disposait d'un riche vocabulaire.

Les dockers éteignirent leurs cigarettes et se déployèrent lentement en demi-cercle. Ils étaient à six contre un. Il y avait de quoi les plaindre. Butler n'en avait pas encore fini avec eux.

– Et maintenant, mesdames, avant de commencer quoi que ce soit, je précise qu'il est interdit de griffer, de cracher et de rapporter à maman.

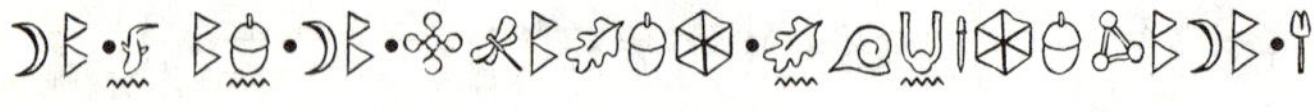

Ce fut la dernière goutte. Les six dockers émirent un hurlement et se précipitèrent comme un seul homme. S'ils avaient porté la moindre attention à leur adversaire en cet instant précédant le contact, ils auraient remarqué qu'il avait changé de position pour abaisser son centre de gravité. Ils auraient aussi pu voir que les mains qu'il sortait de ses poches avaient la taille et la forme approximative d'une grosse pelle. Mais personne ne prêta attention à Butler – chacun d'eux était trop occupé à surveiller ses camarades pour s'assurer qu'il n'était pas le seul à monter à l'assaut.

La raison d'être d'une diversion, c'est de se faire remarquer. Avec évidence. Grossièreté. Pas du tout le style de Butler. Il aurait préféré s'occuper de ces messieurs à l'aide d'un fusil à fléchettes, à cinq cents mètres de distance. A défaut, si le contact direct était absolument nécessaire, quelques pressions du pouce à la base du cou, sur le centre nerveux, auraient été plus à son goût – silencieux comme un murmure.

Mais le but de l'opération aurait été manqué.

Aussi Butler fit-il le contraire de ce que son entraînement lui avait appris, hurlant comme un démon et utilisant les techniques de combat les plus vulgaires.

Vulgaire ne signifiait pas inefficace, cependant. Un prêtre du monastère de Shaolin aurait peut-être anticipé quelques-uns de ses mouvements les plus exagérés mais les dockers étaient des adversaires peu entraînés. Il faut dire à leur décharge qu'ils n'étaient pas complètement à jeun.

Butler abattit le premier d'un crochet à la face. Il attrapa les deux suivants et cogna leurs têtes l'une contre l'autre, comme dans un dessin animé. A sa très grande honte, il expédia le quatrième d'un simple coup de pied circulaire. Mais le grand spectacle fut réservé aux deux derniers. Le serviteur les attrapa par le col de leur blouson, roula sur le dos, et les précipita d'un même mouvement dans les eaux du port de Dublin. Gros « plouf ! » bien sonores, longs cris plaintifs. Parfait.

Deux faisceaux de phares jaillirent alors de l'ombre d'un container et une berline appartenant à l'administration s'arrêta sur le quai dans un crissement de pneus. Comme prévu, il s'agissait d'une patrouille du service des douanes. Butler sourit avec une satisfaction un peu sombre et disparut derrière l'angle d'un mur. Il s'était volatilisé depuis longtemps lorsque les agents des douanes montrèrent leurs badges et commencèrent leurs investigations. Les réponses apportées à leurs questions ne leur permirent guère d'avancer. « Gros comme une maison » n'était pas une description suffisante pour retrouver un suspect.

Lorsque Butler eut regagné la voiture, Artemis était déjà revenu de sa mission.

– Bien joué, mon vieux, commenta celui-ci. Mais j'ai bien peur que votre maître en arts martiaux ne se retourne dans sa tombe. Un vulgaire coup de pied circulaire ? Comment avez-vous pu ?

Butler se mordit la langue, faisant marche arrière pour dégager le 4x4. Lorsqu'ils passèrent sur la bretelle de sortie, il ne put s'empêcher de jeter un coup d'œil au chaos qu'il avait provoqué.

Les fonctionnaires s'affairaient à hisser hors des eaux polluées un docker trempé jusqu'aux os.

Artemis avait eu besoin de cette diversion pour servir un objectif bien précis. Mais Butler savait qu'il était inutile de demander quel était cet objectif. Son employeur ne parlait de ses projets à personne tant qu'il ne jugeait pas le moment venu. Et lorsque Artemis jugeait le moment venu, en général, il ne se trompait pas.

Root tremblait lorsqu'il émergea de la capsule. Il lui semblait que les choses ne se passaient pas comme ça de son temps. Même si, à la vérité, c'était sans doute bien pire à l'époque. Au temps de la vieille Irlande traditionnelle, il n'y avait pas de harnais polymères compliqués, pas de moteurs d'appoint et certainement pas d'écrans de contrôle.

Tout reposait sur l'instinct et une petite touche d'enchantement. D'une certaine manière, Root aurait préféré qu'il en soit toujours ainsi. La science privait toute chose de sa magie.

D'un pas vacillant, il longea le tunnel jusqu'au terminal. Tara étant la destination préférée des voyageurs, elle bénéficiait d'une salle d'attente de bonne dimension. Il y avait six navettes par semaine, pour la seule provenance de Haven-Ville.

Bien entendu, elles n'empruntaient pas les puits à pression. Les touristes payants n'avaient pas envie d'être secoués sauf lorsqu'ils s'offraient une virée illégale à Disneyland.

Le fort de fée était bondé de voyageurs de la pleine lune qui se plaignaient des suspensions de la navette. Un lutin femelle se cachait derrière son comptoir, assiégé par des gremlins en colère.

– Ça ne sert à rien de me lancer des maléfices, couinait le lutin, adressez-vous donc à cet elfe.

Elle pointa un index vert et tremblant en direction du commandant qui approchait. La foule des gremlins se retourna vers Root et, lorsqu'ils virent le pistolet à triple canon accroché à sa hanche, leur agressivité s'évanouit soudain.

Root attrapa derrière le comptoir le micro qui servait à faire les annonces et le tira vers lui aussi loin que le permettait la longueur du câble.

– Maintenant, écoutez-moi bien, grogna-t-il, sa voix rocailleuse résonnant dans tous les haut-parleurs du terminal. Je suis le commandant Root, chef des FAR. Il y a une situation grave en surface et je compte sur la collaboration de tous les civils qui se trouvent ici. Pour commencer, j'aimerais bien que vous cessiez de jacasser pour que je puisse enfin m'entendre réfléchir !

Il s'interrompit afin de s'assurer que son souhait était exaucé. C'était le cas.

– Ensuite, je voudrais que chacun d'entre vous, y compris les enfants braillards, s'asseye sur les bancs destinés au public jusqu'à ce que je sois parti d'ici. Ensuite, vous pourrez recommencer à ronchonner, à vous goinfrer ou je ne sais quoi ; peu m'importe ce que font les civils.

Personne n'avait jamais songé à accuser Root de céder trop facilement au politiquement correct. Et personne n'y songerait jamais.

– Je veux aussi que le responsable de ce terminal me rejoigne ici. Immédiatement !

Root lança le micro sur le comptoir, provoquant un effet Larsen qui transperça tous les tympans alentour. Une fraction de seconde plus tard, un hybride hors d'haleine, moitié elfe, moitié gobelin, sautillait à ses côtés.

– Pouvons-nous faire quelque chose pour vous, commandant ?

Root fit oui de la tête, enfonçant un épais cigare dans la cavité située sous son nez.

– Je veux que vous me dégagiez un tunnel. Et pas question d'avoir des gens des douanes ou de l'immigration dans les pattes. Vous commencerez à renvoyer tout le monde en dessous dès que mes équipes seront arrivées.

Le directeur du terminal déglutit difficilement.

– Tout le monde ?

– Oui, y compris le personnel. Et emportez tout ce que vous pourrez prendre. Évacuation totale.

Il s'interrompit et fixa d'un air mauvais les yeux mauves du responsable.

– Je vous préviens : il ne s'agit pas d'un exercice.

– Vous voulez dire...

– Oui, répondit Root en poursuivant son chemin le long de la rampe d'accès. Le Peuple de la Boue a commis un acte ouvertement hostile envers nous. Qui sait où ça peut nous mener ?

L'elfe-gobelin regarda Root disparaître dans la fumée de son cigare.

Un acte ouvertement hostile ? Cela pouvait signifier la guerre. Il appela son comptable sur son téléphone mobile.

– Bark ? C'est Nimbus, à l'appareil. Je veux que vous vendiez toutes les actions que je possède dans le port des navettes. Oui, toutes. J'ai l'intuition qu'elles ne vont pas tarder à faire le grand plongeon.

Le capitaine Holly Short avait l'impression qu'une limace suceuse cachée dans son oreille lui aspirait le cerveau. Elle s'efforçait de comprendre ce qui pouvait causer une douleur pareille mais sa mémoire n'était pas encore en état de marche. La seule chose qu'elle arrivait encore à faire, c'était respirer en restant allongée.

Le moment était venu d'essayer de dire quelque chose. Quelque chose qui soit à la fois court et judicieux.

Au secours, voilà ce qui convenait, estima-t-elle. Elle prit fébrilement son souffle et ouvrit la bouche :

– Auuummcccou, laissèrent échapper ses lèvres infidèles.

Non, ça n'allait pas. Impossible à comprendre, même par un gnome ivre.

Que se passait-il ? Elle était étendue sur le dos, sans plus de force qu'une racine dans un tunnel humide. Qu'est-ce qui avait bien pu lui faire cet effet-là ? Holly se concentra, essayant d'esquiver la douleur qui l'aveuglait.

Le troll ? Était-ce lui ? L'avait-il estropiée dans ce restaurant ? Voilà qui expliquerait tout. Mais non. Un vague souvenir semblait lui revenir en mémoire, un souvenir concernant le Vieux Pays. Et le Rituel.

Il y avait aussi quelque chose qui s'enfonçait dans sa cheville.

– *Hello* !

Une voix. Pas la sienne. Même pas une voix d'elfe.

– Alors, vous êtes réveillée ?

C'était une langue d'Europe. Du latin. Non. De l'anglais. Était-elle en Angleterre ?

– Je me disais que la fléchette vous avait peut-être tuée. L'intérieur des extraterrestres n'est pas fait comme le nôtre. J'ai vu ça à la télévision.

Qu'est-ce que c'était que ces idioties ? L'intérieur des extraterrestres ? De quoi parlait cette créature ?

– Vous avez l'air en forme. Vous ressemblez à Muchacha Maria – c'est une lutteuse mexicaine lilliputienne.

Holly poussa un grognement. Son don pour les langues devait être en panne. Il était temps de voir à quel genre de folie elle avait affaire. Rassemblant toutes ses forces sur son visage, elle parvint à soulever une paupière. Elle la referma presque aussitôt. Il semblait qu'une mouche blonde géante, debout à côté d'elle, la regardait.

– N'ayez pas peur, dit la mouche. Ce ne sont que des lunettes de soleil.

Cette fois, Holly ouvrit les deux paupières en même temps. La créature tapotait de l'index une sorte d'œil argenté. Non, ce n'était pas un œil. Plutôt une lentille. Une lentille réfléchissante. Comme celles que portaient les deux autres... Tout lui revint d'un coup, rem plissant le trou de sa mémoire, comme la serrure d'un coffre-fort dont la combinaison se met soudain en

place. Elle avait été enlevée par deux humains tandis qu'elle accomplissait le Rituel. Deux humains qui avaient une connaissance étonnante du monde des fées.

Holly essaya à nouveau de parler :

– Où... où suis-je ?

L'humaine gloussa d'un rire réjoui en claquant des mains. La fée remarqua ses ongles longs et vernis.

– Vous parlez anglais ? Quel drôle d'accent ! On dirait un mélange d'un peu de tout.

Holly fronça les sourcils.

Elle avait l'impression que la voix de la fille s'enfonçait comme un tire-bouchon dans son crâne douloureux. Elle leva un bras. Plus de localisateur.

– Où sont mes affaires ?

La fille agita l'index, comme si elle réprimandait un enfant dissipé.

– Artemis vous a enlevé votre petit pistolet et tous vos autres jouets. Vous pourriez vous blesser avec ces engins-là.

– Artemis ?

– Artemis Fowl. Tout ça, c'était son idée. Tout est toujours son idée.

Holly fronça à nouveau les sourcils. Artemis Fowl. Pour une raison qu'elle ignorait, ce nom même suffisait à la faire frissonner. C'était un mauvais présage. L'intuition d'une fée ne se trompait jamais.

– Ils vont venir me chercher, dit-elle, sa voix rauque s'élevant d'entre ses lèvres sèches. Vous ne vous rendez pas compte de ce que vous avez fait.

La jeune fille plissa le front.

– Vous avez parfaitement raison. Je n'ai aucune idée de ce qui se passe. Il n'y a donc aucun intérêt à essayer de me tirer les vers du nez.

Holly réfléchit. De toute évidence, il était inutile de se lancer dans des petits jeux psychologiques avec cette fille.

Le mesmer était son seul espoir, mais il ne pouvait pénétrer les surfaces réfléchissantes. Comment diable ces humains le savaient-ils ? Il faudrait éclaircir la question plus tard. Pour l'instant, elle devait trouver le moyen de séparer cette écervelée de ses lunettes de soleil.

– Vous êtes une belle petite humaine, dit Holly, la voix débordant d'une flatterie mielleuse à souhait.

– Oh, merci, madame...

– Appelez-moi Holly.

– Oh, merci, Holly. Un jour, j'ai eu ma photo dans le journal local. J'ai gagné un concours. Miss betterave sucrière 1999.

– J'en étais sûre. Une beauté naturelle. Je parie que vous avez des yeux magnifiques.

– C'est ce que tout le monde me dit, approuva Juliet. Avec des cils comme des ressorts de montre.

Holly soupira.

– Si seulement je pouvais les voir.

– Pourquoi pas, après tout ?

Les doigts de Juliet se refermèrent autour des branches de ses lunettes. Puis elle hésita.

– Je ne devrais peut-être pas.

– Pourquoi ? Juste un instant.

– Je ne sais pas. Artemis m'a dit de ne jamais les enlever.

– Il ne le saura pas.

Juliet montra du doigt une caméra de surveillance fixée au mur.

– Oh, il s'en apercevra. Artemis voit toujours tout.

Elle se pencha tout près de la fée.

– Parfois, j'ai même l'impression qu'il arrive à voir ce qui se passe dans ma tête.

Holly se renfrogna. Une fois de plus, elle était mise en échec par cet Artemis.

– Allez, juste une seconde. Ça ne peut pas faire de mal.

Juliet fit semblant de réfléchir.

– Non, sans doute. A moins que vous ayez l'intention de me neutraliser à coup de mesmer. Vous me prenez vraiment pour une idiote ?

– J'ai une autre idée, dit Holly, d'un ton beaucoup plus grave. Je pourrais par exemple me lever, t'assommer et t'enlever ces stupides lunettes.

Juliet éclata d'un rire réjoui, comme si c'était la chose la plus ridicule qu'elle eût jamais entendue

– Elle est bien bonne, madame la fée.

– Je suis très sérieuse, petite humaine.

– Si vous êtes sérieuse, soupira Juliet en glissant un doigt fin et délicat derrière ses lunettes pour essuyer une larme, je vais vous donner les deux raisons pour lesquelles vous ne ferez rien du tout. La première c'est que, d'après Artemis, tant que vous êtes dans une maison humaine, vous devez obéir à tout ce qu'on vous dit. Et moi, je vous dis de rester sur ce lit de camp.

Holly ferma les yeux. Là encore, la fille avait raison. D'où avaient-ils pu tirer toutes leurs informations ?

– Et la deuxième, reprit Juliet avec un sourire, mais cette fois on retrouvait quelque chose de son frère dans la façon dont elle montrait les dents, la deuxième, c'est que j'ai suivi le même entraînement que Butler et il y a longtemps que j'ai une envie folle de trouver quelqu'un sur qui exercer ma technique du marteau-pilon.

« On verra ça, ma petite humaine », songea Holly. Le capitaine Short n'était pas au maximum de ses forces et il y avait toujours cette petite chose qui s'enfonçait dans sa cheville.

Elle croyait savoir de quoi il s'agissait et, si elle ne se trompait pas, c'était peut-être le début d'un bon plan.

Le commandant Root avait réglé l'écran récepteur de son casque sur la fréquence du localisateur de Holly. Il mit plus longtemps que prévu pour atteindre Dublin. Le mécanisme des ailes modernes était plus complexe que de son temps et il avait négligé de prendre des cours de formation. Lorsqu'il était à la bonne altitude, il arrivait presque à superposer la carte lumineuse de sa visière avec les rues de Dublin grandeur nature qui s'étalaient au-dessous de lui. Presque.

– Foaly, espèce de centaure outrecuidant ! aboya-t-il dans son micro.

– Un problème, chef ? répondit la voix métallique.

– Un problème ? Oui, vous pouvez appeler ça comme ça. Quand est-ce que vous avez mis à jour les données sur Dublin pour la dernière fois ?

Root entendait dans son écouteur des bruits de succion. On aurait dit que Foaly était en train de déjeuner.

– Désolé, commandant, je finis ma carotte. Mmh... Dublin, voyons... Soixante-quinze... 1875.

– C'est bien ce qui me semblait ! La ville a complètement changé. Les humains ont même réussi à modifier le tracé de la côte.

Foaly resta un bon moment silencieux. Root l'imaginait en train de s'atteler à la question. Le centaure n'aimait pas s'entendre dire qu'un élément de son système, quel qu'il fût, n'était pas à jour.

– O.K., reprit-il enfin. Voici ce que je vais faire. Nous avons un scope sur un satellite télé qui couvre l'Irlande.

– Je vois, marmonna Root, ce qui était fondamentalement un mensonge.

– Je vais envoyer directement par e-mail le balayage de la semaine dernière dans votre visière. Heureusement, il y a une carte vidéo dans tous les nouveaux casques.

– Oui, heureusement.

– Le plus difficile, ce sera de coordonner votre trajectoire de vol avec les données vidéo...

Root en avait entendu assez.

– Vous en avez pour combien de temps, Foaly ?

– Ahm... Deux minutes, peut-être un peu plus.

– Combien en plus ?

– Une dizaine d'années si je me suis trompé dans mes calculs.

– Alors, je vous conseille de ne pas vous tromper. En attendant, je reste en vol stationnaire.

Cent vingt-quatre secondes plus tard, la carte en noir et blanc de Root s'effaça pour laisser place à une image en couleur éclairée comme en plein jour.

Lorsque Root bougeait, l'image bougeait aussi, ainsi que le point rouge qui indiquait l'emplacement du localisateur de Holly.

– Impressionnant, dit Root.

– Vous pouvez répéter, commandant ?

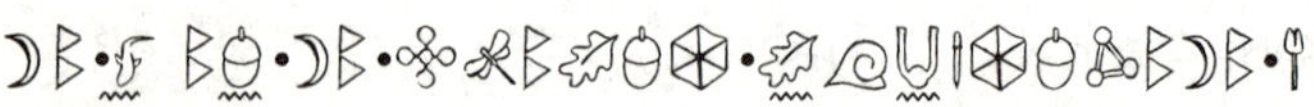

– J'ai dit impressionnant, s'écria-t-il. Et pas la peine de prendre la grosse tête.

Le commandant entendit des éclats de rire et comprit que Foaly l'avait branché sur les haut-parleurs de la salle. Tout le monde l'avait entendu complimenter le centaure pour son travail. Il n'allait plus lui parler pendant au moins un mois. Mais ça en valait la peine. La vidéo qu'il recevait à présent était parfaitement à jour. Si le capitaine Short était retenu dans un immeuble, l'ordinateur lui donnerait instantanément une image en trois dimensions. C'était infaillible. Sauf que...

– Foaly, la balise indique la mer. Qu'est-ce qui se passe ?

– J'imagine qu'elle est sur un bateau, commandant.

Root se maudit de ne pas y avoir pensé lui-même. Ils devaient pouffer de rire dans la salle de contrôle.

Bien sûr qu'elle était sur un bateau ! Root descendit de quelques centaines de mètres jusqu'à ce que la silhouette sombre d'un navire se dessine dans la brume.

Apparemment, c'était un baleinier. La technologie avait peut-être évolué au cours des siècles, mais on n'avait encore rien trouvé de mieux qu'un harpon pour massacrer le plus grand mammifère du monde.

– Le capitaine Short est quelque part là-dedans, Foaly. Dans le ventre du navire. Qu'est-ce que vous pouvez me fournir ?

– Rien, commandant. Ce n'est pas une construction fixe. Lorsque nous aurons retrouvé son immatriculation, il sera trop tard.

– Et une image thermique ?

– Non, commandant. Cette coque doit avoir au moins cinquante ans. Avec un taux de plomb important. Les ondes ne parviendraient même pas à pénétrer la première couche. J'ai bien peur que vous ne soyez obligé de vous débrouiller seul.

Root hocha la tête.

– Avec tous les milliards qu'on a déversés dans votre département ! Faites-moi penser à réduire votre budget quand je reviendrai.

– Oui, commandant, répliqua Foaly, dont le ton était maussade pour une fois.

Il n'aimait pas les plaisanteries budgétaires.

– Mettez le commando de Récupération en alerte maximale. J'aurai peut-être besoin d'eux très vite.

– Je m'en occupe, commandant.

– Je vous le conseille. Terminé.

Root allait devoir se débrouiller seul. Pour dire la vérité, c'était ce qui lui convenait le mieux. Pas de fatras scientifique. Pas de centaure arrogant pour lui hennir dans les oreilles. Rien que son intelligence d'elfe et peut-être un soupçon de magie.

Root inclina ses ailes et descendit sous la couche de brouillard. Inutile de prendre des précautions. Il avait activé son bouclier et n'était pas visible par un œil humain. Même sur les radars capables de détecter les avions furtifs il ne provoquerait qu'une distorsion à peine perceptible. Le commandant fondit vers le plat-bord. C'était un navire d'une très grande laideur. Une odeur de douleur et de mort traînait sur ses ponts imprégnés de sang. Nombre de nobles créatures avaient été tuées ici, tuées et dépecées pour quelques pains de savon et un peu d'huile de chauffage. Root hocha la tête. Les humains étaient décidément des barbares.

Le témoin lumineux émis par le localisateur de Holly clignotait de plus en plus rapidement. Elle était tout près. La silhouette du capitaine Short, toujours vivante, espérait-il, devait se trouver quelque part dans un rayon de deux cents mètres. Mais sans image des lieux pour se repérer, il ne pouvait compter sur aucune aide pour explorer les entrailles du navire.

Root atterrit en douceur sur le pont, ses bottes collant légèrement au mélange de graisse et de savon séché qui s'étalait sur la surface d'acier. Le navire semblait désert. Pas d'homme de quart en vue, pas de bosco sur la passerelle, aucune lumière nulle part. Mais ce n'était pas une raison pour abandonner toute prudence. Les humains pouvaient toujours surgir au moment où l'on s'y attendait le moins, Root en avait déjà fait l'amère expérience. Un jour, alors qu'il aidait un commando de Récupération à ramener les débris d'une capsule écrasée contre la paroi d'un tunnel, un groupe de spéléologues humains les avait repérés. Un désastre ! Hystérie collective, poursuites infernales, effacements de mémoire à haute dose. Toute la panoplie. Root frissonna. Des nuits comme celle-là peuvent faire vieillir une fée de plusieurs décennies d'un coup.

Gardant son bouclier totalement activé, le commandant rangea ses ailes dans leur étui et s'avança à pied sur le pont. Son écran ne signalait aucune présence vivante dans les parages mais, comme l'avait dit Foaly, la coque comportait une grande quantité de plomb. Même la peinture était à base de plomb ! Le navire tout entier était une menace flottante pour l'environnement. Un bataillon de parachutistes aurait pu se cacher sous le pont sans que la caméra de son casque parvienne à le détecter. Très rassurant. Même le témoin lumineux du localisateur de Holly était moins brillant que la normale et pourtant il était alimenté par une batterie nucléaire. Root n'aimait pas ça. Pas du tout. « Du calme, se dit-il sur le ton de la dérision. Tu es protégé par le bouclier et il n'y a pas le moindre humain en vue. »

Root ouvrit la première écoutille. Le panneau pivota sans difficulté. Le commandant renifla. Ces Êtres de la Boue avaient utilisé de la graisse de baleine pour huiler les gonds.

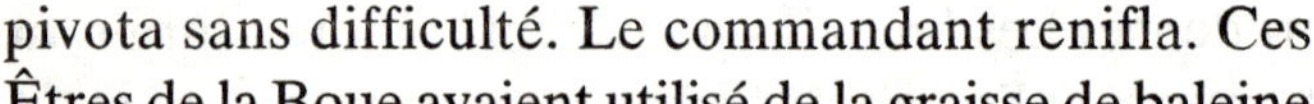

N'y aurait-il jamais de limites à leur dépravation ?

La coursive était plongée dans une obscurité visqueuse et Root dut brancher son filtre infrarouge. Bon, d'accord, parfois, la technologie avait du bon mais il ne l'avouerait jamais à Foaly. L'enchevêtrement de tuyaux et de grillages qui s'étalait devant lui s'éclaira soudain d'une lumière rouge surnaturelle Quelques minutes plus tard, il regretta d'avoir eu une pensée positive pour les prouesses techniques du centaure. Le filtre infrarouge déformait sa perception de l'espace et il s'était déjà cogné deux fois la tête contre des canalisations qui dépassaient d'une cloison.

Il n'y avait toujours aucun signe de vie – humaine ou féerique. Beaucoup d'animaux, en revanche. Surtout des rongeurs. Et quand on mesure soi-même à peine plus d'un mètre, un rat de bonne taille peut constituer une sérieuse menace, surtout qu'ils sont l'une des rares espèces animales capables de voir à travers un bouclier de fée. Root saisit son pistolet et le régla au niveau trois, c'est-à-dire « cuisson moyenne », selon l'expression qu'employaient les elfes dans les vestiaires. Il fit fuir un rat, le derrière fumant, à titre d'avertissement pour les autres. Rien de mortel, juste de quoi lui apprendre à ne pas s'intéresser de trop près à un elfe pressé.

Root accéléra le pas. L'endroit était idéal pour un guet-apens. Le dos tourné à la seule issue possible, il devenait quasiment aveugle. Une mission de cauchemar. Si l'un de ses propres subordonnés s'était livré à ce genre d'exploit, il lui aurait arraché ses galons.

Mais les situations désespérées exigeaient qu'on prenne des risques judicieusement calculés. C'était le principe même du commandement.

Il passa devant plusieurs portes sans chercher à savoir ce qu'il y avait derrière, suivant uniquement le signal sonore du localisateur. Un panneau d'acier fermait la coursive et le capitaine Short, ou son cadavre, se trouvait derrière.

Root pesa de tout son poids contre la porte qui s'ouvrit sans résistance. Mauvaise nouvelle. Si une créature vivante était retenue prisonnière de l'autre côté, le panneau aurait été verrouillé. Le commandant régla son pistolet au niveau cinq et franchit l'ouverture. L'arme bourdonnait faiblement. Elle était à présent assez puissante pour pulvériser un éléphant mâle d'une seule décharge.

Aucune trace de Holly. Et, d'ailleurs, aucune trace de qui que ce soit. Il se trouvait dans une chambre froide. Des stalactites étincelantes pendaient d'un enchevêtrement de tuyaux. L'haleine de Root s'échappait devant lui en nuages glacés. Aux yeux d'un humain, c'était sûrement un spectacle étrange. Comme un souffle désincarné.

– Ah, dit une voix familière. Nous avons un visiteur.

Root se laissa tomber sur un genou, le pistolet brandi.

– Alors, vous êtes venu au secours de votre officier disparu ?

Le commandant cligna des yeux pour chasser une goutte de sueur qui perlait à sa paupière. Une goutte de sueur ? Par cette température ?

– Malheureusement, j'ai bien peur que vous ne vous soyez trompé d'endroit.

C'était une voix métallique. Artificielle. Amplifiée.

Root consulta son écran pour y déceler des signes de vie. Il n'y en avait aucun. Pas dans cette chambre froide, en tout cas. Mais il était observé. Une caméra capable de percer son bouclier était-elle cachée quelque part dans l'écheveau des canalisations ?

– Où êtes-vous ? Montrez-vous !

L'humain pouffa et son rire résonna en un étrange écho sur les parois de la vaste cale.

– Oh, non. Pas encore, mon cher ami féerique. Mais bientôt. Et croyez-moi, quand je me montrerai, vous regretterez de m'avoir vu.

Root essaya de repérer l'origine de la voix. Il fallait faire parler l'humain.

– Qu'est-ce que vous voulez ?

– Humm. Ce que je veux ? Ça aussi, vous le saurez bientôt.

Au centre de la cale, il y avait une caisse basse sur laquelle était posé un attaché-case ouvert.

– Pourquoi m'avez-vous fait venir ici ?

Root tapota la mallette avec son pistolet. Rien ne se produisit.

– Pour une petite démonstration.

Le commandant se pencha sur l'attaché-case. A l'intérieur, soigneusement protégé par du polystyrène, un objet plat était emballé sous vide à côté d'un émetteur VHF à trois bandes. Le localisateur de Holly était posé dessus. Root grogna. Elle n'aurait jamais abandonné son équipement de son plein gré ; aucun officier des FAR ne ferait une chose pareille.

– Quel genre de démonstration, espèce de tordu psychopathe ?

Le même rire glacé retentit.

– La démonstration de ma volonté de parvenir à mes fins.

Root aurait dû commencer à s'inquiéter de sa propre santé, mais il était trop préoccupé par celle de Holly.

– Si vous avez touché à une seule pointe des oreilles de mon officier...

– Votre officier ? Oh, je vois que nous avons affaire à un gros bonnet. Quel honneur ! Ce sera d'autant mieux pour vous exposer ce que je veux.

Une sonnette d'alarme retentit dans la tête de Root.

– Ce que vous voulez ?

La voix qui s'élevait du haut-parleur d'aluminium était aussi sinistre qu'un hiver nucléaire.

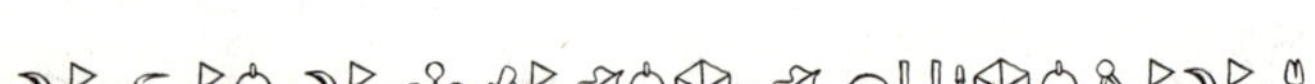

– Mon cher petit être féerique, ce que je veux, c'est vous faire comprendre que je ne suis pas quelqu'un avec qui on peut se permettre de plaisanter. J'aimerais bien que vous examiniez le paquet que vous avez sous les yeux.

Le commandant s'exécuta. La forme n'était pas suffisamment précise pour en tirer une conclusion. L'objet était plat, comme un pain de mastic ou de... Oh, non !

Sous l'emballage, une lumière rouge se mit à clignoter.

– Il va falloir voler à tire-d'aile, ma petite fée, dit la voix. Et transmettre à vos amis le bonjour d'Artemis Fowl II.

A côté de la lumière rouge, des symboles verts s'affichèrent soudain dans une succession régulière. Root les reconnut pour les avoir appris en classe d'études humaines, au temps où il était à l'académie. C'étaient... des chiffres. En ordre décroissant. Un compte à rebours !

– Nom d'un... ! grogna Root (inutile de préciser la suite, elle serait censurée).

Il fit volte-face et s'enfuit dans la coursive, suivi par la voix moqueuse d'Artemis Fowl qui résonnait dans le couloir métallique.

– Trois, lança l'humain. Deux...

– Nom d'un... ! répéta Root.

La coursive paraissait beaucoup plus longue, à présent. Un morceau de ciel étoilé apparaissait par une porte entrebâillée. Il activa ses ailes. Il lui faudrait se lancer dans un vol acrobatique. L'envergure du Colibri était à peine plus étroite que la largeur de la coursive.

– Un.

Des étincelles jaillirent lorsque les ailes éraflèrent un tuyau qui dépassait. Root fit une cabriole et se redressa à une vitesse proche de Mach 1.

– Zéro... dit la voix. Boum !

A l'intérieur de l'emballage sous vide, un détonateur projeta une étincelle, mettant le feu à un kilo de semtex pur. En une nanoseconde, l'intense chaleur dévora l'oxygène environnant et s'engouffra dans l'espace qui offrait la moindre résistance, c'est-à-dire le long de la coursive par laquelle s'enfuyait le commandant des FAR.

Root rabattit sa visière et mit les gaz à fond. La porte n'était plus qu'à quelques mètres. Restait à savoir qui l'atteindrait le premier – l'elfe ou la boule de feu.

Root réussit à la battre de vitesse. Il se lança dans un looping arrière et sentit le souffle de l'explosion sur son torse. Des flammes enveloppèrent sa combinaison, lui léchant les jambes. Root poursuivit sa manœuvre et plongea droit dans l'eau glacée. Il remonta à la surface en poussant des jurons.

Au-dessus de lui, le baleinier avait été entièrement consumé par les flammes délétères.

– Commandant, dit une voix dans son écouteur.

C'était Foaly. La communication était rétablie.

– Commandant, quelle est votre situation ?

Root s'arracha à l'étreinte de la mer et s'éleva dans le ciel.

– Ma situation, Foaly, est extrêmement contrariante. Collez-vous à vos ordinateurs. Je veux que vous me communiquiez tout ce qu'il est possible de savoir sur un certain Artemis Fowl et je veux que vous me trouviez ça avant mon retour à la base.

– Oui, mon commandant. Tout de suite.

Il n'y eut aucune plaisanterie.

Même Foaly se rendait compte que ce n'était pas le moment.

Root monta à trois cents mètres d'altitude et resta un instant en vol stationnaire. Au-dessous, le baleinier en flammes attirait des véhicules de secours comme des papillons de nuit se précipitant sur une lumière. Tandis qu'il époussetait ses coudes d'où pendaient quelques fils carbonisés, il se promit de régler ses comptes avec cet Artemis Fowl. On pouvait compter sur lui pour ça.

CHAPITRE VI

SIÈGE

Artemis s'adossa contre le fauteuil de cuir pivotant de son bureau, souriant par-dessus ses mains jointes. Parfait. Voilà une petite explosion qui devrait guérir ces fées de leur attitude cavalière. Et par la même occasion, on comptait un baleinier de moins dans le monde. Artemis Fowl n'aimait pas les baleiniers. Il existait des moyens moins contestables de fabriquer des produits à base d'huile.

La caméra de la taille d'une tête d'épingle cachée dans le localisateur avait parfaitement fonctionné. Grâce à ses images à haute résolution, il avait pu voir le souffle cristallin typique des fées.

Artemis consulta l'écran de contrôle qui permettait de surveiller la cave. Sa prisonnière était assise sur le lit de camp, la tête entre les mains. Il fronça les sourcils. Il ne s'attendait pas à voir la fée paraître si... humaine. Jusqu'à présent, il avait considéré ces créatures comme des proies. Un gibier à chasser.

Mais maintenant qu'il en voyait une ainsi, dans cette situation très inconfortable, les choses semblaient différentes.

Artemis mit l'ordinateur en veille et se dirigea vers la double porte. Il était temps d'avoir une petite conversation avec son invitée.

Au moment où ses doigts se posaient sur la poignée de cuivre, la porte s'ouvrit à la volée et Juliet apparut dans l'encadrement, les joues rouges d'avoir couru.

– Artemis, dit-elle, le souffle court. Votre mère. Elle...

Le garçon eut l'impression qu'une boule de plomb lui tombait dans l'estomac.

– Oui ?

– Artemis, c'est... C'est votre...

– Juliet, pour l'amour du ciel, de quoi s'agit-il ?

Elle plaqua ses deux mains contre sa bouche, essayant de reprendre contenance. Quelques secondes plus tard, elle écarta ses ongles au vernis pailleté et parla entre scs doigts.

– C'est votre père, monsieur. Artemis senior. Mrs. Fowl dit qu'il est revenu !

Pendant une fraction de seconde, Artemis jura que son cœur avait cessé de battre. Son père ? Revenu ? Était-ce possible ? Bien sûr, il avait toujours cru que son père était encore vivant. Mais ces derniers temps, depuis qu'il avait manigancé le stratagème pour voler l'or des fées, c'était comme si son père avait été relégué dans un coin de son esprit.

Artemis éprouva un sentiment de culpabilité qui lui retourna l'estomac. Il avait abandonné. Abandonné son propre père.

– Tu l'as vu, Juliet ? De tes yeux ?

La jeune fille hocha la tête.

– Non, Artemis, non, monsieur. J'ai simplement entendu des voix. Dans la chambre. Mais votre mère ne m'a pas laissée entrer. Sous aucun prétexte. Pas même pour lui apporter une boisson chaude.

Artemis fit quelques calculs. Il y avait à peine une heure qu'ils étaient revenus. Son père aurait pu se glisser dans la maison à l'insu de Juliet. C'était possible. Simplement possible. Il jeta un coup d'œil à sa montre, synchronisée avec Greenwich. Le temps moyen constamment réglé par signal radio. Trois heures du matin. Le temps passait. Tout son plan dépendait de l'initiative que les fées prendraient avant l'aube.

Artemis eut un sursaut. De nouveau, il mettait sa famille au second plan. Qu'était-il en train de devenir ? La priorité aurait dû être son père, pas une machination destinée à récolter de l'argent.

Juliet, toujours dans l'embrasure de la porte, le regardait de ses immenses yeux bleus. Elle attendait qu'il prenne une décision, comme toujours. Et pour une fois, l'indécision se lisait sur ses traits pâles.

– Bon, finit-il par grommeler. Je ferais bien de monter là-haut tout de suite.

Artemis passa devant la jeune fille, grimpant les marches quatre à quatre. La chambre de sa mère se trouvait deux étages plus haut, dans un grenier aménagé.

Arrivé devant la porte, il hésita. Qu'allait-il dire si son père était miraculeusement revenu ? Qu'allait-il faire ? Il était ridicule de se mettre dans tous ses états pour ça. C'était impossible à prévoir. Il frappa discrètement.

– Mère ?

Il n'y eut pas de réponse, mais il crut entendre glousser et rire et se retrouva instantanément projeté dans le passé. A l'origine, cette pièce avait été le salon de ses parents. Ils restaient assis des heures sur le canapé, à pouffer de rire comme des collégiens, donnant à manger aux pigeons ou regardant les voiliers voguer dans la baie de Dublin. Lorsque Artemis senior avait disparu, Angeline Fowl était devenue de plus en plus attachée à cet endroit et avait fini par refuser de le quitter.

– Mère ? Ça va ?

Il entendit des voix étouffées de l'autre côté de la porte. Des murmures de conspirateurs.

– Mère, j'entre.

– Un instant. Timmy, arrête un peu, tiens-toi bien. Nous avons de la visite.

Timmy ? Le cœur d'Artemis résonna dans sa poitrine comme un coup de caisse claire. Timmy, le surnom qu'elle donnait à son père. Timmy et Arty, les deux hommes de sa vie. Il ne pouvait plus attendre. Artemis ouvrit la double porte à la volée.

Il fut d'abord frappé par la clarté. Sa mère avait allumé les lampes. Un bon signe, sans aucun doute. Artemis savait où elle était, il savait exactement à quel endroit regarder. Mais il ne pouvait s'y résoudre. Que se passerait-il si... si...

– Oui ? Qu'y a-t-il donc ?

Artemis se tourna, les yeux toujours baissés.

– C'est moi.

Sa mère éclata de rire. Un rire léger, insouciant.

– Je vois bien que c'est vous, papy. Vous ne pouvez donc pas laisser une seule nuit de liberté à votre fils ? C'est notre lune de miel, ne l'oubliez pas.

Artemis comprit. C'était une escalade dans la folie. Papy ? Angeline prenait Artemis pour son grand-père. Mort depuis plus de dix ans. Il leva lentement les yeux.

Sa mère était assise sur le canapé, resplendissante dans sa robe de mariée, le visage maladroitement recouvert d'une couche de maquillage. Mais ce n'était pas le pire.

A côté d'elle, il y avait le mannequin de son père, réalisé à l'aide de l'habit qu'il avait porté en ce jour glorieux, dans la cathédrale de Christchurch, quatorze ans auparavant. Les vêtements étaient remplis de mouchoirs en papier et la chemise de smoking surmontée d'une taie d'oreiller rembourrée sur laquelle un visage avait été dessiné avec du rouge à lèvres. C'était presque comique. Artemis étouffa un sanglot, ses espoirs se volatilisant comme un arc-en-ciel d'été.

– Qu'est-ce que tu en dis, papa ? reprit Angeline d'une voix de basse, en remuant l'oreiller comme un ventriloque manipulant sa marionnette. Une nuit de liberté pour ton fils, d'accord ?

Artemis acquiesça d'un signe de tête. Que pouvait-il faire d'autre ?

– D'accord, une nuit. Et la journée de demain, aussi. Soyez heureux.

Le visage d'Angeline rayonnait d'une joie sincère. Elle bondit du canapé pour étreindre son fils qu'elle ne reconnaissait pas.

– Merci, papy. Merci.

Artemis l'étreignit à son tour, bien qu'il eût l'impression de tricher.

– C'est bien naturel, mè... Angeline. Et maintenant, il faut que je m'en aille. J'ai des choses à faire.

Sa mère se rassit à côté de son imitation de mari.

– Oui, papy. Allez-y, ne vous inquiétez pas, nous ne risquons pas de nous ennuyer.

Artemis sortit sans regarder derrière lui. C'était vrai qu'il avait des choses à faire. Extorquer de l'or à des fées, notamment. Il n'avait pas de temps à consacrer au monde fantasmatique de sa mère.

Le capitaine Short se tenait la tête dans les mains. Dans une main pour être précis. L'autre tâtonnait à l'intérieur de sa botte, dans l'angle mort de la caméra de surveillance. En réalité, Holly avait les idées parfaitement claires mais il n'était pas mauvais de faire croire à l'ennemi qu'elle était hors d'état d'agir. Peut-être allaient-ils sous-estimer ses capacités. Ce serait alors la dernière erreur qu'ils auraient l'occasion de commettre au cours de leur vie.

Les doigts de Holly se refermèrent sur l'objet qui s'enfonçait dans sa cheville. En le touchant, elle sut aussitôt ce que c'était. Le gland ! Il avait dû glisser dans sa botte pendant la mêlée qui avait accompagné son enlèvement. Voilà qui pouvait devenir un élément essentiel dans la suite des événements. Elle n'avait plus besoin que d'un petit carré de terre pour que ses pouvoirs soient restaurés.

Holly jeta un coup d'œil furtif autour de la cellule.

Apparemment, c'était du béton neuf. Pas la moindre fissure, des angles de mur bien nets. Nulle part où cacher son arme secrète. La fée tenta de se lever pour voir si elle tenait sur ses jambes. Pas trop mal dans l'ensemble : en dehors de ses genoux un peu tremblants, son équilibre était assez stable. Elle s'approcha du mur et appuya la joue et les paumes de ses mains contre la surface lisse. Le béton était vraiment récent. Il restait même des endroits encore humides. De toute évidence, sa prison avait été construite spécialement pour cet usage.

– Vous cherchez quelque chose ? dit une voix.

Une voix dure, glaciale.

Holly s'écarta brusquement du mur. Le jeune humain se tenait à moins de deux mètres d'elle, les yeux cachés par des lunettes réfléchissantes. Il était entré dans la cellule sans faire le moindre bruit. Extraordinaire.

– Asseyez-vous, s'il vous plaît.

Holly n'avait aucune envie de s'asseoir, s'il vous plaît. Ce qu'elle voulait, c'était neutraliser ce gamin insolent et se servir de sa misérable peau d'humain comme monnaie d'échange. Artemis lisait ses pensées dans ses yeux et semblait s'en amuser.

– Alors, capitaine Short, on a quelques petits projets en tête ?

Holly découvrit ses dents. C'était une réponse suffisante.

– Nous sommes tous les deux pleinement conscients des règles à respecter, capitaine. Ceci est ma maison. Vous devez donc vous soumettre à mes désirs. Ce sont vos lois, pas les miennes. Comme vous pouvez vous en douter, je ne désire nullement que vous me fassiez du mal ou que vous tentiez de vous enfuir d'ici.

Ce fut à ce moment-là que le détail frappa Holly.

– Comment connaissez-vous mon... ?

– Votre nom ? Votre grade ?

Artemis sourit, mais d'un sourire sans joie.

– Quand on porte un badge...

La main de la fée couvrit machinalement le badge argenté fixé à sa combinaison.

– Mais c'est écrit en...

– En gnomique, je sais. Il se trouve que je parle cette langue couramment. Comme tout le monde dans mon organisation.

Holly resta silencieuse un moment, le temps d'assimiler cette révélation capitale.

– Fowl, dit-elle d'un ton pénétré, vous n'avez aucune idée de ce que vous avez fait. Provoquer ainsi la rencontre entre nos deux mondes peut signifier un désastre pour nous tous.

Artemis haussa les épaules.

– Je ne suis pas du tout intéressé par *nous tous*, seulement par moi. Et je n'aurai aucun ennui, vous pouvez me croire. Maintenant, asseyez-vous, s'il vous plaît.

Holly s'assit, gardant ses yeux noisette fixés sur le petit monstre qui se tenait devant elle.

– Alors, c'est quoi ce plan magistral, Fowl ? Laissez-moi deviner : devenir le maître du monde ?

– Rien d'aussi grandiloquent, répondit Artemis en pouffant de rire. Je ne cherche que la richesse.

– Ah, un voleur, lança Holly avec mépris. Vous n'êtes donc qu'un simple voleur ?

Le visage d'Artemis prit une expression agacée qui laissa place à son habituel sourire sardonique.

– Oui. Un voleur, si vous voulez. Mais pas un *simple* voleur. Le premier voleur interespèces du monde.

Le capitaine Short laissa échapper une exclamation dédaigneuse :

– Le premier voleur interespèces ! Le Peuple de la Boue n'a pas cessé de nous voler pendant des millénaires. Pourquoi pensez-vous que nous vivons sous terre ?

– C'est vrai. Mais je serai le premier à réussir le tour de force de séparer une fée de son or.

– L'or ? L'or ? Espèce de stupide petit humain. Vous ne croyez quand même pas à ces balivernes sur les coffres au trésor ? On dit sur nous des choses qui ne sont pas vraies, figurez-vous.

La tête rejetée en arrière, Holly éclata de rire.

Artemis contempla patiemment ses ongles, attendant qu'elle ait fini.

Lorsque son hilarité se fut enfin calmée, il agita l'index.

– Vous avez raison de rire, capitaine Short. Pendant un certain temps, j'ai cru moi aussi à ces bêtises sur les coffres remplis d'or au pied des arcs-en-ciel mais, depuis, j'ai beaucoup appris. A présent, je connais l'existence du fonds de rançon pour les otages.

Holly dut faire un effort pour contrôler l'expression de son visage.

– Quel fonds de rançon ?

– Allons, capitaine. A quoi bon jouer la comédie ? C'est vous-même qui m'en avez parlé.

– Je... je vous en ai parlé ! balbutia la fée. Ridicule !

– Regardez votre bras.

Elle remonta sa manche droite. Il y avait un petit tampon d'ouate fixé avec du sparadrap sur sa veine.

– C'est à cet endroit que nous vous avons administré la piqûre de thiopental sodique, plus connu sous le nom de sérum de vérité. Vous nous avez tout raconté.

Holly savait que c'était vrai. Sinon, comment aurait-il pu être au courant ?

– Vous êtes fou !

Artemis hocha la tête d'un air indulgent.

– Si je gagne, je suis un génie. Si je perds, je suis fou. C'est comme ça que s'écrit l'histoire.

Bien entendu, il n'y avait pas eu la moindre injection de thiopental sodique, simplement une piqûre bénigne avec une aiguille stérilisée. Artemis n'aurait pas pris le risque de causer des dommages cérébraux à sa monnaie d'échange, mais il ne voulait pas non plus révéler qu'il avait tiré ses informations du *Livre des fées.* Il valait mieux laisser croire à son otage qu'elle avait trahi son propre peuple. Son moral en serait atteint et elle deviendrait plus vulnérable à ses jeux psychologiques.

Cette ruse, pourtant, le mettait mal à l'aise. Elle était indéniablement cruelle. Jusqu'où était-il prêt à aller pour obtenir cet or ? Il ne le savait pas lui-même et continuerait à l'ignorer tant que le moment ne serait pas venu. Holly s'affaissa, momentanément vaincue par ce qu'elle venait d'entendre.

Elle avait parlé. Révélé des secrets à caractère sacré. Même si elle parvenait à s'enfuir, elle serait désormais reléguée dans un tunnel glacial, sous le cercle arctique.

– La partie n'est pas terminée, Fowl, dit-elle enfin. Nous avons des pouvoirs que vous n'imaginez même pas. Il faudrait des jours et des jours pour en faire la liste.

A nouveau, le garçon éclata d'un rire exaspérant.

– A votre avis, ça fait combien de temps que vous êtes ici ?

Holly grogna ; elle savait ce qui allait venir.

– Quelques heures ?

Artemis hocha la tête en signe de dénégation.

– Trois jours, mentit-il. Nous vous avons mis un goutte-à-goutte pendant soixante heures... jusqu'à ce que vous nous révéliez tout ce que nous avions besoin de savoir.

Au moment même où les mots s'échappaient de sa

bouche, Artemis se sentit coupable. Ces petits jeux psychologiques avaient sur Holly un effet manifeste, elle en était littéralement retournée. Était-ce bien nécessaire ?

– Trois jours ? Vous auriez pu me tuer. Quel genre d'individu... ?

Ce fut cette incapacité à poursuivre qui répandit le doute dans l'esprit d'Artemis. La fée l'estimait si malfaisant qu'elle n'arrivait même plus à trouver les mots pour le qualifier.

Holly reprit contenance.

– Dans ce cas, monsieur Fowl, lança-t-elle avec un mépris appuyé, si vous en savez tant sur nous, vous devez également savoir ce qui se passera quand on m'aura localisée.

Artemis acquiesça d'un air absent.

– Oh oui, bien sûr, je le sais. D'ailleurs, je compte bien là-dessus.

Ce fut au tour de Holly de sourire.

– Ah, vraiment. Dites-moi un peu, mon garçon, avez-vous déjà eu l'occasion de rencontrer un troll ?

Pour la première fois, l'assurance du jeune humain sembla baisser d'un cran.

– Non. Un troll, jamais.

Le sourire de Holly s'élargit, découvrant un peu plus sa dentition.

– Eh bien, c'est ce qui va vous arriver, Fowl.

Vous pouvez en être sûr. Et j'espère bien assister au spectacle.

Les FAR avaient installé un centre d'opération en surface, à la sortie du conduit E1 : Tara.

– Alors ? dit Root, en repoussant d'une tape un gremlin infirmier qui lui appliquait sur le front une pommade contre les brûlures. Laissez tomber. La magie aura vite fait d'arranger ça.

– Alors quoi ? répliqua Foaly.

– Épargnez-moi vos blagues, Foaly. Aujourd'hui, je ne suis pas d'humeur à m'extasier sur la-merveilleuse-technologie-du-petit-poney. Dites-moi ce que vous avez trouvé sur cet humain.

Foaly se renfrogna, rajustant son chapeau d'aluminium sur sa tête, et ouvrit le couvercle d'un ordinateur portable pas plus épais qu'une gaufre.

– J'ai réussi à me brancher clandestinement sur Interpol. Ce n'est pas très difficile, croyez-moi. Je me suis même demandé s'ils n'allaient pas me souhaiter la bienvenue...

Root pianota avec impatience sur la table de conférence.

– Continuez, s'il vous plaît.

– D'accord. Fowl. Un fichier de dix gigaoctets. Sur papier, ça représenterait la moitié d'une bibliothèque.

Le commandant émit un sifflement.

– Voilà un humain bien occupé.

– Pas un, plusieurs, c'est toute une famille, rectifia Foaly. Les Fowl ont défié la justice pendant des générations. Rackets, trafics, vols à main armée... Au cours du XXe siècle, ils se sont surtout consacrés à la délinquance en col blanc.

– Nous savons où il se trouve ?

– Ça, c'était le plus facile. Le manoir des Fowl. Quatre-vingts hectares près de Dublin. Il est situé à une vingtaine de kilomètres de l'endroit où nous sommes.

Root se mordit la lèvre.

– Vingt seulement ? Ça veut dire que nous pourrions tout régler avant l'aube.

– Ouais. Arranger ce gâchis avant qu'il nous échappe à la lumière du soleil.

Le commandant approuva d'un hochement de tête. C'était l'occasion d'agir. Au cours des siècles, les fées n'avaient jamais opéré à la lumière naturelle. Même quand elles vivaient à la surface, c'étaient essentiellement des créatures nocturnes. Le soleil diluait leurs pouvoirs magiques comme une photographie qui se décolore. S'ils devaient attendre une journée de plus avant d'envoyer une force d'intervention, qui sait quels dégâts Fowl pourrait provoquer ?

Il était même possible que toute cette affaire soit destinée aux médias et que le lendemain soir la photo du capitaine Short se retrouve en couverture de tous les journaux de la planète. Root fut parcouru d'un frisson. Ce serait la fin de tout, à moins que le Peuple de la Boue ait appris à coexister avec d'autres espèces. Mais si l'histoire lui avait enseigné quelque chose, c'était bien que les humains ne pouvaient s'entendre avec personne, même pas avec eux-mêmes.

– Très bien. Tout le monde à son poste. Formation en V. Établissement d'un périmètre dans le parc du manoir.

Les membres du commando de Récupération répondirent par des approbations toutes militaires et s'efforcèrent de faire le plus de bruit possible en entrechoquant leurs armes.

– Foaly, rassemblez les techniciens. Suivez-nous dans la navette. Et amenez les antennes paraboliques. On va isoler le domaine, histoire de nous donner un peu de marge pour respirer.

– Une petite chose, commandant, dit Foaly d'un air songeur.

– Oui ? répondit Root avec impatience.

– Pourquoi cet humain nous a-t-il dit qui il était ? Il devait se douter que nous pourrions le retrouver.

Root haussa les épaules.

– Peut-être qu'il n'est pas aussi intelligent qu'il le pense.

– Non. Je ne crois pas que ce soit l'explication. Je ne le crois pas du tout. Je pense qu'il a une longueur d'avance sur nous depuis le début et que c'est encore le cas maintenant.

– Je n'ai pas de temps à perdre avec des théories, Foaly. L'aube approche.

– Encore une petite chose, commandant.

– C'est important ?

– Je crois que oui.

– Alors ?

Le centaure tapota une touche de son ordinateur portable, faisant défiler sur l'écran les éléments biographiques d'Artemis.

– Le cerveau de cette affaire, celui qui a imaginé ce stratagème très élaboré.

– Oui ? Et alors, quoi ?

Foaly releva la tête, une expression presque admirative dans ses yeux dorés.

– Eh bien, il n'a que douze ans. Et même pour un humain, c'est très jeune.

Root renifla d'un air dédaigneux en logeant une nouvelle batterie dans son pistolet à triple canon.

– Il regarde trop la télé. Il doit se prendre pour Sherlock Holmes.

– Plutôt pour le professeur Moriarty, rectifia Foaly.

– Holmes, Moriarty, ils se ressemblent tous, une fois qu'on leur enlève la peau du crâne.

Sur cette élégante repartie, Root suivit son commando dans le ciel nocturne.

Les membres du commando de Récupération adoptèrent une formation en V dont Root occupait la pointe. Ils volaient en direction du sud-ouest, suivant les images vidéo envoyées par e-mail dans leurs casques. Foaly leur avait même marqué l'emplacement du manoir des Fowl avec un point rouge.

– Infaillible, avait-il marmonné dans son micro, juste assez fort pour que le commandant l'entende.

L'élément central du domaine des Fowl était un château rénové, construit au XVe siècle par lord Hugh Fowl, et dont le style oscillait entre le Moyen Age tardif et le début des temps modernes.

Les Fowl étaient restés fidèles à leur manoir au cours des années, survivant aux guerres, aux émeutes et à divers contrôles fiscaux. Artemis n'avait pas l'intention d'être le premier de la lignée à le perdre.

Le domaine était entouré d'un mur crénelé de cinq mètres de hauteur, avec les tours de guet et les chemins de ronde d'origine. Le commando de Récupération atterrit juste à l'intérieur des limites du manoir et se mit aussitôt à scanner les environs à la recherche d'éventuelles présences hostiles.

– Gardez vingt mètres de distance, ordonna Root.

Ratissez la zone. Contact radio toutes les soixante secondes. C'est clair ?

Les soldats approuvèrent d'un bref signe de tête. Bien sûr que c'était clair. Ils étaient des professionnels.

Le lieutenant Cudgeon, chef des commandos de Récupération, grimpa au sommet d'une des tours de guet.

– Tu sais ce que nous devrions faire, Julius ?

Root et lui avaient été élevés dans le même tunnel ; ils avaient suivi leurs études ensemble à l'académie.

Dans le monde des fées, Cudgeon était l'une des quatre ou cinq personnes qui tutoyaient Root et l'appelaient par son prénom.

– Je sais à quoi tu penses.

– Nous devrions lessiver le domaine tout entier.

– Je m'y attendais.

– C'est le moyen le plus propre. Un rinçage bleu et nos pertes seront réduites au minimum.

« Rinçage bleu » était le terme d'argot qui désignait la bombe biologique dévastatrice que les FAR utilisaient en de rares occasions. L'avantage de la biobombe, c'était qu'elle ne détruisait que la matière vivante.

Le paysage et les bâtiments, eux, restaient intacts.

– Il se trouve que c'est un de mes officiers qui constituerait « les pertes minimum » dont tu parles.

– C'est ça, répliqua Cudgeon d'un air dédaigneux.

Un officier féminin du service de Détection. Le fameux « test ». Je crois que tu n'auras aucun mal à justifier la solution tactique.

Le visage de Root prit la teinte violacée que tout le monde connaissait bien.

– La meilleure chose que tu puisses faire dans l'immédiat, c'est de dégager de mon chemin, sinon je vais être tenté de faire subir un rinçage bleu à cette espèce de bouillie marécageuse que tu appelles ton cerveau.

Cudgeon resta imperturbable.

– Ce n'est pas en m'insultant que tu changeras la réalité, Julius. Tu sais très bien ce que dit le Livre. Nous ne pouvons en aucun cas laisser les éléments souterrains prendre des risques en surface. Tu auras droit à une suspension temporelle, c'est tout, après...

Le lieutenant n'eut pas le temps de finir. Ce n'était pas nécessaire.

– Je sais parfaitement ce que dit le Livre, coupa Root d'un ton sec. Mais j'aimerais mieux que tu ne sois pas aussi va-t-en-guerre. Si je ne te connaissais pas si bien, je jurerais que tu as du sang humain dans les veines.

– Tu n'as aucune raison de dire ça, répondit Cudgeon d'un air boudeur. Je fais simplement mon travail.

– C'est vrai, admit le commandant. Je suis désolé.

Il était rare qu'on entende Root s'excuser mais

il faut dire que l'insulte avait été profondément offensante.

Butler surveillait les écrans de contrôle.

– Il y a quelque chose ? demanda Artemis.

Butler sursauta ; il n'avait pas entendu entrer son jeune maître.

– Non. Une ou deux fois, il m'a semblé voir un frémissement mais ce n'était rien.

– Rien, ça veut dire rien, commenta Artemis d'un air énigmatique. Branchez la nouvelle caméra.

Butler s'exécuta. Pas plus tard que le mois précédent, son maître avait acheté une caméra spéciale sur Internet. Deux mille images seconde, récemment mise au point par la société Lumière et Magie pour les documentaires animaliers, capable de filmer le mouvement des ailes d'un colibri, par exemple. Elle captait les images plus vite que l'œil humain. Artemis l'avait fait installer derrière un angelot qui surmontait l'entrée principale.

Butler activa la manette de commande.

– Où ?

– Essayez l'allée centrale. J'ai l'impression que des visiteurs sont en route.

Le serviteur manipula de ses doigts massifs la manette de la taille d'un cure-dents.

Une image remplit aussitôt l'écran numérique.

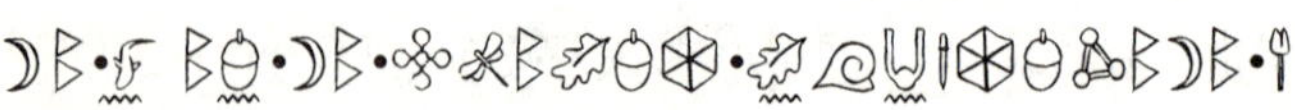

– Rien, marmonna Butler. Plus calme qu'une tombe.

Artemis pointa l'index sur le pupitre de commande.

– Faites un arrêt sur image.

Butler fut sur le point de demander pourquoi. Sur le point. Mais il retint sa langue et pressa la touche. Sur l'écran, le cerisier se figea, ses fleurs suspendues dans les airs. Plus important, une douzaine de silhouettes vêtues de noir apparurent soudain dans l'allée centrale.

– Incroyable ! s'exclama Butler. D'où sortent-ils ?

– Ils ont activé leurs boucliers, expliqua Artemis. Vibrations à hautes fréquences. Trop rapides pour l'œil humain...

– Mais pas pour la caméra, dit Butler en hochant la tête d'un air approbateur.

Maître Artemis. Toujours deux longueurs d'avance.

– Si seulement je pouvais la prendre avec moi.

– Si seulement. Mais nous avons quelque chose qui est presque aussi bien..

Avec des gestes délicats, Artemis prit un casque sur l'établi. C'était celui de Holly, ou plutôt ce qu'il en restait. Impossible de faire entrer la tête de Butler dans le casque d'origine : autant essayer de loger une pomme de terre dans un dé à coudre. Seuls la visière et les boutons de contrôle étaient intacts. Ils avaient été fixés tant bien que mal à une bombe de cavalier pour adapter l'ensemble au crâne du serviteur.

– Cet objet est équipé de plusieurs filtres. Selon toute probabilité, l'un d'eux doit neutraliser l'effet bouclier. Essayons, d'accord ?

Artemis glissa le casque de fortune sur la tête de Butler.

– Bien entendu, étant donné votre champ de vision, il y aura des angles morts, mais cela ne devrait pas trop vous handicaper. Faites tourner la caméra.

Butler réenclencha la caméra tandis qu'Artemis abaissait les filtres l'un après l'autre devant les yeux du serviteur.

– Là ?

– Non.

– Là ?

– Tout devient rouge. Des ultraviolets. Pas de fées.

– Et là ?

– Non. Filtre Polaroid, je crois.

– On arrive au dernier.

Butler sourit.

A la manière d'un requin qui vient d'apercevoir le derrière nu d'un baigneur.

– Ça y est.

Butler voyait le monde dans sa totalité, y compris le commando de Récupération des FAR déployé dans l'allée centrale.

– Hmm, dit Artemis. Variation stroboscopique, j'aurais dû m'en douter. Très hautes fréquences.

– Je vois, mentit Butler.

– C'est une métaphore ou vous les voyez vraiment ? répondit son employeur avec un sourire.

– Je les vois.

Artemis s'ébroua. Encore une plaisanterie. Bientôt, il porterait des chaussures de clown et se livrerait à des acrobaties dans le grand hall.

– Très bien, Butler. Le moment est venu pour vous de faire ce que vous faites le mieux. Il me semble qu'il y a quelques intrus dans le parc...

Le majordome se leva. Il n'avait pas besoin d'instructions supplémentaires. Il rajusta sa bombe puis se dirigea vers la porte à grandes enjambées.

– Ah, heu... Butler.

– Oui, Artemis ?

– Je préfère qu'ils soient morts de peur. Si possible.

Butler approuva d'un signe de tête. Si possible

Le commando Récup 1 était le meilleur et le plus brillant de tous. C'était le rêve de tout enfant fée de pouvoir un jour revêtir la combinaison noire des commandos de Récupération. Ils représentaient l'élite. On les surnommait les Baroudeurs.

Dans le cas du capitaine Kelp, Baroud était même son prénom. Il avait bien insisté sur ce point lors de la cérémonie qui avait marqué son admission à l'académie.

Baroud mena son équipe dans la grande allée centrale.

Comme d'habitude il se plaça en première ligne, bien décidé à être le premier à monter au combat si, comme il l'espérait ardemment, un combat avait lieu

– Vous voyez quelque chose ? murmura-t-il dans le micro qui sortait de son casque en s'enroulant comme un serpent.

– Négatif sur le un.

– Rien, capitaine.

– Ce qui s'appelle rien de rien, Baroud.

Le capitaine Kelp fit la grimace.

– Nous sommes en opération, caporal. Respectez la procédure.

– Mais c'est maman qui l'a dit !

– Je me fiche de ce que maman a dit, caporal ! Le grade, c'est le grade ! Vous devez m'appeler capitaine Kelp.

– Oui, mon capitaine, dit le caporal d'un air boudeur. Mais ne me demande plus de repasser ta tunique.

Baroud régla sa radio sur le canal de son frère, coupant la communication avec le reste du commando.

– Tu arrêtes de parler de maman, d'accord ? Et du repassage. Si tu participes à cette mission, c'est parce que je l'ai demandé ! Alors, maintenant, tu te conduis comme un professionnel ou tu retournes derrière le périmètre !

– O.K., Bard'.

– Baroud ! s'écria le capitaine Kelp. Je m'appelle Baroud, pas Bar ni Bard'. Baroud ! D'accord ?

– D'accord, Baroud. Maman a raison. Tu es encore un bébé.

Jurant d'une manière très peu professionnelle, le capitaine Kelp brancha son casque sur la fréquence ouverte. Juste à temps pour entendre un son étrange :

– Arrkk.

– Qu'est-ce que c'était ?

– Quoi ?

– Sais pas.

– Rien, capitaine.

Mais Baroud avait suivi un stage de reconnaissance des sons avant de passer son examen de capitaine et il était sûr que le « Arrkk » avait été produit par quelqu'un qui venait de recevoir un coup sur la trachée. Il était plus que probable que son frère avait trébuché dans un buisson.

– Grub ? Ça va ?

– Caporal Grub, si ça ne vous ennuie pas.

Kelp donna un féroce coup de pied à une pâquerette.

– Contrôle général. Répondez dans l'ordre.

– Un, O.K.

– Deux, ça va.

– Trois, je m'ennuie mais je suis vivant.

– Cinq, j'approche de l'aile ouest.

Kelp se figea.

– Attendez. Quatre ? Quatre, vous êtes là ? Quelle est votre situation ?

– ...

Rien, à part des parasites.

– Bon, alors, le quatre ne répond plus. Peut-être une panne technique. Mais nous ne pouvons pas prendre de risques. Regroupez-vous devant l'entrée principale.

Le commando Récup 1 se rassembla en faisant un peu moins de bruit qu'une araignée. Kelp compta rapidement les têtes. Onze. Il en manquait une pour faire un commando au complet. Le quatre se promenait sans doute du côté des massifs de roses en se demandant pourquoi personne ne lui parlait.

Baroud remarqua alors deux choses : premièrement, une paire de bottes noires dépassait de sous un buisson, près de la porte ; deuxièmement, un humain à la silhouette massive se tenait dans l'embrasure de cette même porte.

La main posée au creux de son bras, l'homme tenait un pistolet à l'aspect particulièrement redoutable.

– Silence total, murmura Kelp et, aussitôt, onze visières se rabattirent devant les visages, empêchant tout bruit de respiration ou toute communication d'être entendus de l'extérieur.

– Maintenant, pas de panique. Je crois comprendre

ce qui s'est passé. Quatre s'approche de la porte. L'Être de Boue l'ouvre. Quatre prend un coup sur la tête et atterrit dans les buissons. Pas de problème. Notre couverture est intacte. Je répète, intacte. Alors, s'il vous plaît, pas la peine d'avoir des fourmis dans les doigts. Grub... pardon, caporal Kelp, vérifiez la condition du quatre. Les autres, vous restez tranquilles et vous ne faites pas de bruit.

Le commando recula avec précaution, jusqu'au bord de la pelouse soigneusement entretenue. La silhouette qu'ils avaient devant les yeux était véritablement impressionnante, sans nul doute le plus grand humain qu'ils aient jamais vu.

– Nom d'un... murmura le numéro deux.

– Gardez le silence radio sauf en cas d'urgence, ordonna Kelp. Les jurons n'ont aucun caractère d'urgence.

En son for intérieur, cependant, il comprenait cette réaction. Dans un moment comme celui-là, il était content que son bouclier soit activé. Cet homme paraissait capable d'écraser une douzaine d'elfes d'un seul coup de son poing massif.

Grub revint prendre sa place parmi les autres.

– La condition du quatre est stable. Simple commotion, à mon avis. Sinon, tout est O.K. Mais son bouclier est désactivé, alors je l'ai caché dans les buissons.

– Vous avez bien fait, caporal. Bonne initiative.

Ce n'était vraiment pas le moment que quelqu'un repère les bottes du quatre.

Le pas lourd, l'homme s'avança dans l'allée d'un air dégagé. Il était difficile de savoir s'il jetait des coups d'œil à gauche ou à droite à cause du capuchon qui dissimulait son visage. Étrange pour un humain de sortir encapuchonné par une si belle nuit.

– Otez les crans de sûreté, ordonna Baroud.

Les membres du commando devaient lever les yeux au ciel, pensa-t-il. Comme s'ils n'avaient pas déjà ôté les crans de sûreté depuis une bonne demi-heure. Mais il fallait respecter le règlement, au cas où un tribunal s'en mêlerait par la suite. Il y avait eu une époque où les commandos de Récupération tiraient d'abord et ne répondaient jamais aux questions qu'on leur posait après. Mais ce n'était plus le cas.

Maintenant, il se trouvait toujours un civil bien pensant pour brandir les droits du citoyen. Même en faveur des humains, aussi incroyable que cela puisse paraître !

La montagne humaine s'arrêta au beau milieu du commando. S'ils n'avaient pas été invisibles, sa position tactique aurait été idéale pour les attaquer. Leurs propres armes à feu étaient pratiquement inutiles, elles auraient sans doute provoqué plus de dégâts dans leurs propres rangs que chez leur adversaire.

Fort heureusement, le commando tout entier était

invisible, à l'exception du quatre, soigneusement dissimulé sous ce qui semblait être un rhododendron

– Activez les électrotriques.

A tout hasard. Il n'y avait pas de mal à être prudent.

Ce fut lorsque les officiers des FAR changèrent d'armes, au moment précis où ils avaient la main dans le holster, que l'Être de Boue s'adressa à eux :

– Bonsoir, messieurs, dit-il en retirant son capuchon.

« Curieux », pensa Baroud.

C'était presque comme si... Puis il vit la visière rafistolée.

– A couvert ! hurla-t-il. A couvert !

Mais il était trop tard. La seule solution, c'était de se battre. Ce qui n'avait rien d'une solution.

Butler aurait pu les prendre à distance, un par un, avec le fusil du chasseur d'ivoire. Mais ce n'était pas le plan prévu. Il fallait impressionner. Transmettre un message. Il s'agissait d'une tactique courante dans toutes les armées du monde : envoyer d'abord la chair à canon avant d'ouvrir les négociations. On estimait presque normal qu'ils se heurtent à une résistance et Butler n'était que trop heureux de répondre à cette attente.

Il jeta un coup d'œil par la fente de la boîte aux lettres et, ô heureuse coïncidence, il se trouva face à une paire de grosses lunettes qui regardait dans l'autre sens. L'occasion était trop belle.

– C'est l'heure d'aller au lit, dit-il en ouvrant la porte à la volée d'un puissant coup d'épaule.

La créature fit un vol plané de plusieurs mètres avant d'atterrir dans les buissons. Juliet en serait malade. Elle adorait les rhododendrons. Un adversaire au sol. Les autres allaient bientôt suivre.

Butler s'enveloppa la tête dans le capuchon de son blouson et s'avança sur le perron. Ils étaient là, déployés comme un commando d'Action Men. S'ils n'avaient pas disposé de tout un arsenal apparemment très efficace, accroché à leurs ceinturons, ils auraient été presque comiques.

Glissant négligemment un doigt dans le pontet de son pistolet, Butler s'avança au milieu d'eux. C'était le petit costaud sur la droite qui donnait les ordres. On le devinait en voyant les autres têtes tournées vers lui.

Le chef ordonna quelque chose et le commando abandonna les pistolets au profit d'armes de combat rapproché. C'était plus raisonnable : avec leurs armes à feu, ils n'auraient réussi qu'à se tirer dessus les uns les autres. Le moment était venu de passer à l'action.

– Bonsoir, messieurs, dit Butler.

Il n'avait pas pu s'en empêcher et il ne le regretta pas en voyant l'expression de consternation qui apparut sur leurs visages. Il sortit alors son pistolet et tira.

Le capitaine Kelp fut le premier touché, une fléchette à la pointe de titane transperçant sa combinaison à hauteur du cou.

Il s'effondra mollement, comme si l'air s'était soudain transformé en eau. Deux autres membres du commando tombèrent avant d'avoir compris ce qui se passait.

« Ce doit être traumatisant, songea froidement Butler, de perdre soudain un avantage qu'on avait réussi à conserver pendant des siècles. »

A présent, ce qui restait du Récup 1 brandissait les électrotriques activées.

Mais les combattants commirent l'erreur de ne pas bouger, attendant un ordre qui ne venait pas. Butler eut ainsi l'occasion de passer à l'attaque. Comme s'il avait eu besoin d'un avantage supplémentaire.

Pourtant, le serviteur hésita un instant. Ces êtres étaient si petits. On aurait dit des enfants. A ce moment, Grub lui donna un coup de son électrotrique sur le coude et une décharge de mille volts traversa la poitrine de Butler. Toute compassion pour le petit Peuple s'évanouit aussitôt.

Il attrapa la matraque insolente et fit tournoyer l'arme et son propriétaire à la manière d'un lasso. Lorsqu'il lâcha le tout, Grub poussa un cri aigu et fut projeté dans les airs avant d'atterrir directement sur trois de ses camarades.

Continuant de faire des moulinets avec les bras, Butler distribua des coups de poing dévastateurs, frappant deux créatures en pleine poitrine. Une autre grimpa sur son dos, lui infligeant des décharges d'électrotrique. Butler se laissa tomber sur son attaquant. Il y eut un craquement et les décharges cessèrent.

Puis soudain, il se retrouva avec un canon sous le menton. L'un des combattants avait réussi à sortir son arme.

– Ne bouge plus, ver de vase, bourdonna une voix filtrée par un casque. (Le pistolet n'était pas à prendre à la légère, il était rempli d'un liquide coloré qui bouillonnait sur toute la longueur du canon.) Donne-moi une raison de tirer et tu y as droit.

Butler leva les yeux au ciel. L'espèce avait beau être différente, on y employait les mêmes vieux clichés macho. Il frappa son adversaire du plat de la main. Pour la petite créature, c'était sans doute comme si le ciel lui était tombé sur la tête.

– Ça vous convient comme raison ?

Butler se releva. Il y avait des corps étalés un peu partout autour de lui, dans divers états de choc et d'inconscience. Ils avaient eu peur, sans aucun doute mais, apparemment, ils n'en étaient pas morts. Mission accomplie.

L'un d'eux cependant simulait l'évanouissement. On le voyait à ses genoux minuscules qui s'entrechoquaient. Butler le saisit par le cou, son pouce et son médius se rejoignant facilement.

– Nom ?

– G... Grub... heu..., je veux dire caporal Kelp.

– Eh bien, caporal, il faudra annoncer à votre commandant que si je revois des forces armées entrer ici, elles seront reçues à coups de fusil. Et, cette fois, il ne s'agira plus de fléchettes mais de balles perforantes.

– Oui, monsieur, des coups de fusil. Compris. Ce ne serait que justice.

– Bien. Je vous donne cependant l'autorisation d'évacuer vos blessés.

– C'est très gentil de votre part.

– Mais si jamais j'aperçois le moindre petit bout d'arme sur l'un de vos infirmiers, je pourrais bien être tenté de faire sauter quelques-unes des mines que j'ai plantées dans le parc.

Grub déglutit avec difficulté, son teint devenant de plus en plus pâle derrière sa visière.

– Des infirmiers sans armes. C'est clair comme le cristal.

Butler reposa la créature sur le sol puis épousseta ses vêtements de ses doigts massifs.

– Bien, une dernière chose. Vous m'écoutez ?

Signes de tête empressés.

– Je veux un négociateur. Quelqu'un qui puisse prendre des décisions. Pas un sous-fifre qui soit obligé de courir consulter ses chefs chaque fois qu'on formule une exigence. Compris ?

– Très bien. C'est-à-dire que... ça ne devrait pas poser de problème, j'en suis sûr. Malheureusement, je suis moi-même un de ces sous-fifres, je ne peux donc pas vous garantir que ça n'en posera pas...

Butler éprouva une furieuse envie de renvoyer d'un coup de pied le petit bonhomme dans son camp.

– D'accord, je comprends. Et maintenant... taisez-vous !

Grub ouvrit la bouche pour exprimer son approbation puis la referma aussitôt et se contenta d'acquiescer d'un signe de tête.

– Parfait. Bon, avant de partir, vous allez ramasser toutes vos armes et tous vos casques et en faire un petit tas, ici, devant moi.

Grub prit une profonde inspiration. Après tout, autant disparaître en héros.

– Ça, c'est impossible, dit-il.

– Ah, vraiment ? Et pourquoi ?

Grub se redressa de toute sa taille.

– Un officier des FAR n'abandonne jamais son arme.

– Ça se comprend. Je posais simplement la question. Vous pouvez partir, maintenant.

N'en croyant pas sa chance, Grub fila vers le centre d'opérations. Parmi tous ses camarades, il était le seul encore debout. Baroud ronflait dans les graviers de l'allée mais lui, Grub Kelp, avait tenu tête au Monstre de Boue.

Quand maman saurait ça !

Holly était assise au bord de son lit, les doigts serrés sur le cadre métallique. Elle le souleva lentement, faisant porter le poids sur ses bras. L'effort menaça de lui déboîter les coudes. Elle maintint le cadre un instant en l'air puis le laissa retomber violemment sur le sol de ciment d'où s'éleva un nuage de poussière, d'une épaisseur satisfaisante, qui tournoya autour de ses genoux

– Très bien, grogna-t-elle.

Holly jeta un coup d'œil à la caméra. Ils l'observaient, sans aucun doute. Pas de temps à perdre.

Elle serra à nouveau les doigts, répétant l'opération à plusieurs reprises jusqu'à ce que le cadre d'acier imprime des marques profondes dans ses phalanges. Chaque impact arrachait au sol encore frais des éclats de ciment de plus en plus nombreux

Au bout d'un moment, la porte de la cellule s'ouvrit à la volée et Juliet fit irruption dans la pièce.

– Qu'est-ce que vous fabriquez ? haleta-t-elle. Vous essayez de démolir la maison ?

– J'ai faim ! s'écria Holly. Et j'en ai assez de faire des signes à cette stupide caméra. Vous ne nourrissez pas vos prisonniers, ici ? Je veux manger !

Juliet serra les poings.

Artemis lui avait recommandé d'être courtoise mais il y avait des limites.

– Pas la peine de monter sur vos grands... ou vos petits chevaux, je ne sais pas sur quoi vous montez chez vous. Qu'est-ce que ça mange, une fée ?

– Vous avez du dauphin ? demanda Holly d'un ton sarcastique.

Juliet eut un frisson.

– Non, je n'ai pas de dauphin, espèce de bête sauvage !

– Des fruits, alors. Ou des légumes. Et veillez à les laver. Je ne veux pas que vos horribles poisons chimiques entrent dans mon sang.

– Ha, ha, très drôle, vous êtes irrésistible. Ne vous inquiétez pas, tous nos produits sont biologiques.

Juliet se retourna vers la porte puis s'arrêta.

– Et n'oubliez pas les règles. Interdiction d'essayer de vous enfuir de la maison. Et inutile de casser les meubles. Ne m'obligez pas à vous faire une démonstration de mes talents de lutteuse.

Dès que les pas de Juliet se furent éloignés, Holly recommença à défoncer le ciment avec le cadre du lit.

Les engagements que devaient respecter les fées étaient soumis à certaines conditions : il fallait que les instructions soient très précises et données les yeux dans les yeux. Se contenter de dire qu'il était inutile de faire quelque chose ne constituait pas une interdiction formelle pour un elfe.

D'autre part, Holly n'avait pas l'intention de s'enfuir de la maison.

Ce qui ne voulait pas dire qu'elle ne chercherait pas à sortir de la cellule.

Artemis avait encore ajouté un écran dans sa salle de contrôle.

Celui-ci était relié à une caméra installée dans la chambre d'Angeline Fowl. Il consacra quelques instants à regarder ce que faisait sa mère. Il se sentait parfois gêné d'avoir mis une caméra dans sa chambre ; il avait presque l'impression de l'espionner. Mais c'était pour son bien. Elle risquait toujours de se faire mal.

Pour l'instant, elle dormait paisiblement, après avoir avalé les somnifères que Juliet avait laissés sur son plateau. Tout cela faisait partie du plan. Et allait même se révéler d'une importance vitale.

Butler entra dans la salle de contrôle. Il tenait à la main une poignée d'accessoires sortis tout droit du monde des fées et se massait le cou.

– De sacrés petits malins, ces gens-là.

Artemis leva les yeux.

– Des problèmes ?

– Rien de très grave. Mais leurs petits bâtons électriques font quand même de l'effet. Comment va notre prisonnière ?

– A merveille. Juliet est allée lui chercher quelque chose à manger. J'ai bien peur que l'enfermement ne soit pas très bon pour la santé mentale du capitaine Short.

Sur l'écran, Holly continuait de fracasser le ciment avec les pieds du lit.

– Ça se comprend, commenta le serviteur. J'imagine qu'elle doit être contrariée. Elle ne peut même pas creuser un tunnel pour s'enfuir.

Artemis sourit.

– Non. Le domaine tout entier est construit sur une couche calcaire. Même un nain n'arriverait pas à creuser un tunnel pour sortir d'ici. Ni pour y entrer.

Ce qui devait se révéler faux.

Complètement faux.

Et marquer un tournant important pour Artemis Fowl.

Les FAR avaient établi des procédures d'urgence pour des cas comme celui-ci. Mais il faut reconnaître qu'elles ne prévoyaient pas qu'un commando de Récupération puisse se faire assommer par un seul adversaire. Ce qui ne rendait que plus urgente la mise en œuvre de l'étape suivante, d'autant que de très légères lueurs orangées commençaient à s'insinuer dans le ciel nocturne.

– On peut passer à l'action ? rugit Root dans son micro, oubliant qu'il était sensible au moindre murmure.

« On peut passer à l'action », pensa Foaly, occupé à brancher la dernière antenne parabolique sur une des tours de guet. Ces militaires et leurs phrases toutes faites : « passer à l'action », « tout le monde à son poste », « je n'en sais rien mais j'en ai entendu parler »... Un besoin de se rassurer.

A haute voix, il répondit :

– Pas la peine de hurler, commandant. Ce micro pourrait capter le bruit d'une araignée en train de se gratter à Madagascar.

– Et est-ce qu'une araignée est en train de se gratter à Madagascar ?

– Heu... je ne sais pas. Ils ne peuvent pas vraiment...

– Bon, alors, ne détournez pas la conversation, Foaly, et répondez à ma question !

Le centaure se renfrogna. Le commandant prenait toujours tout à la lettre. Il brancha le modem de l'antenne parabolique sur son ordinateur portable.

– O.K. On peut... passer à l'action.

– Il était temps. Allez-y, appuyez sur le bouton.

Pour la troisième fois en très peu de temps, Foaly grinça des dents. Il était en fait le type même du génie méconnu. Appuyez sur le bouton, s'il vous plaît. Root n'avait pas la capacité intellectuelle d'apprécier ce qu'il était en train de faire.

Arrêter le temps ne consistait pas simplement à appuyer sur un bouton : il fallait mener avec la plus extrême précision toute une série d'opérations délicates. Sinon, la zone de suspension temporelle pouvait se transformer en un petit tas de cendres et de boue radioactive.

Il était vrai que les fées pratiquaient des arrêts de temps depuis des millénaires mais, de nos jours, avec l'Internet et les communications satellites, les humains étaient capables de s'apercevoir qu'une zone quelconque de la planète avait échappé au temps pendant une heure ou deux. A une certaine époque, on pouvait faire subir à tout un pays une suspension temporelle sans que les Êtres de la Boue n'y voient d'autre cause que la colère des dieux. Mais ce n'était plus le cas. Aujourd'hui, les humains disposaient d'instruments pour tout mesurer et si l'on devait procéder à une telle opération, il fallait le faire avec le plus grand soin.

Jadis, il suffisait de cinq elfes qui formaient un pentagramme autour de l'objectif et y déployaient un bouclier magique, arrêtant provisoirement le temps à l'intérieur de ce périmètre ensorcelé.

Le procédé marchait très bien tant que les elfes sorciers n'avaient pas besoin d'aller aux toilettes. Malheureusement, de nombreux sièges s'étaient soldés par un échec parce qu'un elfe avait bu un verre de trop. Sans compter que les sorciers se fatiguent vite et qu'ils attrapent des crampes dans les bras. Les bons jours, on pouvait faire durer l'opération une heure et demie, ce qui n'était pas suffisant pour justifier tous ces efforts.

C'était Foaly qui avait eu l'idée de mécaniser le processus. Il demandait aux sorciers de diriger leurs incantations sur des batteries au lithium puis il établissait un réseau d'antennes paraboliques autour de la zone désignée. Simple en apparence ? Et pourtant beaucoup plus compliqué qu'il n'y paraissait.

Mais la méthode présentait des avantages certains. Pour commencer, il n'y avait plus de montées en puissance intempestives. Les batteries n'éprouvaient pas le besoin de faire étalage de leurs pouvoirs. Il était possible de calculer avec précision la quantité d'énergie nécessaire et les sièges pouvaient ainsi durer jusqu'à huit heures consécutives.

Dans le cas présent, le domaine des Fowl était l'endroit parfait pour une suspension temporelle – un lieu isolé entouré de limites bien précises. Par une chance incroyable, il disposait même de tours sur lesquelles installer les antennes paraboliques. C'était comme si Artemis Fowl avait absolument voulu qu'on arrête le temps autour de lui... Le doigt de Foaly hésita au moment où il allait appuyer sur le bouton.

Était-ce vraiment possible ? Après tout, ce jeune humain avait une longueur d'avance sur eux depuis le début.

– Commandant ?

– Ça y est, nous sommes branchés ?

– Pas tout à fait. Il y a quelque chose...

La réplique de Root fit presque exploser les écouteurs du centaure.

– Non, Foaly ! Il n'y a pas quelque chose ! Gardez vos brillantes idées pour vous, merci bien. La vie du capitaine Short est en danger, alors vous poussez ce bouton, sinon c'est moi qui vais venir le pousser avec votre nez !

– Nerveux, murmura Foaly, et il appuya sur le bouton.

Le lieutenant Cudgeon consulta son lunomètre.

– Tu as huit heures devant toi.

– Je sais combien j'ai de temps, grogna Root. Et arrête de me suivre. Tu n'as rien d'autre à faire ?

– Tiens, c'est vrai, maintenant que tu m'y fais penser, j'ai une biobombe à armer.

Root se retourna vers lui.

– Ne commence pas à m'énerver, lieutenant. Entendre tes commentaires incessants n'aide pas à ma concentration. Alors prends les décisions que tu crois devoir prendre. Mais tiens-toi prêt à les justifier devant un tribunal. Si cette opération échoue, il y a des têtes qui vont tomber.

– Sûrement, marmonna Cudgeon comme pour lui-même. Mais pas la mienne.

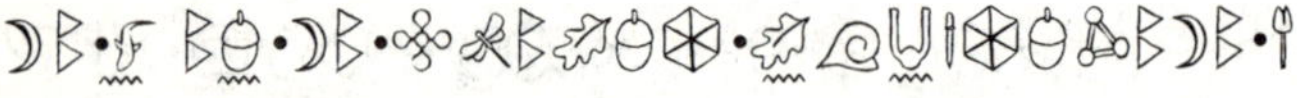

Root regarda le ciel. Un champ d'azur scintillant s'étendait sur le domaine des Fowl. Très bien.

Ils venaient de tomber dans l'oubli. Derrière les murs, la vie suivait son cours à un rythme exagéré mais, si quelqu'un parvenait à franchir l'enceinte fortifiée et le grand portail, il trouverait un manoir désert, tous ses occupants prisonniers du passé.

Ainsi, pendant les huit prochaines heures, une lumière d'aube naissante se maintiendrait sur le domaine.

Une fois ce délai écoulé, Root ne pourrait plus garantir la sécurité de Holly.

Étant donné la gravité de la situation, il était plus que probable que Cudgeon obtiendrait le feu vert pour lancer la biobombe dans tout le manoir. Root avait déjà assisté à un rinçage bleu. Aucun être vivant n'avait survécu, pas même les rats.

Root rejoignit Foaly au pied de la tour nord. Le centaure avait garé une navette près de la muraille d'un mètre d'épaisseur. Déjà, l'endroit s'était transformé en un enchevêtrement de câbles et de fibres optiques palpitantes.

– Foaly ? Vous êtes là ?

La tête du centaure coiffé de son chapeau d'aluminium émergea d'un lecteur de disque dur éventré.

– Ici, commandant. J'imagine que vous êtes venu pousser un bouton avec mon nez.

Root faillit éclater de rire.

– Ne me dites pas que vous vous attendez à des excuses, Foaly. J'ai déjà épuisé mon quota pour aujourd'hui. Et encore, c'était par égard pour un ami de longue date.

– Cudgeon ? Pardonnez-moi, commandant, mais à votre place, je ne gaspillerais pas mes excuses pour le lieutenant. Lui, il ne s'excusera pas quand il vous aura poignardé dans le dos.

– Vous vous trompez sur son compte. Cudgeon est un bon officier. Un peu impatient, sans doute, mais il fera ce qui convient quand le moment sera venu.

– Ce qui convient pour lui-même. Et je ne crois pas que Holly soit en tête de ses priorités.

Root ne répondit rien. Il ne le pouvait pas.

– Autre chose. J'ai la vague impression que le jeune Artemis Fowl voulait que nous arrêtions le temps. Jusqu'à présent, il a toujours su profiter de tout ce que nous avons fait.

Root se massa les tempes.

– C'est impossible. Comment un humain pourrait-il être au courant des suspensions temporelles ? De toute façon, ce n'est pas le moment de vous lancer dans des théories, Foaly. Je dispose de moins de huit heures pour arranger ce désastre. Alors, qu'est-ce que vous pouvez me donner ?

Dans un bruit de sabots, Foaly s'approcha d'une

étagère fixée au mur, sur laquelle était disposé du matériel.

– Pas d'armement lourd, ça, c'est sûr. Pas après ce qui est arrivé au Récup 1. Pas de casque non plus. Cette grosse brute d'Homme de Boue a l'air de les collectionner. Non, pour montrer notre bonne foi, nous allons vous envoyer là-bas sans armes et sans protection.

Root eut un air pincé.

– Vous avez pris ça dans quel manuel ?

– C'est une procédure habituelle. Créer la confiance encourage la communication.

– Ça suffit, arrêtez de faire des citations et donnez-moi quelque chose avec quoi je puisse tirer.

– Comme vous voudrez, soupira Foaly en prenant sur l'étagère un objet semblable à un doigt.

– Qu'est-ce que c'est que ça ?

– C'est un doigt. A quoi ça ressemble d'après vous ?

– A un doigt, en effet, admit Root.

– Mais il ne s'agit pas d'un doigt ordinaire.

Le centaure jeta un regard autour de lui pour s'assurer que personne ne les observait.

– L'extrémité contient une fléchette sous pression. Un seul coup. Il suffit d'appuyer à l'endroit de la jointure pour que votre adversaire fasse un bon petit somme.

– Pourquoi ne m'avez-vous jamais montré ce truc-là auparavant ?

– C'est du genre top secret.

– Et alors ? dit Root d'un air soupçonneux.

– Et alors, il y a eu des accidents...

– Racontez-moi ça, Foaly.

– Nos agents oublient qu'ils l'ont sur le doigt.

– Et ils finissent par se tirer dessus.

Foaly acquiesça d'un air navré.

– L'un de nos meilleurs lutins s'est mis le doigt dans le nez, par inadvertance. Trois jours de coma.

Root enroula sur son index le doigt en latex qui prit immédiatement la forme et la couleur de son vrai doigt.

– Ne vous inquiétez pas, Foaly. Je ne suis pas complètement idiot. Qu'est-ce que vous avez d'autre ?

Le centaure décrocha de l'étagère quelque chose qui ressemblait à un faux postérieur.

– Vous plaisantez ? Qu'est-ce que c'est que ça ?

– Rien, avoua-t-il. Mais ça amuse beaucoup dans les soirées.

Root pouffa de rire. Deux fois de suite. Ce qui constituait pour lui une forme de défaillance.

– Bon, fini la rigolade. Vous allez me brancher ?

– Bien entendu. Avec une caméra-iris. Quelle couleur ?

Il scruta les yeux du commandant.

– Mmm. Marron. Couleur de boue exactement.

Il choisit un petit flacon sur l'étagère et retira d'une capsule une lentille de contact électronique. Il écarta les paupières de Root avec le pouce et l'index et lui colla sur l'œil la caméra-iris.

– Ça va peut-être vous irriter. Essayez de ne pas frotter, sinon elle risque de glisser derrière l'œil. Résultat, on verrait l'intérieur de votre tête et Dieu sait qu'il n'y a rien d'intéressant là-dedans.

Root battit des paupières, résistant à l'envie de se frotter l'œil.

– Ça y est ? Vous avez terminé ?

Foaly acquiesça d'un signe de tête.

– Nous ne pouvons pas prendre de risque supplémentaire.

Le commandant approuva à contrecœur. Ses hanches lui paraissaient étrangement légères sans pistolet à triple canon accroché à son ceinturon.

– Très bien, j'imagine que cet extraordinaire doigt à fléchette suffira. Mais je vous préviens tout de suite, Foaly, si ce machin me saute à la figure, vous prenez la prochaine navette pour Haven-Ville.

Le centaure eut un petit hennissement amusé.

– Faites quand même attention quand vous irez aux toilettes.

Root n'esquissa pas le moindre sourire. Il y avait des choses avec lesquelles il ne fallait pas plaisanter.

La montre d'Artemis s'était arrêtée. C'était comme si Greenwich avait disparu. Ou alors, songea Artemis, c'est nous qui avons disparu. Il consulta CNN. L'image s'était figée. On voyait Riz Khan tressauter légèrement sur l'écran. Artemis ne put s'empêcher d'avoir un sourire réjoui. Ils l'avaient donc fait, comme dans le Livre.

Les FAR avaient arrêté le temps. Tout marchait selon le plan prévu.

Le moment était venu de vérifier une théorie. Artemis se tourna vers le mur d'écrans et brancha la caméra de sa mère sur le grand écran central de soixante-dix centimètres. Angeline Fowl n'était plus sur le canapé. Artemis prit une vue panoramique de la pièce. Elle était vide. Sa mère était partie. Elle avait disparu. Son sourire s'élargit. Parfait. Exactement comme il s'y attendait.

Il reporta son attention sur Holly Short. Elle continuait de taper par terre avec son lit. De temps à autre, elle se levait et frappait le mur à coups de poing. Peut-être était-ce plus que de la simple contrariété. Y avait-il une forme de méthode dans sa folie ? D'un doigt fin, il tapota l'écran.

– Qu'est-ce que vous fabriquez, capitaine ? Vous avez un petit plan derrière la tête ?

Il fut distrait par un mouvement sur l'écran qui montrait l'allée centrale.

– Enfin, dit-il dans un souffle. Le jeu commence.

Une silhouette s'avançait dans l'allée. Petite, mais

quand même imposante. Et sans bouclier. La comédie était donc terminée.

Artemis appuya sur le bouton de l'interphone.

– Butler ? Nous avons un invité. Je vais l'accueillir. Vous, vous revenez ici et vous surveillez les écrans de contrôle.

La voix métallique de Butler répondit dans le haut-parleur :

– Compris, Artemis. J'arrive.

Artemis boutonna sa veste taillée par un grand couturier et s'arrêta devant le miroir pour resserrer sa cravate. Le secret de la négociation, c'était d'avoir toutes les cartes en main ou, même si ce n'était pas le cas, de faire semblant de les avoir.

Il arbora son expression la plus sinistre. « L'expression du Mal, se dit-il. Du Mal mais aussi d'une haute intelligence. Et déterminée, ne pas oublier la détermination. » Il posa la main sur la poignée de la porte. Du calme, maintenant. Respirer profondément et s'efforcer de chasser l'idée qu'on ait pu commettre une erreur de jugement et que le risque existe de se retrouver abattu d'un coup de pistolet. Un, deux, trois… Il ouvrit la porte.

– Bonsoir, dit-il, en hôte courtois jusqu'au bout des ongles, mais sinistre, maléfique, intelligent et déterminé.

Root se tenait sur le seuil, les paumes en l'air, le

geste universel signifiant : « Vous voyez bien que je ne porte aucune arme meurtrière. »

– C'est vous, Fowl ?

– Artemis Fowl, pour vous servir. A qui ai-je l'honneur ?

– Commandant Root, chef des FAR. Bon, maintenant qu'on s'est présentés, on pourrait peut-être parler affaires ?

– Certainement.

Root voulut tenter d'utiliser son faux doigt.

– Alors, sortez, que je vous voie un peu mieux.

Les traits d'Artemis se durcirent.

– Mes démonstrations n'ont donc servi à rien ? Le baleinier ? Votre commando ? Faudra-t-il que je tue quelqu'un ?

– Non, répondit précipitamment Root. J'avais simplement...

– Vous aviez simplement l'intention de m'attirer au-dehors pour tenter de me capturer et de vous servir de moi comme monnaie d'échange. S'il vous plaît, commandant Root, montrez-vous à la hauteur ou alors envoyez-moi quelqu'un d'intelligent.

Root sentit le sang lui monter aux joues comme sous l'action d'une pompe.

– Écoutez-moi bien, espèce de jeune...

Artemis sourit, à nouveau dominateur.

– Ce n'est pas une très bonne technique, commandant, de perdre son sang-froid avant même de s'être assis à la table des négociations.

Root respira profondément à plusieurs reprises.

– Très bien. Faisons comme vous dites. Où voulez-vous que nous discutions ?

– A l'intérieur, bien entendu. Je vous autorise à entrer, mais souvenez-vous, la vie du capitaine Short est entre vos mains. Faites-y bien attention.

Root suivit son hôte dans le hall au plafond voûté, sous le regard noir des générations de Fowl dont les austères portraits s'alignaient le long des murs. Ils franchirent une porte de chêne verni qui ouvrait sur une salle de conférence toute en longueur où deux places avaient été aménagées de part et d'autre d'une table ronde, avec blocs-notes, cendriers et carafes d'eau.

Root fut ravi de voir les cendriers et sortit aussitôt de son gilet un cigare à moitié mâchonné.

– Après tout, vous n'êtes peut-être pas si barbare que ça, grommela-t-il en exhalant un immense nuage de fumée verte.

Indifférent aux carafes d'eau, le commandant prit une flasque dans sa poche et versa dans un verre un liquide violet. Il but longuement, laissa échapper un rot, puis s'assit.

– Prêt ?

Artemis étala quelques notes devant lui, comme un journaliste s'apprêtant à lire les nouvelles.

– Voici la situation telle que je la vois. J'ai les moyens de révéler au grand jour votre existence souterraine et vous n'avez pas le pouvoir de m'en empêcher. Donc, fondamentalement, quel que soit le prix que je demande, ce ne sera pas cher payé.

Root cracha un brin de tabac de champignon.

– Vous pensez pouvoir diffuser vos informations sur Internet ?

– Pas tout de suite, pas tant que durera la suspension temporelle.

Root s'étrangla en avalant la fumée de son cigare. Leur carte maîtresse. L'atout dans la manche. Découvert.

– Très bien, si vous êtes au courant de la suspension temporelle, vous devez aussi savoir que vous êtes complètement coupé du monde extérieur. En réalité, vous n'avez aucun pouvoir.

Artemis griffonna quelque chose sur son bloc-notes.

– Essayons de gagner du temps. Épargnez-moi vos bluffs grossiers, ils deviennent agaçants. En cas d'enlèvement, les FAR envoient tout d'abord un commando d'élite du service de Récupération pour reprendre ce qui a été perdu. C'est ce que vous avez fait. Excusez-moi, mais il y a de quoi sourire. Un commando d'élite ? Franchement... Une patrouille de louveteaux armés de pistolets à eau aurait pu le vaincre facilement.

Root enrageait en silence, passant sa colère sur le mégot du cigare.

– L'étape suivante, selon les textes officiels, c'est la négociation. Et enfin, lorsque les huit heures sont sur le point d'être écoulées, si aucune solution n'a été trouvée, on fait exploser une biobombe dont les effets se limitent à l'espace où le temps a été arrêté.

– Il semble que vous connaissiez beaucoup de choses sur nous, monsieur Artemis. J'imagine que vous ne me direz pas comment vous avez appris tout ça ?

– En effet.

Root écrasa ce qui restait de son cigare dans le cendrier de cristal.

– Très bien, alors, allons-y, quelles sont vos exigences ?

– Il n'y en a qu'une. Une seule.

Artemis glissa son bloc-notes sur la table vernie. Root lut ce qui y était écrit.

– Une tonne d'or vingt-quatre carats. En petits lingots sans aucune marque. Vous n'êtes pas sérieux ?

– Oh, mais si.

Root se pencha en avant.

– Vous ne comprenez donc pas ? Votre position est intenable. Ou bien vous nous rendez le capitaine Short, ou bien nous allons être obligés de vous tuer tous. Il n'y a pas de compromis possible. Nous ne sommes pas en train de négocier. Pas vraiment. Je suis simplement venu vous exposer les faits.

Artemis sourit, de son sourire de vampire.

– Mais vous allez négocier avec moi, commandant.

– Vraiment ? Et qu'est-ce qui vous fait croire que vous êtes si exceptionnel ?

– Je suis exceptionnel parce que je sais comment échapper à la suspension temporelle.

– Impossible, répliqua Root d'un ton dédaigneux. On ne peut pas y arriver.

– Oh, mais si. Faites-moi confiance, je ne me suis pas trompé jusqu'à maintenant.

Le commandant arracha la page du bloc-notes, la plia et la glissa dans sa poche.

– Il va falloir que j'y réfléchisse.

– Prenez votre temps. Nous avons huit heures devant nous... Pardon, sept heures et demie, ensuite, le moment sera venu pour tout le monde.

Root resta longtemps silencieux, pianotant sur la table. Il prit une inspiration comme s'il allait parler puis il changea d'avis et se leva brusquement.

– Nous resterons en contact. Inutile de me raccompagner, je connais le chemin.

Artemis repoussa son fauteuil.

– Allez-y. Mais souvenez-vous, personne parmi vous n'a le droit d'entrer ici tant que je suis vivant.

Le commandant traversa le hall dans l'autre sens, lançant à son tour des regards noirs aux portraits accrochés au mur. Il valait mieux partir maintenant et examiner les nouvelles données de la situation. Ce jeune Fowl était un adversaire difficile à saisir.

Mais il commettait une erreur fondamentale : il s'imaginait que Root allait respecter les règles. Or, ce n'était pas en suivant les pages d'un manuel que Julius Root avait gagné ses galons de commandant.

Il était temps de recourir à des méthodes un peu moins orthodoxes.

Des experts examinaient la bande vidéo obtenue grâce à la caméra-iris de Root.

– Regardez ça, dit le professeur Cumulus, un spécialiste du comportement. Cette contraction... Elle prouve qu'il ment.

– Absurde, s'indigna le docteur Argon, un psychologue venu du sous-sol des États-Unis. Ça le démange, c'est tout. Ça le démange et donc, il se gratte. Rien de menaçant là-dedans.

Cumulus se tourna vers Foaly.

– Non mais, vous l'entendez ? Et vous voudriez que je travaille avec ce charlatan ?

– Espèce de sorcier de carnaval, répliqua Argon.

Foaly leva ses mains velues.

– Messieurs, s'il vous plaît. Il faut vous mettre d'accord. Nous avons besoin d'établir un profil concret.

– Inutile de continuer, dit Argon. Je ne peux pas travailler dans ces conditions.

Cumulus croisa les bras.

– S'il ne peut pas travailler, moi non plus.

Root franchit la double porte de la navette.

Le teint violacé qui constituait son image de marque était encore plus foncé qu'à l'ordinaire.

– Cet humain fait joujou avec nous et je n'ai pas l'intention de tolérer ça. Alors, vous avez regardé la bande ? Quel est l'avis des experts ?

Foaly s'écarta légèrement, laissant le commandant face aux soi-disant experts.

– Apparemment, ils ne peuvent pas travailler dans ces conditions.

Les yeux de Root se plissèrent jusqu'à n'être plus que deux fentes fixées sur ses proies.

– Vous dites ?

– Ce bon docteur n'est qu'un sot, dit Cumulus qui n'était pas accoutumé au caractère du commandant.

– Je... moi... un... un sot ? balbutia Argon, tout aussi ignorant en la matière. Et vous, espèce de fée des cavernes ? Toujours prêt à plaquer vos interprétations aberrantes sur le geste le plus innocent.

– Innocent ? Ce garçon est un paquet de nerfs. De toute évidence, il ment. C'est élémentaire.

Root abattit son poing sur la table, provoquant des craquelures qui s'étendirent à la surface comme une toile d'araignée.

– Silence !

Et le silence se fit. Instantanément.

– Écoutez-moi bien, les experts ! Il me semble qu'on vous verse des honoraires plutôt coquets pour établir ce profil. C'est bien ça ?

Les deux autres acquiescèrent d'un signe de tête, n'osant pas parler de peur de briser le silence... imposé !

– C'est sans doute le dossier de votre vie, alors je veux que vous soyez totalement concentrés. Compris ?

Nouveaux signes de tête approbateurs.

Root arracha la caméra de son œil larmoyant.

– Avancez la bande, Foaly. Allez vers la fin.

L'image s'accéléra et les mouvements devinrent saccadés.

On voyait Root suivre l'humain dans la salle de conférence.

- Ici. Arrêtez. Vous pouvez faire un zoom sur son visage ?

– Si je peux faire un zoom ? dit Foaly d'un air dédaigneux. Est-ce qu'un nain est capable de voler une toile d'araignée sous les pattes de sa propriétaire ?

– Oui, répondit Root.

– C'était une simple question rhétorique.

– Je n'ai pas besoin de vos leçons de grammaire, Foaly, je veux un zoom, c'est tout.

Le centaure fit grincer ses dents en forme de pierres tombales.

– O.K., chef, tout de suite.

Ses doigts effleurèrent le clavier à la vitessc de l'éclair. Le visage d'Artemis grandit jusqu'à occuper toute la surface de l'écran à plasma.

– Je vous conseille de bien m'écouter, reprit Root en saisissant les deux experts par l'épaule. Nous arrivons à un moment clé dans l'évolution de votre carrière.

– Je suis exceptionnel, dit la bouche sur l'écran, parce que je sais comment échapper à la suspension temporelle.

– Et maintenant, dites-moi, poursuivit Root, est-ce qu'il ment ou pas ?

– Repassez-le, demanda Cumulus. Montrez-moi ses yeux.

Argon approuva.

– Oui, c'est ça, simplement les yeux.

Foaly enfonça quelques touches et les yeux bleu foncé d'Artemis emplirent tout l'écran.

– Je suis exceptionnel, tonna la voix humaine, parce que je sais comment échapper à la suspension temporelle.

– Alors ? Il ment ou pas ?

Cumulus et Argon échangèrent un regard débarrassé de toute trace d'hostilité.

– Non, répondirent-ils d'une même voix.

– Il dit la vérité, ajouta le spécialiste du comportement.

– Ou en tout cas, il en est convaincu, nuança le psychologue.

Root se tamponna l'œil avec un liquide désinfectant.

– C'est bien ce que je pensais. Quand j'ai eu cet humain en face de moi, j'ai pensé que c'était un génie ou un fou.

Sur l'écran, les yeux froids d'Artemis leur lançaient un regard mauvais.

– Et alors, finalement ? C'est un génie ou un fou ? demanda Foaly.

Root prit son pistolet à triple canon sur le râtelier d'armes.

– Quelle différence ? lança-t-il en attachant son fidèle pistolet à sa ceinture. Donnez-moi une ligne extérieure pour le E1. Ce jeune Fowl semble connaître toutes nos règles, il est donc temps d'en violer quelques-unes.

CHAPITRE VII
MULCH

Le moment est venu d'ajouter un nouveau personnage à ce tableau d'un autre monde. En fait, il ne s'agit pas, à proprement parler, d'un nouveau personnage. Nous l'avons déjà rencontré dans la file d'attente des délinquants, au poste des FAR. Incarcéré à diverses reprises pour de nombreux vols, il s'appelle Mulch Diggums, le nain kleptomane. Un individu qui, même aux yeux d'Artemis Fowl, aurait paru douteux. Comme si ce récit ne comportait pas suffisamment d'êtres dépourvus de moralité.

Né dans une famille typique de nains des cavernes, Mulch avait estimé dès son plus jeune âge qu'il n'était pas fait pour le travail de la mine et avait décidé d'utiliser ses talents d'une tout autre manière : c'est-à-dire en creusant des trous pour entrer chez les autres et plus généralement dans des maisons appartenant aux Êtres de la Boue. Bien entendu, cela signifiait le renoncement à tous ses pouvoirs magiques. Toute demeure était en effet sacrée. Si l'on violait cette règle, il fallait en accepter les conséquences. Mais, aux yeux de Mulch, ce n'était pas très important. D'une manière générale, il ne se souciait guère de magie. On n'y avait pas souvent recours, au fond des mines.

Pendant quelques siècles, les choses s'étaient plutôt bien passées et il avait fondé un petit commerce de souvenirs récoltés en surface, qui s'était révélé très lucratif. Jusqu'à ce qu'il essaye de vendre la coupe Jules Rimet à un agent déguisé des FAR. A compter de ce jour, sa chance avait tourné et il avait été arrêté une bonne vingtaine de fois depuis lors, passant un total de trois cents ans à faire des séjours réguliers en prison.

Mulch manifestait un appétit prodigieux lorsqu'il s'agissait de creuser des tunnels et c'est malheureusement une expression qu'il convient de prendre au pied de la lettre. A ceux qui ne seraient pas très familiers du mécanisme d'excavation des nains, je vais m'efforcer de fournir les explications les moins malséantes possibles. Comme certains membres de la classe des reptiles, les nains ont la faculté de se décrocher la mâchoire, ce qui leur permet d'avaler plusieurs kilos de terre à la seconde. Cette matière est alors transformée grâce à un métabolisme d'une remarquable efficacité qui en conserve les minéraux les plus utiles avant d'en... expulser le reste à l'autre extrémité, si l'on peut dire. Charmant.

Pour le moment, Mulch se languissait dans une cellule aux murs de pierre du poste central des FAR. Ou en tout cas, il essayait de donner l'image d'un nain languissant et impassible. Mais en fait, il tremblait dans ses bottes à bouts ferrés.

La guerre des gangs qui opposait les nains aux gobelins faisait rage et un elfe des FAR particulièrement brillant avait jugé utile de le mettre dans une cellule où était déjà enfermée une bande de gobelins surexcités. Une négligence, peut-être. Ou plus vraisemblablement, une petite vengeance de l'officier dont il avait essayé de vider les poches dans la file d'attente.

– Alors, le nain, lança d'un air méprisant le chef des gobelins, une créature au visage couvert de verrues et au corps tatoué de haut en bas. Comment ça se fait que tu n'as pas encore creusé un tunnel pour filer d'ici ?

Mulch tapota le mur.

– C'est de la pierre dure.

Le gobelin éclata de rire.

– Et alors ? Elle ne doit pas être plus dure que ton crâne de nain.

Ses camarades s'esclaffèrent à leur tour. Mulch également. Il pensait que ce serait habile. Il avait tort.

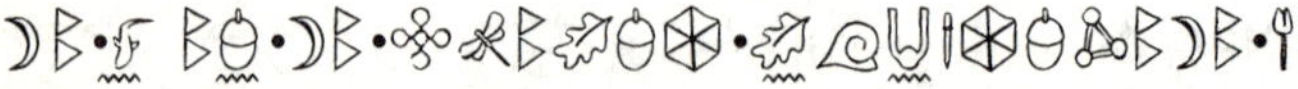

– Tu te moques de moi, le nain ?

Mulch cessa de rire.

– Je ne me moque pas, rectifia-t-il, je ris parce que c'est drôle, la blague sur mon crâne.

Le gobelin s'approcha de lui jusqu'à ce que son nez sale et gluant ne soit plus qu'à un centimètre de celui de Mulch.

– C'était un rire condescendant, le nain ?

Mulch déglutit avec peine en évaluant la situation S'il décrochait sa mâchoire tout de suite, il parviendrait sans doute à avaler le chef avant que les autres aient le temps de réagir. Mais les gobelins étaient terriblement difficiles à digérer. Trop d'os.

Le gobelin fit apparaître une boule de feu autour de son poing.

– Je t'ai posé une question, rase-mottes.

Mulch sentit ses glandes sudoripares passer la vitesse supérieure. Les nains n'aiment pas le feu. Le simple fait d'en parler leur déplaît. A l'inverse des autres communautés du Peuple des fées, ils n'ont aucun désir de vivre en surface. Trop proche du soleil. Ironie du sort pour quelqu'un qui avait fait son fonds de commerce de la Libération des Objets Appartenant aux Êtres de la Boue.

– P... pas la peine de se fâcher, bredouilla Mulch. J'essayais simplement d'être amical.

– Amical ! répliqua Face de Verrue avec mépris. Les

gens de ton espèce ne connaissent pas la signification de ce mot. Vous êtes tous des lâches prêts à poignarder tout le monde dans le dos.

Diplomate, Mulch approuva d'un signe de tête.

– En effet, nous sommes connus pour être un peu perfides.

– Un peu perfides ! Un peu perfides ! Mon frère Flegme est tombé dans une embuscade tendue par une bande de nains déguisés en tas de crottin ! Il est toujours dans le plâtre !

Mulch eut un hochement de tête compatissant.

– La vieille ruse du tas de crottin. Honteux. C'est une des raisons pour lesquelles je me tiens à l'écart de la communauté.

Face de Verrue fit tournoyer la boule de feu entre ses doigts.

– Il y a deux choses au monde que je méprise profondément.

Mulch eut l'impression qu'il n'allait pas tarder à découvrir de quoi il s'agissait.

– La première, c'est un sale petit nain.

Rien de surprenant.

– La deuxième, ce sont les gens qui trahissent leurs semblables. Et, apparemment, tu appartiens à ces deux catégories.

Mulch eut un faible sourire.

– C'est bien ma chance...

– La chance n'a rien à voir là-dedans. C'est le destin qui t'a envoyé entre mes mains.

En temps normal, Mulch aurait pu faire remarquer qu'il existait des liens étroits entre la chance – ou la malchance – et le destin. Mais, aujourd'hui, ce n'était pas le moment.

– Tu aimes le feu, le nain ?

Mulch secoua la tête en signe de dénégation.

Face de Verrue eut un sourire.

– C'est bien dommage parce que j'ai justement l'intention de te faire avaler cette boule de feu.

Le nain eut soudain la gorge sèche. C'était typique des gens de son espèce ! Qu'est-ce que les nains ont le plus en horreur ? Le feu. Quelles sont les seules créatures capables de faire apparaître des boules de feu entre leurs doigts ? Les gobelins. Et donc, avec qui les nains ont-ils choisi de se battre ? Quelle bande d'idiots !

Mulch recula jusqu'au mur.

– Attention. On pourrait tous brûler.

– Pas nous, dit Face de Verrue avec un sourire en aspirant la boule de feu dans ses longues narines. Nous sommes totalement insensibles aux flammes.

Mulch savait parfaitement ce qui allait arriver maintenant. Il en avait été trop souvent le témoin dans des allées obscures. Une bande de gobelins cernaient un de ses congénères isolé et lui tiraient un double coup de feu – au sens propre – en pleine tête.

Les narines de Face de Verrue frémirent : il se préparait à souffler la boule de feu qu'il venait d'inhaler. Mulch se recroquevilla de terreur. Il ne restait plus qu'une seule possibilité. Les gobelins avaient fait une erreur fondamentale. Ils avaient oublié de lui immobiliser les bras.

Le gobelin prit une profonde inspiration par la bouche puis la referma. Il accumulait de l'air pour augmenter la pression du jet de feu. Il rejeta la tête en arrière, le nez pointé vers le nain et souffla. Rapide comme l'éclair, Mulch enfonça alors ses pouces dans les narines de Face de Verrue. Répugnant, certes, mais c'était quand même mieux que d'être transformé en nain grillé.

La boule de feu ne pouvait plus sortir. Elle rebondit sur les pouces de Mulch et remonta dans la tête du gobelin. La moindre résistance des conduits lacrymaux lui permit de s'y engouffrer et les flammes sous pression jaillirent des yeux du gobelin. Une langue de feu se répandit sur toute la surface du plafond.

Mulch retira ses pouces et, après les avoir rapidement essuyés, les mit dans sa bouche pour soulager la brûlure grâce au baume naturel contenu dans sa salive. Bien sûr, s'il avait toujours disposé de ses pouvoirs magiques, il lui aurait suffi d'un simple souhait pour que toute trace de brûlure disparaisse de ses doigts. Mais la perte de la magie était le prix à payer pour une vie passée dans l'illégalité.

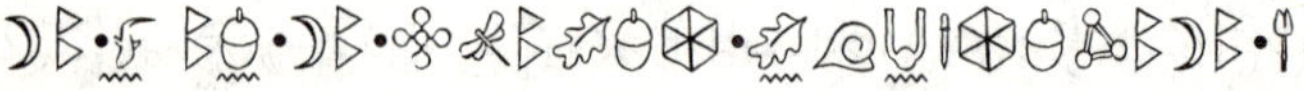

Face de Verrue n'avait pas l'air en très grande forme. De la fumée sortait par tous les orifices de sa tête. Les gobelins étaient peut-être insensibles aux flammes, mais la boule de feu avait quand même fait subir un bon nettoyage à ses conduits. Il vacilla comme une herbe aquatique agitée par le courant puis s'abattit face contre terre sur le sol de ciment. Quelque chose craqua. Sans doute un gros nez de gobelin.

La réaction des autres membres de la bande ne fut guère favorable.

– Regardez ce qu'il a fait au chef !

– Ce nabot puant !

– On va le passer à la broche !

Mulch recula encore un peu plus. Il avait espéré que les autres gobelins seraient désemparés une fois leur chef mis hors circuit. Apparemment, il n'en était rien. Bien que ce ne fût pas du tout dans sa nature, Mulch n'avait plus d'autre choix que de passer à l'attaque.

Il décrocha sa mâchoire, se rua en avant et attrapa entre ses dents la tête du gobelin le plus proche.

– Et 'ainte'ant, recu'ez, hurla-t-il la bouche pleine. Recu'ez ou 'otre co'ain est 'ichu !

Les autres se figèrent sur place, ne sachant comment réagir. Aucun d'entre eux n'ignorait ce que des molaires de nain pouvaient faire à une tête de gobelin. Triste spectacle en vérité.

Ils firent tous surgir une boule de feu entre leurs doigts.

– 'e 'ous 'ré'iens !

– Tu ne pourras pas nous avoir tous, nabot.

Mulch résista à son envie de donner un bon coup de dents. C'est le mouvement le plus naturel chez les nains, la mémoire génétique de millénaires passés à creuser des tunnels. Le fait de sentir le gobelin gluant se tortiller sous sa morsure ne l'aidait guère à se contrôler. Ses possibilités d'action étaient de plus en plus réduites. Les autres avançaient vers lui et il ne pouvait rien faire tant qu'il avait la bouche pleine. Il ressentit alors une angoisse dévorante. Pardon pour le jeu de mots.

Soudain, la porte de la cellule s'ouvrit dans un cliquetis et il sembla qu'un bataillon entier d'agents des FAR envahissait les lieux. Mulch sentit le contact froid d'un canon de pistolet contre sa tempe.

– Recrache le prisonnier, ordonna une voix.

Mulch fut ravi d'obéir. Un gobelin couvert de bave et secoué de haut-le-cœur s'effondra sur le sol.

– Et vous, les gobelins, vous éteignez ça.

Une par une, les boules de feu s'évanouirent.

– Ce n'est pas ma faute, gémit Mulch en montrant Face de Verrue qui se convulsait sur le sol. Il s'est mis en boule.

L'officier rangea son arme dans son holster et sortit une paire de menottes.

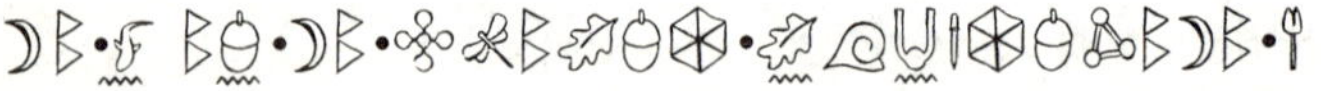

– Je me fiche éperdument de ce que vous vous faites les uns aux autres, dit-il en faisant pivoter Mulch pour lui passer les menottes. Si ça dépendait de moi, je vous mettrais tous dans une grande salle et je reviendrais une semaine plus tard pour tout nettoyer au jet d'eau. Mais le commandant Root veut te voir en surface le plus tôt possible.

– Le plus tôt possible ?

– C'est-à-dire tout de suite et même un peu avant.

Mulch connaissait Root.

Le commandant était responsable de plusieurs de ses séjours dans des résidences d'État. Si Julius voulait le voir, ce n'était sans doute pas pour lui offrir un verre et l'emmener au cinéma.

– Tout de suite ? Mais on est en pleine lumière du jour. Je vais être carbonisé.

L'officier des FAR éclata de rire.

– Il n'y a pas de lumière du jour là où tu vas, mon bonhomme. Là où tu vas, il n'y a plus rien du tout.

Root attendait le nain à l'intérieur du portail de la zone de suspension temporelle. Le portail était encore une des inventions de Foaly. Il permettait aux fées d'entrer et de sortir de la zone sans que l'altération du flux temporel en soit affectée. Ainsi, bien que le voyage de Mulch jusqu'à la surface eût duré près de six heures, il fut introduit auprès de Root quelques instants seulement après que celui-ci eut décidé de le faire venir.

C'était la première fois que Mulch pénétrait dans une zone de suspension temporelle. Il regarda la vie suivre son cours à un rythme exagéré au-delà de la couronne scintillante. Des voitures filaient à des vitesses impossibles et des nuages se précipitaient dans le ciel comme poussés par des vents de force dix.

– Mulch, espèce de petit dépravé, rugit Root. Vous pouvez enlever votre combinaison, à présent. La zone de suspension temporelle filtre les UV, c'est ce qu'on m'a dit en tout cas.

On avait donné au nain une combinaison antiradiation à l'entrée du E1. Malgré leur peau très épaisse, les nains étaient extrêmement sensibles à la lumière du soleil et pouvaient brûler en moins de trois minutes. Mulch se glissa hors de la combinaison moulante comme s'il s'extrayait d'une deuxième peau.

– Content de vous voir, Julius.

– Appelez-moi commandant Root si ça ne vous ennuie pas.

– Ah oui, c'est vrai que vous êtes commandant, maintenant. J'ai entendu dire ça. Une erreur administrative, j'imagine ?

Les dents de Root réduisirent son cigare en charpie.

– Je n'ai pas le temps d'écouter vos impertinences, monsieur le bagnard. Et la seule raison pour laquelle vous n'avez pas déjà pris mon pied au derrière, c'est que j'ai du travail pour vous.

Mulch fronça les sourcils.

– Bagnard ? Dites donc, Julius, j'ai un nom, je crois ?

Root se pencha pour se mettre au niveau du nain.

– Je ne sais pas dans quel monde merveilleux vous vivez, bagnard, mais, dans le monde réel, vous êtes un malfaiteur et mon travail consiste à vous rendre la vie la plus désagréable possible. Alors, si vous vous attendez à des ronds de jambe sous prétexte que j'ai témoigné contre vous une quinzaine de fois, vous allez déchanter !

Mulch se massa les poignets à l'endroit où les menottes avaient laissé des marques rouges.

– D'accord, commandant. Pas la peine d'entrer en éruption. Je suis simplement un petit délinquant, pas un assassin.

– D'après ce qu'on m'a dit, vous avez failli le devenir dans votre cellule.

– Pas ma faute. C'est eux qui m'ont attaqué.

Root vissa un nouveau cigare entre ses lèvres.

– Bon, peu importe. Suivez-moi et ne volez rien au passage.

– Bien, mon commandant, répondit Mulch d'un ton innocent.

Il n'avait pas besoin de voler quoi que ce soit d'autre. Il avait déjà subtilisé à Root sa carte magnétique d'accès à la zone lorsque celui-ci avait commis l'erreur de se pencher vers lui.

Ils franchirent le périmètre établi par le commando de Récupération autour de l'allée centrale.

– Vous voyez ce manoir ?

– Quel manoir ?

Root se tourna vers lui.

– J'ai autre chose à faire qu'à écouter ce genre de plaisanterie, bagnard. Ma suspension temporelle est presque à moitié écoulée. Encore quelques heures et l'un de mes meilleurs officiers sera victime d'un rinçage bleu !

Mulch haussa les épaules.

– Ça ne me regarde pas. Je ne suis qu'un malfaiteur, ne l'oubliez pas. En fait, je sais très bien ce que vous attendez de moi et ma réponse est non.

– Je ne vous ai encore rien demandé.

– C'est évident. J'ai la réputation de cambrioler les maisons. Or, ceci est une maison. Vous, vous ne pouvez pas entrer, parce que vous perdriez vos pouvoirs magiques, mais mes pouvoirs à moi ont déjà disparu. Donc...

Root cracha son cigare.

– Vous n'avez donc aucun sens civique ? C'est toute notre société, toute notre culture, qui sont en cause.

– Ce n'est pas ma culture à moi. La prison chez les fées ou chez les humains, c'est la même chose à mes yeux.

Le commandant réfléchit.

– O.K., espèce de vermisseau. Je réduis votre peine de cinq ans.

– Je veux une amnistie totale.

– Vous rêvez, Mulch.

– A prendre ou à laisser.

– Soixante-quinze ans en régime souple. A prendre ou à laisser.

Mulch fit semblant de réfléchir. C'était pour la forme puisqu'il avait de toute façon l'intention de s'enfuir.

– En cellule individuelle ?

– Oui, oui, en cellule individuelle. Alors, vous acceptez ?

– D'accord, Julius. Mais seulement parce que c'est vous.

Foaly cherchait une caméra-iris de la bonne couleur.

– Noisette, je crois. Ou peut-être marron clair. Vous avez des yeux vraiment étonnants, Mr. Mulch.

– Merci, Foaly. Ma mère m'a toujours dit que c'était ce que j'avais de mieux.

Root faisait les cent pas dans la navette.

– Est-ce que vous vous rendez compte, tous les deux, que nous disposons de très peu de temps ? On se fiche de la couleur. Donnez-lui une caméra, c'est tout.

Foaly prit avec ses pincettes une des lentilles plongées dans son flacon rempli de liquide désinfectant.

– Ce n'est pas seulement une question de vanité,

commandant. Plus les couleurs sont semblables, moins il y a d'interférences avec la vision réelle.

– Peu importe, dépêchez-vous, c'est tout.

Foaly immobilisa le menton de Mulch entre le pouce et l'index

– Et voilà. Avec ça, nous ne vous quitterons pas.

Puis il entortilla un minuscule cylindre dans les épaisses touffes de poils qui sortaient des oreilles de Mulch.

– Nous serons également en contact sonore. Au cas où vous auriez besoin d'appeler à l'aide.

Le nain eut un sourire désabusé.

– Excusez-moi si je ne déborde pas de confiance en vous, mais je me suis toujours mieux débrouillé tout seul.

– Pour vous, mieux se débrouiller, ça signifie récolter dix-sept condamnations ? lança Root en pouffant de rire.

– Ah tiens, je croyais que nous n'avions pas le temps de plaisanter ?

Le commandant saisit le nain par l'épaule.

– Vous avez raison. On n'a pas le temps du tout. Allons-y.

Il entraîna Mulch sur une pelouse, en direction d'un bosquet de cerisiers.

– Je veux que vous creusiez un tunnel pour vous introduire là-dedans et que vous trouviez comment ce jeune Fowl s'y est pris pour en savoir autant sur nous. Il y a probablement un système de surveillance. Quel qu'il soit, détruisez-le. Essayez de repérer le capitaine Short et voyez ce que vous pouvez faire pour elle. Si elle est morte, au moins, on pourra lancer la biobombe sans regrets.

Mulch plissa les yeux en observant le paysage.

– Je n'aime pas beaucoup ça.

– Qu'est-ce que vous n'aimez pas ?

– La configuration du terrain. Ça sent le calcaire. Des fondations de roche dure. Il n'y a peut-être pas moyen de creuser là-dedans.

Foaly trotta jusqu'à eux.

– J'ai scanné les lieux. Le bâtiment d'origine est entièrement construit sur du roc mais les dépendances bâties par la suite reposent sur un sol d'argile. Apparemment, la cave à vin de l'aile sud a un plancher en bois. Ça ne devrait pas poser de problème pour quelqu'un qui a des dents comme les vôtres.

Mulch estima qu'il valait mieux prendre cette remarque comme une constatation plutôt que comme une insulte. Il ouvrit le rabat postérieur de son pantalon.

– Bon, alors, attention, reculez.

Root et les officiers qui l'entouraient coururent se mettre à couvert mais Foaly, qui n'avait jamais vu un nain creuser un tunnel, préféra rester pour jeter un coup d'œil.

– Bonne chance, Mulch.

Le nain décrocha sa mâchoire.

– 'er'i, marmonna-t-il en se penchant, prêt à mordre.

Le centaure regarda autour de lui.

– Où sont passés les... ?

Il n'eut pas le temps de finir sa phrase : une motte d'argile récemment avalée et encore plus récemment recyclée s'écrasa sur son visage. Lorsqu'il se fut essuyé les yeux, Mulch avait déjà disparu dans un trou encore frémissant et de grands éclats de rire secouaient les cerisiers.

Mulch suivit une veine de bonne terre meuble qui s'insinuait dans un repli volcanique du sol rocheux. Consistance moelleuse, pas trop de cailloux. Beaucoup d'insectes. Très important pour garder des dents saines et robustes, l'attribut essentiel des nains – la première chose qu'on regardait avant d'envisager un mariage. Mulch descendit vers le calcaire, son ventre frottant presque contre la surface dure. Plus le tunnel était profond, moins il y avait de risque d'affaissement en surface. On n'était jamais trop prudent, de nos jours, avec tous les capteurs et les mines enterrés ici ou là. Les Êtres de la Boue prenaient des mesures inimaginables pour protéger leurs biens. Et, dans le cas présent, ils n'avaient pas tort.

Mulch sentit une vibration sur sa gauche. Des lapins.

Le nain grava dans sa mémoire l'endroit exact grâce à sa boussole interne. Il était toujours utile de savoir où se situait la vie animale souterraine. Il contourna le terrier, suivant les fondations du manoir qui décrivaient une longue boucle nord-ouest.

La cave était très facile à localiser. Au cours des siècles, des résidus s'étaient infiltrés dans le sol, imprégnant la terre de la personnalité du vin. Celui-ci avait du corps, pas le genre léger. Une note fruitée, mais pas suffisante pour en assouplir la saveur. Un vin à conserver tout en bas du porte-bouteilles uniquement pour les grandes occasions. Mulch se délecta. C'était de la bonne argile.

Le nain dirigea ses mâchoires tranchantes vers la surface, mordant les lattes du plancher dans lequel il creusa un trou. Il se hissa par l'ouverture aux contours déchiquetés, secouant son pantalon pour le débarrasser de la terre recyclée qui s'y était accrochée.

Il avait émergé dans une pièce dont l'obscurité était la bienvenue, parfaite pour un œil de nain. Son sonar naturel l'avait amené vers une surface nue du plancher. Un mètre plus à gauche et il se serait retrouvé dans un énorme tonneau de rouge italien.

Mulch raccrocha sa mâchoire et s'approcha du mur à pas feutrés. Il colla contre la brique rouge une oreille en forme de conque et resta immobile un bon moment, s'imprégnant des vibrations de la maison. Une fréquence basse, comme un bourdonnement. Il y avait un générateur quelque part et un flot d'électricité parcourait les câbles.

Des bruits de pas, aussi. Peut-être au troisième étage. Puis, plus près, un coup sourd. Du métal sur du ciment. Le son se répéta. Quelqu'un était en train de construire quelque chose. Ou de le casser.

Il sentit un frôlement à ses pieds. Instinctivement, Mulch écrasa sa semelle contre le sol. C'était une araignée. Une simple araignée.

– Désolé, ma jolie, dit-il à la tache grisâtre. Je suis un peu nerveux, ces temps-ci.

Les marches de l'escalier étaient en bois, bien entendu. Et devaient avoir plus d'un siècle à en juger par l'odeur. Des marches comme celles-ci, il suffisait de les regarder pour qu'elles se mettent à grincer. Plus efficaces que n'importe quel système d'alarme pour annoncer les intrus. Mulch les escalada en restant tout au bord, les pieds dans le prolongement l'un de l'autre. Le long du mur, le bois était mieux soutenu, moins sensible aux craquements.

Ce n'était pas si simple qu'il y paraissait. Les pieds de nain sont adaptés aux travaux de terrassement, et non pas aux délicates complexités de la danse classique ou de l'équilibre sur des marches de bois. Mulch parvint cependant à atteindre la porte sans incident. Il y eut bien un ou deux légers grincements, mais rien qui fût détectable par une oreille humaine ou un système d'alarme.

Bien entendu, la porte était verrouillée mais c'était comme si elle avait été ouverte, car la résistance qu'elle offrait était négligeable pour un nain kleptomane.

Mulch s'arracha un solide poil de barbe. Les poils de nain sont totalement différents de ceux des humains. Les cheveux et la barbe de Mulch constituaient en réalité un réseau d'antennes qui lui permettaient de s'orienter sous terre et d'éviter les dangers. Une fois arraché, le poil durcissait comme par un phénomène de rigidité cadavérique. Mulch recourba l'extrémité du poil quelques secondes avant qu'il ne se raidisse entièrement. Excellent crochet.

Il lui suffit de le faire tourner légèrement dans la serrure pour la faire céder. Deux gorges seulement. Lamentable comme sécurité. Typique des humains, ils ne s'attendent jamais à une attaque venant du sous-sol. Mulch s'avança dans un couloir au sol recouvert de parquet. Cet endroit sentait l'argent de tous les côtés. Il pourrait ramasser une fortune, ici, pour peu qu'il en ait le temps.

Il y avait des caméras juste au-dessous du linteau de la porte Dissimulées avec goût dans les ombres des moulures. Mais néanmoins vigilantes. Mulch resta là un moment, calculant les angles morts possibles. Trois caméras balayaient le couloir dans un mouvement panoramique qui se répétait toutes les quatre-vingt-dix secondes. Impossible de passer.

– Vous pouvez demander de l'aide, dit une voix dans l'oreille de Mulch.

– Foaly ?

Le nain dirigea son faux iris vers la caméra la plus proche.

– On peut faire quelque chose contre ça ? murmura-t-il.

Il entendit alors un bruit de clavier sur lequel on tapotait et, soudain, son œil droit fit un zoom avant à la manière d'un objectif d'appareil photo.

– Pratique, dit-il dans un souffle. Il faudrait que je m'en procure un pour mon usage personnel.

La voix de Root crépita dans le minuscule écouteur :

– Aucune chance, bagnard. C'est un matériel uniquement fourni par l'administration. Et d'ailleurs, à quoi ça vous servirait en prison ? A regarder le mur d'en face en gros plan ?

– Toujours aimable, Julius. Qu'est-ce qu'il y a ? Vous êtes jaloux parce que je réussis là où vous avez échoué ?

L'horrible juron de Root fut couvert par la voix de Foaly.

– Ça y est, je l'ai. Simple circuit vidéo. Pas même numérique. Je vais diffuser par antenne parabolique dans toutes les caméras une image en boucle des dix

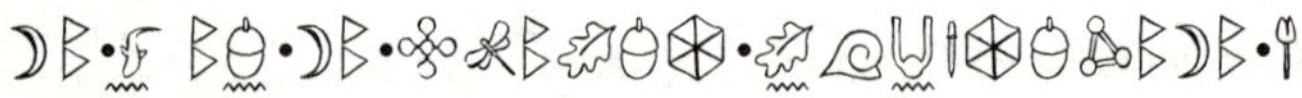

dernières secondes. Ça devrait vous donner quelques minutes de tranquillité.

Mulch remua les pieds, visiblement mal à l'aise.

– Il vous faut combien de temps pour ça ? Je suis un peu exposé, ici.

– C'est déjà commencé, répliqua Foaly. Vous pouvez y aller.

– Vous êtes sûr ?

– Bien sûr que je suis sûr. Simple question d'électronique élémentaire. Je bricolais déjà les systèmes de surveillance des humains quand j'étais au jardin d'enfants. Faites-moi confiance.

« Faire confiance à un expert des FAR ? Autant espérer que les humains cesseront un jour d'exterminer les espèces animales à coups de fusil », songea Mulch. Mais il se contenta de répondre à haute voix :

– D'accord. J'y vais. Terminé.

Il traversa le hall à pas feutrés. Même ses mains étaient feutrées, ondulant dans l'air comme s'il avait pu se rendre plus léger. Les manipulations du centaure avaient sans doute bien fonctionné car aucun Être de Boue surexcité ne s'était rué dans l'escalier en brandissant un pistolet primitif à base de poudre à canon.

Les escaliers. Ah, les escaliers ! Mulch aimait tant les escaliers ! Ils étaient comme un puits de mine déjà creusé, au sommet duquel il pensait trouver à coup sûr un excellent butin.

Et quel escalier que cet escalier-là ! Tout en chêne verni avec ces moulures compliquées que l'on associe généralement au XVIIIe siècle ou à la richesse la plus obscène. Mulch caressa une rampe ornementée. Dans le cas présent, les deux étaient sans doute associés.

Mais il n'avait pas le temps de traînasser. Les escaliers restaient rarement déserts très longtemps, surtout lorsque la maison était assiégée. Qui pouvait dire combien de soldats assoiffés de sang attendaient derrière chaque porte, avides d'ajouter une tête de fée ou de nain à leurs trophées accrochés au mur.

Mulch monta avec précaution, toujours sur ses gardes. Même le chêne massif pouvait craquer. Il resta tout au bord des marches, évitant le tapis. Il savait depuis sa huitième condamnation combien il était facile de cacher un capteur de système d'alarme sous l'épaisseur d'un tapis d'époque.

Il parvint à atteindre le palier supérieur en conservant la tête sur les épaules. Mais il devait subir une autre pression, au sens exact du terme. En raison de sa rapidité, la digestion des nains peut se révéler explosive. La terre meuble qu'on trouvait sous le manoir des Fowl était très aérée et cet air avait pénétré dans le tube digestif de Mulch en même temps que tout le reste, argile et minéraux. Et à présent, l'air accumulé cherchait à s'échapper.

Le savoir-vivre des nains exigeait que les gaz soient

expulsés à l'intérieur même du tunnel, mais Mulch n'avait pas eu le temps de respecter les bonnes manières. Il regrettait maintenant de ne pas avoir pris quelques instants pour se débarrasser de ces ballonnements intempestifs pendant qu'il était encore dans la cave. Le problème, chez les nains, c'est que leurs gaz ne peuvent sortir que par le bas, non par le haut. Imaginons, si c'est possible, les effets catastrophiques qu'aurait un renvoi en pleine digestion d'une grosse motte d'argile.

Débordement total du système. Pas très beau à voir. Aussi l'anatomie des nains assurait-elle la descente systématique des gaz, aidant ainsi à l'expulsion des excès de terre. Bien entendu, il y aurait une manière plus simple d'expliquer les choses, mais cette version-là ne pourrait figurer que dans un livre exclusivement réservé aux adultes.

Mulch serra les bras autour de son ventre. Il aurait mieux valu qu'il sorte au-dehors. Une explosion dans un endroit comme celui-ci pourrait faire voler les vitres en éclats.

Il longea le couloir en traînant les pieds et franchit la première porte qu'il trouva sur son chemin.

Encore des caméras. Et en grand nombre. Mulch observa le mouvement des appareils. Quatre d'entre eux balayaient la pièce d'un bout à l'autre, trois autres étaient fixes.

– Foaly ? Vous êtes là ? murmura le nain.

– Non ! répondit le centaure de son ton typiquement sarcastique. J'ai beaucoup mieux à faire que de m'inquiéter de l'effondrement de notre civilisation.

– C'est ça, merci. Je ne voudrais pas que le danger qui pèse sur ma vie interrompe votre allégresse.

– Aucun risque.

– J'ai un problème à vous soumettre.

Foaly se montra aussitôt intéressé.

– Vraiment ? Je vous écoute.

Mulch dirigea son regard vers les caméras dissimulées dans les moulures du linteau de la porte.

– Je voudrais savoir sur quoi exactement sont pointées ces trois caméras.

Foaly éclata de rire.

– Vous appelez ça un problème ? Ces vieux systèmes vidéo émettent de faibles rayonnements ionisants. Invisibles à l'œil nu, bien entendu, mais pas avec votre caméra oculaire.

Le faux iris de Mulch tremblota puis émit une étincelle.

– Aïe !

– Désolé, ce n'est qu'une petite décharge.

– Vous auriez pu me prévenir.

– Vous aurez droit à un gros bisou plus tard, mon bébé. Je croyais que les nains étaient des durs.

– Nous sommes des durs. Je vous montrerai ça quand je serai de retour.

La voix de Root interrompit les rodomontades :

– Vous ne montrerez rien à personne, bagnard, sauf peut-être l'endroit où se trouvent les toilettes dans votre cellule. Et maintenant, dites-moi un peu ce que vous voyez.

Mulch regarda à nouveau la pièce à travers son œil devenu sensible aux rayonnements ionisants. Chaque caméra émettait un mince trait lumineux, semblable aux derniers rayons du soleil couchant. Les trois rayons étaient braqués sur un portrait d'Artemis Fowl senior.

– Oh, non, pas derrière un tableau, s'il vous plaît, quand même pas !

Mulch colla son oreille contre la vitre qui recouvrait le portrait. Il n'y avait rien d'électrique. Donc, pas de système d'alarme. Pour être plus sûr, il renifla le cadre. Pas de plastique, ni de cuivre. Rien que du bois, de l'acier et du verre. Un peu de plomb dans la peinture. Il glissa un ongle derrière le cadre et tira. Le tableau se détacha du mur en douceur, pivotant sur des gonds. Derrière, il y avait un coffre-fort.

– C'est un coffre, dit Foaly.

– Je le sais bien, espèce d'idiot. J'essaie de me concentrer, figurez-vous ! Si vous tenez à m'aider, indiquez-moi donc la combinaison.

– Pas de problème. Mais il va encore y avoir une petite décharge. Peut-être que le gros bébé va vouloir sucer son pouce pour se consoler.

– Foaly, je vais vous... Aïe !

– Voilà. J'ai branché les rayons X.

Mulch examina le coffre en plissant les yeux. Incroyable. Il arrivait à voir le mécanisme de la serrure. Les gorges et les mentonnets se détachaient nettement de l'ombre. Il souffla sur ses doigts velus et tourna le bouton central de la serrure à combinaison. En quelques secondes le coffre s'ouvrit devant lui.

– Oh, dit-il, déçu.

– Qu'est-ce que c'est ?

– Rien. Simplement de l'argent humain. Rien qui ait de la valeur.

– Laissez tomber, ordonna Root. Essayez une autre pièce. Allez, remuez-vous.

Mulch acquiesça d'un signe de tête. Une autre pièce. Avant que le temps soit écoulé. Mais quelque chose le tracassait. Si ce personnage était si intelligent, pourquoi avait-il caché son coffre-fort derrière un tableau ? C'était tellement banal. Totalement contraire au bon goût.

Non. Il y avait quelque chose qui n'allait pas. Ils étaient en train de se faire berner.

Mulch referma le coffre et repoussa le portrait pour le remettre en place. Il pivota en douceur, léger sur ses gonds. Léger.

Il tira à nouveau le tableau vers lui, puis le repoussa encore une fois.

– Qu'est-ce que vous faites, bagnard ?

– Fermez-la, Julius ! Je veux dire, un peu de silence, commandant.

Le nain regarda le cadre de profil. Il était un peu plus épais que la normale. Beaucoup plus épais, en fait. Même en tenant compte du coffrage. Cinq centimètres de plus. Il passa un ongle dans la rainure du panneau arrière et parvint à le détacher du coffrage, révélant...

– Un autre coffre-fort.

Plus petit, celui-ci. Fait sur mesure, de toute évidence.

– Foaly, cette fois, je n'arrive pas à voir au travers.

– Il est doublé de plomb. Le roi de la cambriole va devoir se débrouiller seul. Allez-y, faites ce que vous savez le mieux faire.

– Typique, marmonna Mulch en collant son oreille contre l'acier glacé.

Il tourna le bouton central au jugé. Belle mécanique.

Le cliquetis était étouffé par le plomb. Il devrait se concentrer. Le bon côté, c'était qu'un coffre aussi étroit ne pouvait avoir qu'une combinaison à trois chiffres maximum.

Le nain retint son souffle et continua de tourner le bouton, un cran à la fois. Pour une oreille normale, même si on avait amplifié le son, tous les déclics auraient semblé les mêmes. Mais pour Mulch, chacun d'eux possédait sa propre signature et lorsqu'un cliquet s'enclencha enfin, il produisit un bruit qui lui parut assourdissant.

– Et d'un, murmura-t-il.

– Dépêchez-vous, bagnard. Le temps passe.

– C'est pour me dire ça que vous m'interrompez ? Je comprends maintenant comment vous avez réussi à vous faire nommer commandant, Julius.

– Bagnard, je vais vous...

Mais c'était inutile. Mulch avait enlevé son écouteur pour le glisser dans sa poche. Maintenant, il pouvait se consacrer entièrement à sa tâche.

– Et de deux.

Il y eut du bruit à l'extérieur de la pièce. Dans le hall. Quelqu'un approchait. De la taille d'un éléphant à en juger par la lourdeur de ses pas. C'était sûrement la montagne humaine qui avait haché menu le commando de Récupération.

Mulch battit des paupières pour chasser une goutte de sueur. Se concentrer. Se concentrer. Les dents du mécanisme continuaient de cliqueter. Millimètre par millimètre. Rien ne s'enclenchait. Le parquet semblait tressauter doucement, mais c'était peut-être un effet de son imagination.

Clic, clic. Allez. Allez. Ses doigts moites glissaient sur le bouton central. Mulch les essuya sur son gilet.

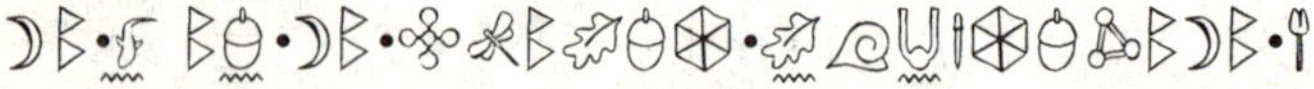

– Allez, vas-y, ma jolie. Dis-moi un mot gentil.

Clic. Clank.

– Oui !

Mulch tourna la poignée. Rien. Il y avait toujours quelque chose qui bloquait. Il effleura du bout des doigts la surface de métal. Là. Une petite irrégularité. Un minuscule trou de serrure. Trop petit pour un crochet moyen. Il était temps de recourir à un truc qu'il avait appris en prison. Mais il fallait faire vite, ses entrailles bouillonnaient comme un ragoût dans une cocotte et le bruit de pas se rapprochait.

Mulch choisit un poil de barbe particulièrement solide et le glissa doucement dans le trou minuscule. Lorsque l'extrémité se recourba et réapparut, il l'arracha de son menton. Le poil se durcit aussitôt, prenant la forme de l'intérieur de la serrure.

Le nain retint son souffle et tourna. En moins de temps qu'il n'en faut à un gobelin pour inventer un mensonge, la serrure s'ouvrit. Magnifique ! Des moments comme celui-ci valaient presque la peine d'avoir passé toutes ces années en prison.

Le nain kleptomane tira vers lui la petite porte du coffre. De la belle ouvrage. Presque digne des doigts d'une fée. Légère comme une pâte feuilletée. A l'intérieur, il y avait un minuscule compartiment. Et dans le compartiment...

– Par tous les dieux du ciel, murmura Mulch.

Les choses alors se précipitèrent. Le choc que Mulch venait d'éprouver se communiqua à ses entrailles qui estimèrent urgent d'expulser l'excès d'air qu'elles renfermaient. Mulch reconnaissait les symptômes : jambes en coton, crampes et gargouillements, postérieur tremblotant.

Il mit à profit les quelques secondes qui lui restaient pour saisir l'objet déposé dans le coffre puis, se penchant en avant, il s'appuya sur ses genoux.

Le vent comprimé avait atteint la force d'un minicyclone impossible à retenir plus longtemps. Il s'échappa donc. Et d'une manière plutôt brutale. Relevant de son souffle puissant le rabat postérieur du pantalon, il frappa de plein fouet le gentleman à la forte carrure qui s'était silencieusement glissé derrière Mulch.

Artemis avait le nez collé à ses écrans. C'était le moment où, traditionnellement, les choses tournaient mal pour les kidnappeurs – lorsqu'on arrivait au troisième quart des opérations. Tout ayant bien marché jusque-là, les ravisseurs ont tendance à se détendre, à allumer quelques cigarettes, à bavarder avec leurs otages. Et voilà comment on se retrouve tout d'un coup à plat ventre par terre avec une douzaine de pistolets pointés sur la nuque. Mais ce ne serait pas le cas d'Artemis Fowl. Il ne commettait jamais d'erreurs.

Les fées devaient sans doute examiner en détail la

bande vidéo de leur première séance de négociations, cherchant le moindre élément qui leur donnerait un moyen d'entrer. Il y en avait un, il leur suffisait de regarder. Dissimulé avec suffisamment d'habileté pour qu'on croie à un hasard.

Il était possible que le commandant Root essaye une nouvelle ruse. C'était un vieux renard, aucun doute à ce sujet. Quelqu'un qui n'accepterait pas de bonne grâce de voir un enfant le surpasser. Il fallait se méfier de lui.

Le simple fait de penser à Root donna des frissons à Artemis. Il décida de procéder à une nouvelle vérification, examinant les écrans.

Juliet était toujours dans la cuisine, occupée à laver des légumes dans l'évier.

Le capitaine Short était allongée sur son lit. Silencieuse comme la tombe. Elle avait renoncé à taper par terre. Peut-être s'était-il trompé à son sujet. Peut-être n'avait-elle aucun plan.

Butler était à son poste, devant la porte de la cellule de Holly. Étrange. Il aurait dû faire sa ronde en ce moment. Artemis prit un talkie-walkie.

– Butler ?

– Oui, je vous reçois.

– Vous devriez avoir commencé votre ronde, non ?

Il y eut un instant de silence.

– Je suis en train de la faire, Artemis. Je me trouve

en ce moment dans le couloir principal. Je me dirige vers la salle des coffres. Vous me voyez ? Je vous adresse un signe de la main en ce moment même.

Artemis regarda l'écran correspondant. Le couloir était désert. Quel que soit l'angle sous lequel on l'observait. Pas trace d'un serviteur en train de faire un signe de la main. Il scruta les écrans en comptant à voix basse... Là ! Toutes les dix secondes, une légère saute d'image. Sur chaque écran.

– Une boucle ! s'écria-t-il en bondissant de son fauteuil. Ils nous passent des boucles !

Dans le haut-parleur, il entendit Butler accélérer le pas et se mettre à courir.

– La salle des coffres !

Artemis sentit une terrible nausée lui secouer l'estomac. Berné ! Lui, Artemis Fowl, avait été berné. Pourtant, il savait bien qu'ils allaient agir. Inconcevable. C'était la faute de son arrogance. Elle l'avait aveuglé et tout son plan allait peut-être s'effondrer lamentablement.

Il régla le talkie-walkie sur la fréquence de Juliet. Dommage qu'il ait débranché l'interphone de la maison, mais la fréquence sur laquelle il fonctionnait n'était pas sûre.

– Juliet ?

– Je vous reçois.

– Où es-tu en ce moment ?

– Dans la cuisine. En train de me détruire les ongles avec cet épluche-légumes.

– Laisse tomber, Juliet ! s'écria Artemis. Laisse tout tomber et va voir la prisonnière !

Obéissante, Juliet laissa tout tomber, y compris le talkie-walkie. Elle allait bouder pendant des jours et des jours, à présent. Mais peu importait. Ce n'était pas le moment de se soucier de l'ego froissé d'une adolescente. Il y avait des questions plus urgentes à traiter.

Artemis appuya sur la touche centrale du système de surveillance informatisé. Sa seule chance d'effacer les boucles, c'était de procéder à une réinitialisation complète. Après un moment angoissant passé à regarder la neige tomber sur les écrans, les images réapparurent enfin. Elles ne ressemblaient plus du tout à ce qu'il avait vu quelques secondes auparavant.

Une chose grotesque avait pénétré dans la salle des coffres. Apparemment, l'intrus avait découvert le compartiment secret. Et, en plus, il avait réussi à ouvrir la serrure invisible. Stupéfiant !

Mais Butler l'avait repéré. Il s'était glissé silencieusement derrière lui et, d'un moment à l'autre, la créature allait se retrouver face contre terre, le nez dans le tapis.

Artemis reporta son attention sur Holly. L'elfe avait recommencé à donner des coups de lit dans le sol. Elle frappait inlassablement la surface de ciment à l'aide du cadre métallique, comme si elle espérait...

L'idée frappa Artemis de plein fouet, comme le jet d'un canon à eau. Si Holly avait réussi à introduire un gland dans sa cellule, il suffirait alors d'un centimètre carré de terre. Et si Juliet laissait la porte ouverte...

– Juliet ! hurla-t-il dans le talkie-walkie. Juliet ! N'entre pas là-dedans !

Mais c'était inutile. Le talkie-walkie de la jeune fille grésillait sur le carrelage de la cuisine et Artemis ne pouvait que regarder, impuissant, la sœur de Butler se diriger à grands pas vers la porte de la cellule en marmonnant quelque chose à propos de ses carottes.

– La salle des coffres ! s'exclama Butler en accélérant le pas.

Son instinct l'aurait poussé à ouvrir le feu tous azimuts mais l'entraînement l'emporta sur l'impulsion. Les armes des fées étaient très nettement supérieures aux siennes et qui pouvait dire combien de canons étaient pointés de l'autre côté de la porte. Non, décidément, la prudence était la seule attitude raisonnable en la circonstance.

Il posa la paume de sa main contre le panneau de la porte pour sentir d'éventuelles vibrations. Rien. Donc pas de machinerie à l'intérieur. Butler referma les doigts sur la poignée et la tourna doucement. De son autre main, il tira de son holster un automatique Sig Sauer. Pas le temps d'aller chercher le fusil à fléchettes, ce serait du tir à balles réelles.

La porte s'ouvrit sans bruit, comme Butler s'y attendait, puisque c'était lui qui s'était chargé d'huiler tous les gonds de la maison. Il vit alors devant lui... Pour dire la vérité, il ne savait pas très bien de quoi il s'agissait. S'il s'était fié à sa première impression, il aurait juré que la chose, énorme et tremblotante, ressemblait à un...

A cet instant, la *chose* explosa, projetant une phénoménale quantité de terre recyclée sur le malheureux serviteur ! Ce fut comme si une centaine de gros marteaux l'avaient frappé simultanément. Butler fut soulevé du sol et précipité hors de la pièce.

Affalé par terre, sombrant peu à peu dans l'inconscience, il pria le ciel pour que maître Artemis n'ait pas assisté à la scène sur son écran vidéo.

Holly faiblissait. Le cadre du lit faisait presque le double de son poids et le bord métallique creusait des marques cruelles et douloureuses dans les paumes de ses mains. Mais elle n'allait pas s'arrêter maintenant. Elle était trop près du but.

Elle abattit une nouvelle fois le lit sur le sol de ciment. Un nuage de poussière grise s'éleva autour de ses jambes. Il se pouvait à tout moment que Fowl comprenne où elle voulait en venir ; elle aurait alors droit à un nouveau traitement hypodermique. Mais en attendant...

Elle serra les dents pour lutter contre la douleur, soulevant le cadre du lit à hauteur de ses genoux.

Ce fut à ce moment qu'elle le vit enfin. Un point marron dans le gris du ciment. Était-ce vraiment ça ?

Oubliant sa douleur, le capitaine Short lâcha le lit et se laissa tomber à genoux. Elle ne s'était pas trompée : une petite surface de terre apparaissait à travers le ciment. D'un geste fébrile, Holly prit le gland dans sa botte en le serrant très fort entre ses doigts sanglants.

– Je replante la graine, murmura-t-elle en enfonçant le poing dans le minuscule espace, pour que soit rendu ailleurs à la terre le cadeau offert près de la rivière.

Holly entendit son cœur battre une fois, peut-être deux, sans que rien ne se produise. Puis elle sentit le flot de magie jaillir le long de son bras comme si elle avait reçu une secousse électrique en essayant de franchir une clôture antitroll. Le choc l'envoya virevolter à travers la cellule. Pendant un moment, le monde tournoya autour d'elle en un étrange kaléidoscope de couleurs et, lorsqu'il se stabilisa à nouveau, Holly n'avait plus rien de l'elfe vaincue qu'elle était encore quelques instants auparavant.

– Et voilà, monsieur Fowl.

Elle sourit en regardant les étincelles bleues qui refermaient ses blessures par la grâce de la magie.

– Voyons maintenant ce que je dois faire pour obtenir votre permission de quitter les lieux.

– Laisse tomber, ronchonna Juliet. Laisse tout tomber et va voir la prisonnière.

D'un geste étudié, elle rejeta ses tresses blondes derrière son épaule.

– Il croit que je suis sa bonne, ou quoi ?

Du plat de la main, elle cogna à la porte de la cellule.

– Attention, madame la fée, je vais entrer, alors si vous faites quelque chose qu'il vaut mieux ne pas voir, c'est le moment d'arrêter.

Juliet composa la combinaison qui permettait d'ouvrir la serrure.

– Et je n'ai pas vos légumes, ni vos fruits bien lavés, mais ce n'est pas ma faute, Artemis a insisté pour que je vienne tout de suite...

Juliet s'interrompit car il n'y avait personne pour l'écouter. Elle s'adressait à une pièce vide. Elle attendit que son cerveau lui fournisse une explication mais rien ne vint.

Enfin, l'idée de regarder une deuxième fois s'insinua dans son esprit.

Elle fit un pas prudent à l'intérieur du cube de béton. Rien. Un simple frémissement dans l'ombre.

Comme une légère brume. C'était sans doute à cause de ces stupides lunettes. Comment pouvait-on voir quoi que ce soit en portant des lunettes de soleil sous terre ? En plus, elles avaient une forme typiquement années 1990, elles n'étaient même pas encore rétro.

Avec un léger sentiment de culpabilité, Juliet tourna la tête vers la caméra de surveillance. Juste un rapide coup d'œil dans la cellule, quel mal pouvait-il y avoir à cela ? Elle releva ses lunettes et lança un regard circulaire dans la pièce.

Au même instant, une silhouette se matérialisa devant elle. Comme surgie de nulle part.

C'était Holly. Avec un grand sourire.

– Oh, vous voilà. Comment avez-vous fait pour... ?

La fée l'interrompit d'un geste de la main.

– Pourquoi n'enlevez-vous pas ces lunettes, Juliet ? Elles ne vous vont vraiment pas.

« Ça, c'est vrai », songea la jeune fille. Et quelle voix magnifique. On dirait un chœur à elle toute seule. Comment refuser quelque chose à une voix pareille ?

– Bien sûr, je vais les enlever, ces lunettes de pithécanthrope. Au fait, vous avez une voix cool, vous. *Do ré mi*, c'est joli, *fa sol la*, c'est extra.

Holly préféra ne pas essayer de comprendre les commentaires de Juliet. C'était déjà suffisamment difficile lorsque la jeune fille était en pleine possession de ses facultés.

– Et maintenant, une simple question.

– Pas de problème.

Une question ? Quelle bonne idée !

– Il y a combien de personnes dans la maison ?

Juliet réfléchit. Une plus une plus une.

Et encore une ? Non, Mrs. Fowl n'était pas vraiment là.

– Trois, dit-elle enfin. Moi et Butler et, bien sûr, Artemis. Mrs. Fowl est là aussi, mais c'est une personne un peu frappée, alors quand on frappe, il n'y a personne.

Juliet pouffa de rire. Elle avait fait une plaisanterie. Et une bonne, en plus.

Holly fut sur le point de demander des explications un peu plus claires mais elle y renonça. Ce qui devait se révéler une erreur.

– Est-ce que quelqu'un d'autre est venu ici ? Quelqu'un comme moi ?

Juliet se mordit la lèvre.

– Il y a eu un petit bonhomme. Avec un uniforme comme le vôtre. Mais lui, il n'était pas mignon. Pas mignon du tout. Il passait son temps à crier et à fumer un cigare puant. En plus, il avait un teint horrible. Rouge comme une tomate.

Holly faillit sourire. Root était venu en personne. A n'en pas douter, la négociation avait dû être désastreuse.

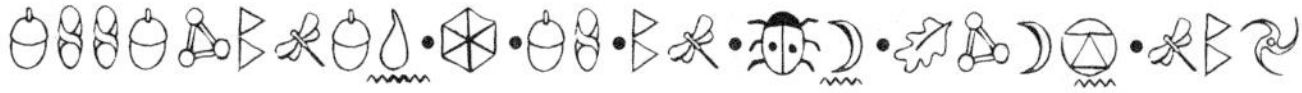

– Personne d'autre ?

– Pas à ma connaissance. Si vous revoyez ce bonhomme, dites-lui donc de laisser tomber la viande rouge. C'est un infarctus ambulant, ce type.

Holly réprima de nouveau un sourire. Juliet était sans doute le seul être humain que l'influence du mesmer rendait plus lucide.

– D'accord, je lui transmettrai le message. Et maintenant, Juliet, je veux que vous restiez dans cette pièce. Quoi qu'on vous dise, n'en sortez pas.

Juliet fronça les sourcils.

– Dans cette pièce ? Mais je vais m'y ennuyer terriblement. Il n'y a même pas de télé. Je ne pourrais pas plutôt aller dans le salon ?

– Non. Il faut que vous restiez ici. D'ailleurs, on vient justement d'installer une télévision murale. Avec un écran de cinéma. Et des matchs de lutte vingt-quatre heures sur vingt-quatre.

Juliet faillit s'évanouir de plaisir. Elle se précipita dans la cellule, bouche bée, tandis que son imagination se chargeait de lui fournir des images.

Holly hocha la tête. « En voilà au moins une qui est heureuse », pensa-t-elle.

Mulch tortilla les hanches pour se débarrasser des dernières mottes de terre.

Si seulement sa mère avait pu le voir en cet instant,

en train de couvrir de boue les Êtres de la Boue ! Ironie du sort, c'était comme ça qu'on disait, non ? A l'école, Mulch n'avait jamais été très bon en grammaire. Ni en poésie. Il n'en avait jamais vu l'utilité.

Au fond de la mine, il n'existait que deux phrases qui avaient une quelconque importance : « Regardez, de l'or ! » et : « Sauve qui peut, un éboulement ! » Aucun sens caché là-dedans, aucune rime.

Le nain reboutonna son rabat postérieur que la bourrasque issue de ses régions inférieures avait soufflé. Il était temps de prendre ses jambes à son cou. L'espoir qu'il avait eu de pouvoir s'échapper en passant inaperçu avait volé en éclats. Littéralement.

Mulch récupéra son écouteur dans sa poche et le vissa dans son oreille. On ne savait jamais, même les FAR pourraient se révéler utiles.

– ... Et quand je vous aurai sous la main, bagnard, vous regretterez de ne pas être resté dans vos mines...

Le nain soupira. Décidément, rien de nouveau.

Serrant dans son poing le trésor arraché au coffre-fort, il revint sur ses pas. A sa très grande stupéfaction, il vit alors un humain enchevêtré dans la rampe de l'escalier. Mulch n'était pas surpris le moins du monde que son système de recyclage ait pu projeter l'éléphantesque Être de Boue à travers les airs. On avait déjà vu dans les Alpes des avalanches provoquées par des gaz de nain. Non, ce qui l'étonnait, c'était que l'homme ait réussi à s'approcher si près de lui sans qu'il s'en aperçoive.

– Tu es très fort, dit Mulch en agitant l'index vers le garde du corps inconscient, mais quand Mulch Diggums passe en coup de vent, personne ne peut lui résister.

L'Être de Boue remua, le blanc de ses yeux apparaissant derrière ses paupières papillonnantes.

La voix de Root crépita dans les oreilles du nain :

– Bougez-vous un peu, Mulch Diggums, avant que l'humain se relève et vous redresse les entrailles. Je vous signale qu'à lui tout seul, il a mis hors de combat un commando entier de Récupération.

Mulch déglutit ; il se sentait soudain beaucoup moins enclin à la fanfaronnade.

– Un commando entier ? Je ferais peut-être bien de retourner sous terre... dans l'intérêt de la mission.

Contournant en hâte le garde du corps qui poussait des grognements, Mulch dévala l'escalier quatre à quatre. Il ne servait plus à rien de se soucier du craquement des marches après avoir fait souffler l'équivalent d'un ouragan tropical dans les couloirs de la maison.

Il avait presque atteint la porte de la cave lorsqu'une silhouette apparut devant lui dans un frémissement. Mulch reconnut l'officier qui l'avait arrêté dans l'affaire du vol de tableaux des maîtres de la Renaissance.

– Capitaine Short.

– Mulch. Je ne m'attendais pas à tomber sur toi.

Le nain haussa les épaules.

– Julius avait un sale boulot à faire. Il fallait bien que quelqu'un s'en charge.

– Je comprends, dit Holly en hochant la tête. Tu as déjà perdu tes pouvoirs magiques. Pas bête. Tu as trouvé quelque chose ?

Il montra sa découverte à Holly.

– C'était dans son coffre.

– Une copie du Livre ! s'exclama-t-elle. Pas étonnant qu'on soit dans ce pétrin. Il nous tenait depuis le début.

Mulch ouvrit la porte de la cave.

– On y va ?

– Je ne peux pas. Il m'a donné l'ordre de ne pas quitter la maison.

– Vous autres avec vos histoires de magie ! Vous ne pouvez pas savoir à quel point on se sent libre quand on est débarrassé de toutes ces calembredaines.

Une suite de bruits secs et sonores retentit à l'étage supérieur. On aurait dit un troll dans un magasin de porcelaine.

– On discutera philosophie plus tard. Pour l'instant, je suggère qu'on se fasse le plus petit possible.

Mulch approuva d'un signe de tête.

– D'accord. Il paraît que ce type a mis hors de combat un commando entier de Récupération.

Holly, qui était en train d'activer son bouclier, s'interrompit, à moitié invisible.

– Un commando entier ? Humm. Avec tout l'équipement ? Je me demande...

Elle continua de s'effacer peu à peu. Bientôt, il ne resta plus d'elle qu'un large sourire qui disparut à son tour.

Mulch fut tenté de rester un peu. Il n'y avait rien de plus amusant que de regarder un officier du service de Détection tomber par surprise sur le dos d'une bande d'humains. Lorsque le capitaine Short en aurait fini avec le dénommé Fowl, il la supplierait de quitter son manoir.

Le dénommé Fowl était justement en train d'observer tout cela depuis son poste de surveillance. Inutile de le nier : les choses tournaient mal. Très mal. Mais il n'y avait rien d'irrémédiable. L'espoir subsistait.

Artemis récapitula les événements qui s'étaient déroulés au cours des dernières minutes. La sécurité du manoir avait été compromise. La salle des coffres était en ruines, dévastée par une sorte de flatulence féerique. Butler était inconscient, peut-être paralysé par cette anomalie gazeuse. Sa prisonnière se promenait en liberté dans la maison et disposait à nouveau de tous ses pouvoirs magiques. Une créature disgracieuse, vêtue d'un pantalon de cuir, creusait des trous sous les fondations de la maison et ne se souciait apparemment pas de respecter les lois du monde des fées. Le petit Peuple avait également réussi à récupérer une copie du Livre, mais il en possédait plusieurs autres, dont une gravée sur disque et déposée dans un coffre en Suisse.

D'un doigt, Artemis écarta une mèche folle de cheveux bruns. Il fallait creuser en profondeur pour découvrir des éléments positifs dans cette situation. Il respira longuement à plusieurs reprises, retrouvant son *ki*, son énergie vitale, comme Butler le lui avait enseigné.

Après un moment de réflexion, il estima que ces nouveaux facteurs n'avaient finalement pas grande importance par rapport aux stratégies mises en œuvre dans les deux camps. Le capitaine Short était toujours prisonnière du manoir. Et la période de suspension temporelle approchait de sa fin. Bientôt, les FAR n'auraient plus d'autre choix que de lancer leur biobombe et c'est alors qu'Artemis Fowl leur porterait le coup de grâce. Bien entendu, tout dépendait du commandant Root. Si, comme il semblait, les capacités intellectuelles de Root n'étaient pas à la hauteur du défi, il se pouvait très bien que son plan s'effondre entièrement. Artemis espérait avec ferveur que quelqu'un, dans l'équipe des fées, serait suffisamment intelligent pour s'apercevoir de la « gaffe » qu'il avait commise au cours de la séance de négociation.

Mulch déboutonna son rabat postérieur. Le moment était venu de « gober de la terre », comme on disait dans les mines. L'ennui avec les tunnels de nain, c'était qu'ils se refermaient d'eux-mêmes si bien que, lorsqu'on voulait parcourir le chemin en sens inverse, il fallait recommencer à creuser. Certains suivaient exactement le même tracé, avalant une terre moins compacte et prédigérée. Mulch, pour sa part, préférait creuser un nouveau tunnel. D'une certaine manière, manger deux fois la même terre ne lui disait rien.

Décrochant sa mâchoire, il s'engouffra telle une torpille à travers le trou du plancher de la cave. Les battements précipités de son cœur se calmèrent dès que l'arôme des minéraux souterrains monta dans ses narines. Sauvé, il était sauvé. Rien ni personne ne pouvait attraper un nain sous terre, même pas un ver de roc écossais. Encore fallait-il atteindre la terre...

Soudain, dix doigts puissants saisirent Mulch par les chevilles. Ce n'était décidément pas son jour de chance. D'abord, Face de Verrue, maintenant cet humain meurtrier. Il y a des gens qui n'apprennent jamais rien. En général, ce sont des Êtres de la Boue.

– 'âchez-'oi, marmonna-t-il, sa mâchoire décrochée s'agitant en vain.

– Sûrement pas, répondit l'homme. Quand tu sortiras d'ici, ce sera dans un sac-poubelle.

Mulch se sentit tiré en arrière. Cet humain était

décidément très fort. Il n'existait pas beaucoup de créatures capables d'arracher un nain agrippé à quelque chose. Il gratta la terre de ses mains, enfournant de pleines poignées d'argile dans sa bouche caverneuse. Il n'y avait qu'une seule chance de s'en sortir.

– Allez, espèce de petit gobelin, sors de là.

Gobelin ! Mulch aurait été scandalisé s'il n'avait été occupé à mastiquer de la terre pour la rejeter sur son ennemi.

L'humain s'interrompit. Il avait peut-être remarqué le rabat postérieur et sans doute le postérieur lui-même. Ce qui s'était produit dans la salle des coffres lui revenait probablement en mémoire.

– Oh...

Ce qui aurait dû suivre ce « Oh... » restera un mystère mais on peut raisonnablement parier qu'il s'agissait d'un mot à ne pas mettre entre toutes les lèvres. En tout cas, Butler n'eut pas le temps d'achever son exclamation. Il préféra relâcher précipitamment sa prise. Sage décision car elle intervint à l'instant précis où Mulch lançait son offensive très terre à terre.

Une motte d'argile compacte vola comme un boulet de canon à l'endroit précis où la tête de Butler s'était trouvée un peu moins d'une seconde auparavant. Si elle y était restée, nul doute que l'impact l'aurait séparée des épaules de son propriétaire. Une fin indigne d'un garde du corps de cette envergure. En l'occurrence, le missile lui effleura seulement l'oreille, mais avec une force suffisante pour le faire tourner sur lui-même à la manière d'un patineur artistique. Pour la deuxième fois en très peu de temps, Butler se retrouva assis par terre.

Lorsque sa vision fut redevenue normale, le nain avait disparu dans un tourbillon de gadoue. Butler estima inutile de se lancer à sa poursuite. Mourir sous terre ne faisait pas partie de ses priorités. « Mais nous nous retrouverons un jour, mon petit bonhomme », songea-t-il d'un air sinistre. Et, en effet, ce jour arriva. Mais c'est une autre histoire.

L'élan de Mulch le propulsa dans les profondeurs. Il parcourut plusieurs mètres dans l'argile avant de se rendre compte que personne ne le poursuivait. Lorsque le goût de la terre eut calmé ses battements de cœur, il estima qu'il était temps de mettre en œuvre le plan qu'il avait imaginé pour s'enfuir.

Il changea de direction, creusant son tunnel vers le terrier de lapin qu'il avait repéré à l'aller. Avec un peu de chance, le centaure n'avait pas installé de sismographes dans le parc du manoir, sinon sa ruse pourrait bien être découverte. Il comptait sur le fait qu'ils devaient s'inquiéter de choses beaucoup plus importantes que de la disparition d'un prisonnier. Tromper

Julius ne présentait aucune difficulté, mais le centaure était beaucoup plus intelligent.

La boussole interne de Mulch le guida avec efficacité et, quelques minutes plus tard, il sentit les faibles vibrations produites par les lapins qui parcouraient les tunnels de leur terrier. A partir de maintenant, le minutage était crucial si l'on voulait que l'illusion soit parfaite. Il ralentit le rythme de sa progression et enfonça doucement ses doigts dans l'argile jusqu'à ce qu'ils atteignent un des tunnels du terrier. Mulch prit bien soin de tourner la tête de l'autre côté car tout ce qu'il voyait apparaissait sur l'écran de contrôle, dans le Q.G. des FAR.

Mulch posa sa main ouverte sur le sol du tunnel, comme une araignée sur le dos, et attendit. Pas très longtemps. Quelques secondes plus tard, il sentit le rythme des pas d'un lapin qui approchait. A l'instant où les pattes arrière de l'animal effleurèrent le piège, Mulch resserra ses doigts puissants autour du cou de sa victime. Le malheureux lapin n'avait aucune chance de lui échapper.

« Désolé, l'ami, pensa le nain. Si je pouvais faire autrement... » Tirant le lapin vers lui, il raccrocha sa mâchoire et se mit à hurler :

– Éboulement ! Éboulement ! Au secours ! A l'aide !

Venait à présent la phase la plus délicate. D'une main, il agita l'argile autour de lui, provoquant des chutes de terre sur sa tête. De l'autre main, il fit sauter la caméra-iris de son œil et la glissa sur celui du lapin. Étant donné l'obscurité totale et la confusion provoquée par le faux éboulement, il devait être impossible de s'apercevoir de la substitution.

– Julius ! Au secours !

– Mulch ! Qu'est-ce qui se passe ? Quelle est votre situation ?

« Quelle est ma situation ? » songea le nain, incrédule. Même en pleine crise, le commandant ne pouvait se défaire de son précieux jargon militaire.

– Je... Argh...

Le nain poussa un cri ultime qui s'évanouit dans un gargouillement déchirant.

Sans doute un peu mélodramatique, mais Mulch ne pouvait résister aux effets théâtraux. Avec un dernier regard désolé au lapin agonisant, il décrocha sa mâchoire et fila vers le sud-est. La liberté lui faisait signe.

CHAPITRE VIII

TROLL

Root se pencha en avant, rugissant dans le micro.

– Mulch ! Qu'est-ce qui se passe ? Quelle est votre situation ?

Foaly tapait fébrilement sur son clavier.

– Nous n'avons plus aucun son. Ni aucun mouvement.

– Mulch, bon Dieu, dites-moi quelque chose !

– Je scanne ses fonctions vitales... Oh, là, là !

– Quoi ? Qu'est-ce qu'il y a ?

– Son cœur bat à une vitesse folle. Comme celui d'un lapin...

– Un lapin ?

– Non, attendez, c'est...

– Quoi ? dit le commandant dans un souffle, terrifié à l'idée d'apprendre ce qu'il devinait déjà.

Foaly se laissa aller contre le dossier de son fauteuil.

– C'est fini. Son cœur s'est arrêté.

– Vous êtes sûr ?

– Les écrans ne mentent pas. Ses fonctions vitales peuvent être captées par la caméra-iris. Plus le moindre signal. Il est mort.

Root ne parvenait pas à le croire. Mulch, l'une des constantes de la vie quotidienne. Mort ? C'était impossible.

– Il a quand même réussi, Foaly. Il a récupéré une reproduction du Livre, ce n'est pas rien, et il a confirmé que Short était toujours vivante.

Le large front de Foaly se plissa.

– Simplement...

– Quoi ? dit Root, soudain soupçonneux.

– Pendant un instant, juste avant la fin, son rythme cardiaque semblait anormalement élevé.

– C'était peut-être une erreur de vos appareils.

Le centaure n'était guère convaincu.

– J'en doute. Il n'y a jamais de pépin dans mes noyaux.

– Vos noyaux ?

– De communication.

– Je ne vois pas d'autre explication. Vous recevez toujours l'image ?

– Ouais. A travers des yeux morts, aucun doute à ce sujet. Pas la moindre étincelle d'électricité dans ce cerveau. La caméra continue de fonctionner sur sa propre pile.

– Alors, c'est fini. Je ne vois pas d'autre explication.

Foaly hocha la tête.

– C'est ce qu'il semble. A moins que... Non, ce serait trop extraordinaire.

– N'oubliez pas qu'il s'agit de Mulch Diggums. Rien n'est trop extraordinaire avec lui.

Foaly ouvrit la bouche pour formuler son incroyable hypothèse mais, avant qu'il ait eu le temps de prononcer un mot, la porte coulissante de la navette s'ouvrit.

– On le tient ! dit une voix triomphante.

– Oui, approuva une deuxième voix. Fowl a commis une erreur !

Root pivota sur son fauteuil. C'étaient Argon et Cumulus, les soi-disant spécialistes du comportement.

– Alors, vous vous êtes décidés à mériter vos honoraires ?

Mais les deux professeurs n'étaient pas d'humeur à se laisser intimider. L'excitation de leur découverte les avait réconciliés. Cumulus se montra même assez téméraire pour repousser d'un geste désinvolte le sarcasme de Root. Ce fut cela, plus que toute autre chose, qui incita le commandant à se redresser sur son siège et à les écouter attentivement.

Argon passa devant Foaly et glissa un disque laser dans le lecteur de la console. Le visage d'Artemis Fowl apparut, filmé par la caméra-iris de Root.

– Nous resterons en contact, dit la voix enregistrée

du commandant. Inutile de me raccompagner, je connais le chemin.

Le visage de Fowl disparut momentanément lorsqu'il quitta son fauteuil.

Root avait levé les yeux juste à temps pour le filmer à nouveau tandis qu'il déclarait d'un ton glacial :

– Allez-y. Mais souvenez-vous, personne parmi vous n'a le droit d'entrer ici tant que je suis vivant.

L'air réjoui, Argon enfonça la touche « pause ».

– Là, regardez !

Le teint de Root perdit les dernières petites traces blanches qu'on pouvait encore voir de-ci de-là.

– Là ? Où ça, là ? Qu'est-ce qu'il y a à regarder ?

Cumulus eut une petite exclamation condescendante, comme devant un enfant un peu lent à comprendre. Ce qui se révéla une erreur, rétrospectivement.

L'instant d'après, le commandant l'avait attrapé par sa barbiche.

– Maintenant, dit-il avec un calme trompeur, faites comme si nous étions pressés et expliquez-moi ce que vous voulez dire sans prendre de poses et sans commentaires inutiles.

– L'humain a dit que nous n'avions pas le droit d'entrer tant qu'il était vivant, couina Cumulus.

– Et alors ?

Argon prit le relais.

– Alors, si nous ne pouvons pas entrer tant qu'il est vivant...

Root respira profondément.

– Nous pourrons entrer quand il sera mort.

Cumulus et Argon avaient le visage rayonnant.

– Exactement, dirent-ils d'une même voix.

Root se gratta le menton.

– Je ne sais pas. D'un point de vue légal, nous sommes sur des sables mouvants.

– Pas du tout, protesta Cumulus. C'est une question de grammaire élémentaire. L'humain a déclaré précisément que l'entrée nous était interdite tant qu'il était vivant. Ce qui équivaut à une invitation quand il sera mort.

Le commandant ne paraissait guère convaincu.

– Au mieux, l'invitation est implicite.

– Non, intervint Foaly. Ils ont raison. C'est un argument de poids. Si Fowl meurt, la porte est grande ouverte. C'est lui-même qui l'a dit.

– Peut-être.

– Pas peut-être ! s'exclama Foaly. Voyons, Julius, pour l'amour du ciel, que vous faut-il de plus ? Nous avons une crise à régler au cas où vous ne l'auriez pas remarqué.

Root hocha lentement la tête en signe d'approbation.

– *Primo*, vous avez raison. *Secundo*, je vais me servir

de ça. *Tertio*, bien joué, tous les deux. Et *quarto*, si jamais vous recommencez à m'appeler Julius, je vous ferai manger vos sabots, Foaly. Maintenant, appelez-moi le Grand Conseil. Il faut que j'aie leur accord pour avoir cet or.

– Tout de suite, commandant Root, je suis à votre disposition, Votre Seigneurie, répondit Foaly avec un grand sourire, renonçant, dans l'intérêt de Holly, à relever la réflexion sur la consommation de ses sabots.

– Donc, nous livrons l'or, marmonna Root, en réfléchissant à haute voix. Ils relâchent Holly, on fait un rinçage bleu dans toute la maison et on récupère la rançon. Très simple.

– Si simple que c'en est tout bonnement brillant, s'enthousiasma Argon. Un coup d'éclat pour notre profession tout entière, ne pensez-vous pas, professeur Cumulus ?

Cumulus était pris de vertige devant les perspectives qui s'ouvraient.

– Tournées de conférences, contrats d'édition. Les droits cinématographiques à eux seuls rapporteront une fortune.

– Et tous ces sociologues devront se fourrer ça dans le crâne une bonne fois pour toutes. Voilà qui met un terme aux balivernes sur la relation directe entre les milieux défavorisés et la délinquance. Ce Fowl n'a jamais souffert de la faim au cours de son existence.

– On peut être affamé de différentes manières, fit remarquer Argon.

– C'est vrai. Affamé de réussite. Affamé de pouvoir. Affamé de...

– Sortez ! lança Root. Sortez avant que je vous étrangle tous les deux. Et si jamais j'entends répéter dans une émission de télévision un seul mot de ce qui s'est dit ici, je saurai d'où ça vient.

Les experts battirent prudemment en retraite, estimant préférable de ne pas appeler leurs agents littéraires avant d'être hors de portée du commandant.

– Je ne sais pas si le Grand Conseil va donner son accord, confessa Root lorsqu'ils eurent disparu. Ça représente beaucoup d'or.

Foaly leva les yeux de sa console.

– Combien exactement ?

Le commandant fit glisser un morceau de papier vers lui.

– Tout ça.

– C'est énorme, dit Foaly avec un sifflement. Une tonne. En petits lingots sans aucune marque. Vingt-quatre carats. Enfin, au moins, c'est un chiffre rond.

– Belle consolation. Je ne manquerai pas de le faire remarquer au Grand Conseil. Vous avez obtenu la ligne ?

Le centaure émit un grognement. Un grognement négatif. Très insolent, en vérité, de répondre par un grognement à un officier supérieur.

Root n'avait pas suffisamment d'énergie pour le rappeler à l'ordre, mais il se promit quelque chose : lorsque tout serait terminé, il diminuerait le salaire de Foaly pendant quelques décennies. Épuisé, il se frotta les yeux. Le décalage de temps commençait à produire ses effets. Même si son cerveau refusait de le laisser dormir puisqu'il était éveillé lorsque la suspension temporelle avait été déclenchée, son corps réclamait à grands cris un peu de repos.

Il se leva de son fauteuil, ouvrant grand la porte pour laisser entrer un peu d'air. Un air confiné. Un air de suspension temporelle. Les molécules elles-mêmes ne pouvaient quitter la zone, encore moins un jeune humain.

Il y avait de l'agitation du côté du portail. Beaucoup d'agitation.

Un essaim de soldats entourait une aérocage qui se déplaçait sur un coussin d'air. Cudgeon marchait en tête et toute la troupe se dirigeait vers Root. Celui-ci sortit de la navette pour aller à leur rencontre.

– Qu'est-ce que c'est que ça ? demanda-t-il d'un ton peu aimable. Un cirque ?

Le visage de Cudgeon était pâle mais déterminé.

– Non, Julius. Justement, c'est la fin du cirque.

Root hocha la tête.

– Je vois. Et ça, ce sont les clowns ?

La tête de Foaly apparut dans l'encadrement de la porte.

– Excusez-moi d'interrompre vos variations métaphoriques sur le cirque, mais qu'est-ce que c'est que ce truc-là ?

– Oui, lieutenant, dit Root en montrant l'aérocage qui flottait en l'air. Qu'est-ce que c'est que ce truc-là ?

Cudgeon rassembla son courage en respirant profondément à plusieurs reprises.

– J'ai pris exemple sur toi, Julius.

– Vraiment ?

– Oui. Vraiment. Tu as envoyé dans la maison une créature douteuse. Eh bien, je vais en faire autant.

Root eut un sourire menaçant.

– Tu ne vas rien faire du tout, *lieutenant*, tant que je n'en aurai pas donné l'ordre.

Machinalement, Cudgeon recula d'un pas.

– Je suis allé voir le Grand Conseil, Julius. J'ai leur entier soutien.

Le commandant se tourna vers Foaly.

– C'est vrai ?

– Apparemment. Ça vient d'être annoncé par la ligne extérieure. C'est Cudgeon qui dirige les opérations, à présent. Il a parlé au Grand Conseil de la demande de rançon et de l'ordre que vous avez donné de libérer Mr. Diggums. Vous savez comment sont les anciens quand il s'agit de se séparer de leur or.

Root croisa les bras.

– Certaines personnes m'ont dit des choses sur toi,

Cudgeon. Par exemple, que tu n'hésiterais pas à me poignarder dans le dos. Je ne les ai pas crues. J'ai été idiot.

– Ce n'est pas une affaire personnelle, Julius. Il s'agit de l'intérêt de la mission. Ce qui se trouve dans cette cage représente notre plus grande chance de succès.

– Alors ? Qu'est-ce qu'il y a dans la cage ? Non, ne me dis rien. Elle doit contenir la seule autre créature dénuée de pouvoirs magiques qu'on puisse trouver dans le monde souterrain. C'est-à-dire le premier troll que nous ayons réussi à capturer vivant en plus d'un siècle.

– Exactement. La parfaite créature pour anéantir notre adversaire.

Les joues de Root se mirent à briller sous l'effort qu'il fit pour réprimer sa colère.

– Je n'arrive pas à croire que tu puisses envisager une chose pareille.

– Regarde la situation en face, Julius, fondamentalement, c'est la même idée que la tienne.

– Non, pas du tout. Mulch Diggums avait pris la décision lui-même. Il connaissait les risques.

– Diggums est mort ?

Root se frotta à nouveau les yeux.

– Oui. Apparemment. Un éboulement.

– Ça prouve que j'ai raison. Un troll ne se laissera pas si facilement éliminer.

– Mais enfin, c'est un animal complètement stupide ! Comment un troll peut-il obéir à des instructions ?

Cudgeon sourit, une assurance de fraîche date perçant derrière son appréhension.

– Quelles instructions ? Il suffit de le diriger vers la maison et de s'écarter de son chemin. Je te garantis que ces humains nous supplieront de venir à leur secours.

– Et mon officier ?

– Nous aurons ramené le troll dans sa cage bien avant que le capitaine Short ait eu le temps de courir le moindre danger.

– Tu peux me l'assurer ?

Cudgeon resta un instant silencieux.

– C'est un risque que je suis prêt... que le Grand Conseil est prêt à prendre.

– De la politique, tout ça, lança Root avec mépris. Pour toi, tout n'est que politique. Une action d'éclat, c'est toujours utile pour obtenir un siège au Conseil. Tu me dégoûtes.

– Quoi qu'il en soit, c'est la stratégie qui a été adoptée. Le Grand Conseil m'a nommé commandant temporaire pour cette mission et, si tu es incapable de mettre notre histoire personnelle de côté, alors dégage de mon chemin et laisse-moi agir.

Root s'écarta d'un pas.

– Ne t'inquiète pas, *commandant*. Je ne veux rien avoir à faire avec cette boucherie. Tout l'honneur sera pour toi.

Cudgeon s'efforça d'avoir l'air le plus sincère possible.

– Julius, quoi que tu penses, il n'y a que les intérêts du Peuple qui me tiennent à cœur.

– Et surtout ceux d'une personne en particulier, répliqua Root d'un air dédaigneux.

Cudgeon décida de le prendre de haut :

– Je n'ai pas l'intention d'en entendre davantage. Chaque seconde que je passe à te parler est une seconde perdue.

Root le regarda droit dans les yeux.

– Dans ce cas, on a perdu six cents ans ensemble, pas vrai, mon *ami* ?

Cudgeon ne répondit pas. Que pouvait-il dire ? L'ambition avait un prix et ce prix, c'était l'amitié.

Il se tourna vers sa troupe composée de lutins sélectionnés avec soin, qui lui étaient entièrement dévoués.

– Amenez l'aérocage dans l'allée. Ne faites rien tant que je n'aurai pas donné le feu vert.

Il passa devant Root, regardant de tous côtés, sauf en direction de son ami de toujours. Foaly n'allait pas se priver d'un commentaire.

– Hé, Cudgeon.

Le commandant temporaire ne pouvait tolérer

un tel ton, certainement pas au premier jour de sa mission.

– Faites attention à ce que vous dites, Foaly. Personne n'est indispensable.

Le centaure pouffa de rire.

– Ça, c'est vrai. C'est justement ce qui est important, en politique : on n'a droit qu'à un seul essai.

Cudgeon ne put s'empêcher de paraître vaguement intéressé.

– Si c'était à moi qu'on donnait une chance de coller mon derrière sur un siège du Grand Conseil, poursuivit Foaly, je ne confierais certainement pas mon avenir à un troll.

Cudgeon perdit soudain son assurance de fraîche date qui laissa place à une pâleur saisissante. Il s'épongea le front et se hâta de rejoindre l'aérocage.

– A demain ! lui cria le centaure. J'aurai besoin de vous pour ramasser mes ordures.

Root s'esclaffa. C'était sans doute la première fois qu'une réflexion de Foaly le faisait rire.

– Bien dit, Foaly, commenta-t-il avec un sourire. Il faut frapper ce traître là où ça peut lui faire le plus mal, en plein dans son ambition.

– Merci, Julius.

Le sourire de Root disparut plus vite qu'une limace frite à la cantine des FAR.

– Je vous ai déjà dit de ne pas m'appeler Julius. Et

maintenant, rétablissez-moi cette ligne extérieure. Je veux que l'or soit prêt quand le plan de Cudgeon aura échoué. Rassemblez tous mes supporters au sein du Conseil. Je suis à peu près certain que Lope sera de mon côté, Cahartez aussi, peut-être même Vinyaya. Elle a toujours été sensible à mon charme diabolique.

– Vous plaisantez, bien sûr ?

– Je ne plaisante jamais, répliqua Root, le visage impassible.

Holly avait un vague plan. Se faufiler dans la maison à l'abri de son bouclier, récupérer quelques-unes de ses armes et provoquer un tel chambardement que Fowl serait obligé de la relâcher. Et si les dégâts qui en résultaient atteignaient plusieurs millions de livres irlandaises, ce serait d'autant mieux.

Il y avait des années que Holly n'avait pas eu cette impression de bien-être. Ses yeux flamboyaient de puissance magique et des étincelles d'énergie parcouraient chaque centimètre carré de sa peau. Elle avait oublié à quel point on se sentait bien lorsqu'on était chauffé au rouge.

Le capitaine Short sentait qu'elle dominait la situation, à présent, tel un prédateur sur la piste de son gibier. C'était à cela que son entraînement l'avait préparée.

Au début, les Êtres de la Boue avaient pris l'avantage. Maintenant, le vent avait tourné. C'était elle le chasseur et ils étaient devenus sa proie.

Holly monta le grand escalier, toujours sur ses gardes, au cas où le serviteur géant serait apparu. Elle ne voulait prendre aucun risque avec lui. Si jamais ses doigts se refermaient sur sa tête, on parlerait d'elle au passé, casque ou pas ; d'ailleurs, il n'était pas du tout sûr qu'elle trouve un casque.

La vaste maison ressemblait à un mausolée – pas le moindre signe de vie dans ses grandes pièces au plafond voûté.

Seuls d'inquiétants portraits la regardaient passer. Chacun d'eux avait le regard des Fowl, soupçonneux et scintillant. Holly se promit de les carboniser tous lorsqu'elle aurait récupéré son Neutrino 2000. Ce serait peut-être une basse vengeance, mais parfaitement justifiée compte tenu de ce qu'Artemis Fowl lui avait fait subir.

Elle monta rapidement les marches, suivant la courbe de l'escalier jusqu'à l'étage supérieur. Un rai de lumière pâle filtrait sous la porte située tout au fond du couloir. Holly posa la paume de sa main contre le panneau de bois pour sentir les vibrations. Grosse activité.

Des cris, des bruits de pas. Qui martelaient le sol dans sa direction.

Holly fit un bond en arrière, se plaquant contre le papier peint satiné. Il était temps. Une silhouette massive surgit dans l'encadrement de la porte et se rua dans le couloir, provoquant des tourbillons d'air dans son sillage.

– Juliet ! s'écria Butler, et le nom de sa sœur résonna encore bien après qu'il eut disparu dans l'escalier.

« Ne t'inquiète pas pour elle, Butler, songea Holly. Elle est en train de passer le plus beau moment de sa vie, le nez collé aux images de *Luttomania.* » La porte ouverte lui offrait une belle occasion. Elle se glissa par l'entrebâillement avant que le bras mécanique ait eu le temps de la refermer.

Artemis Fowl attendait, des filtres antiboucliers attachés tant bien que mal à ses lunettes de soleil.

– Bonsoir, capitaine Short, lança-t-il, en paraissant toujours aussi sûr de lui. Au risque d'employer une formule banale, je vous dirais que je vous attendais.

Holly ne réagit pas. Elle ne regarda même pas son geôlier dans les yeux. Son entraînement lui permit en revanche d'analyser rapidement le contenu de la pièce, son regard s'arrêtant un bref instant sur chaque chose.

– Bien entendu, vous restez liée par les promesses que vous avez faites il y a quelques heures...

Mais Holly ne l'écoutait pas. Elle s'était précipitée vers un établi en acier fixé au mur du fond.

– Donc, fondamentalement, la situation n'a pas changé. Vous êtes toujours ma prisonnière.

– C'est ça, c'est ça, marmonna-t-elle, ses doigts courant sur les rangées d'accessoires confisqués au commando de Récupération.

Elle choisit un casque indétectable par les radars et le glissa sur ses oreilles pointues. Les coussinets pneumatiques s'adaptèrent exactement à la forme de son crâne. Elle était en sécurité, à présent. Tout ordre donné par Fowl resterait désormais sans effet grâce à sa visière réfléchissante. Un micro se mit automatiquement en place.

Le contact fut aussitôt établi :

– ... sur toutes les fréquences. Appel sur toutes les fréquences. Holly, si vous m'entendez, mettez-vous à couvert.

Holly reconnut la voix de Foaly. Au moins quelque chose de familier dans cette situation délirante.

– Je répète : mettez-vous à couvert. Cudgeon va envoyer un...

– Une information qui me concerne ? dit Artemis.

– Silence, siffla-t-elle, en se rendant compte avec inquiétude que le ton du centaure avait perdu son habituelle désinvolture.

– Je répète, ils vont envoyer un troll pour assurer votre libération.

Holly sursauta. C'était Cudgeon qui décidait, à présent. Mauvaise nouvelle.

Fowl l'interrompit à nouveau :

– Ce n'est pas très poli de faire comme si votre hôte n'était pas là.

– Ça suffit, maintenant, gronda-t-elle.

Elle serra le poing et ramena le bras en arrière. Artemis resta impassible. Pourquoi s'inquiéter ? Butler intervenait toujours avant que les coups ne pleuvent. Quelque chose attira alors son regard : une silhouette imposante qui dévalait l'escalier devant la caméra du premier étage. C'était Butler.

– Eh oui, gosse de riche, tu es tout seul, cette fois, dit Holly d'un air mauvais.

Et avant qu'Artemis ait eu le temps d'écarquiller les yeux, elle contracta ses muscles et écrasa son poing sur le nez de son ravisseur.

– Ouille ! dit-il, en tombant assis par terre.

– Moi, ça m'a fait du bien !

Holly se concentra sur la voix qui bourdonnait dans son oreille.

– ... on a fait passer une boucle dans les caméras extérieures, les humains ne verront donc pas ce qui arrive dans la grande allée. Mais c'est en route, croyez-moi.

– Foaly, Foaly, répondez.

– Holly ? C'est vous ?

– La seule, l'unique. Foaly, il n'y a pas de boucle. Je vois tout ce qui se passe sur les écrans.

– L'affreux petit monstre... Il a dû réinitialiser le système.

L'allée centrale était devenue une véritable ruche de fées. Cudgeon, l'air supérieur, donnait des ordres à sa troupe de lutins. Au centre de la mêlée se dressait l'aérocage de cinq mètres de haut qui flottait sur son coussin d'air. La cage se trouvait juste en face de la porte d'entrée et les techniciens étaient en train d'installer un sas de dislocation. Lorsqu'on l'activerait, des pointes en alliage spécial, aménagées dans le châssis, seraient mises à feu simultanément et désintégreraient la porte. Une fois la poussière dissipée, le troll n'aurait plus qu'une seule direction où aller : à l'intérieur du manoir.

Holly regarda les autres écrans. Butler avait réussi à traîner Juliet hors de la cellule. Ils étaient remontés du sous-sol et traversaient à présent le hall du rez-de-chaussée. Juste dans la ligne de feu.

– Nom de nom ! jura-t-elle en se précipitant vers l'établi.

Artemis, toujours par terre, était appuyé sur ses deux coudes.

– Vous m'avez frappé, dit-il, incrédule.

Holly attacha à ses épaules les ailes d'un Colibri.

– Exact, Fowl. Et il y en a plein d'autres en réserve. Alors, reste où tu es si tu tiens à ta santé.

Pour une fois dans sa vie, Artemis s'aperçut qu'il n'avait pas de réplique cinglante à lancer. Il ouvrit la bouche, attendant que son cerveau lui fournisse la repartie spirituelle qui convenait. Mais rien ne vint.

Holly glissa le Neutrino 2000 dans son holster.

– C'est mieux comme ça, petit Être de Boue. Le jeu est terminé, maintenant. Les professionnels vont prendre le relais et, si tu es bien sage, je t'achèterai une sucette à mon retour.

Holly était partie depuis longtemps, s'envolant sous les antiques poutres de chêne, lorsque Artemis répondit :

– Je n'aime pas les sucettes.

Une réponse tristement inadéquate qui consterna Artemis. Vraiment lamentable : « Je n'aime pas les sucettes. » Aucun esprit du Mal digne de ce nom n'aurait toléré qu'on le surprenne ne serait-ce qu'à prononcer le mot « sucette ». Il faudrait qu'il pense à créer une base de données rassemblant des répliques mordantes à utiliser dans des occasions comme celle-ci.

Artemis aurait pu rester assis par terre un certain temps, complètement détaché du monde extérieur, si la porte d'entrée n'avait pas explosé, ébranlant tout le manoir jusque dans ses fondations. Le genre de chose qui suffit à arracher quiconque à ses rêves éveillés.

Un lutin atterrit devant le commandant temporaire Cudgeon.

– Le sas est en place, mon commandant.

Cudgeon fit un signe de tête approbateur.

– Vous êtes sûr qu'il est bien étanche, capitaine ? Je n'ai pas du tout envie que le troll prenne une mauvaise direction.

– Plus étanche qu'un portefeuille de gobelin. Il n'y a pas la moindre bulle d'air qui puisse entrer dans ce sas. Il est plus étanche que l'intestin d'un...

– Très bien, capitaine, l'interrompit Cudgeon, avant que le lutin ait eu le temps d'entrer dans le détail de sa comparaison.

A côté d'eux, l'aérocage trembla violemment, manquant presque de tomber de son coussin d'air.

– On ferait bien de balancer ce zigoto vite fait, commandant. Si on ne le lâche pas bientôt, mes gars vont passer la semaine à ramasser à la petite cuillère les...

– C'est ça, capitaine, très bien, balancez-le. Allez-y, balancez, qu'est-ce que vous attendez ?

Cudgeon se réfugia en hâte derrière le bouclier anti-explosion et nota quelque chose sur son écran de poche à cristaux liquides. « Ne pas oublier : rappeler aux lutins d'employer un langage moins vulgaire en ma présence. Après tout, je suis *commandant,* maintenant. »

Le capitaine au vocabulaire peu choisi se tourna vers le conducteur de l'aérocage.

– Vas-y, Chix, balance-moi ça. Arrache-moi cette bon Dieu de porte de ses fichus gonds.

– Bien, capitaine. On arrache la bon Dieu de porte. C'est parti.

Cudgeon fit une grimace. Demain, il y aurait une grande réunion. A la première heure. Mais cette fois, il aurait l'insigne de commandant accroché à son revers.

Même un lutin serait moins enclin à dire des grossièretés en voyant un triple gland étinceler sous son nez.

Chix mit ses lunettes antishrapnel bien que la cabine de commande eût un pare-brise en quartz. Les lunettes étaient « cool ». Les filles adoraient ça. C'était en tout cas ce qu'il pensait. Il se voyait lui-même comme un aventurier au regard sombre et romantique. Les lutins étaient ainsi. Il suffit de donner une paire d'ailes à un être du petit Peuple pour qu'il se croie irrésistible auprès des filles.

Mais, là encore, les tentatives malheureuses de Chix Verbil pour séduire les dames sont une autre histoire. Dans le cas présent, son seul rôle consistait à appuyer sur la touche déclenchant le mécanisme.

Ce qu'il fit d'un geste théâtral et avec une assurance inébranlable.

Deux douzaines de charges explosèrent dans leurs cylindres, projetant autant de pointes en alliage métallique à une vitesse supérieure à mille cinq cents kilomètres heure. A son point d'impact, chaque projectile pulvérisa une surface d'environ quinze centimètres de côté, arrachant effectivement la porte de ses fichus gonds. Comme aurait dit le capitaine.

Lorsque la poussière se fut dissipée, les techniciens soulevèrent à l'aide d'un treuil la cloison qui fermait la cage et tapèrent sur les flancs du plat de la main.

Cudgeon passa la tête derrière le bouclier anti-explosion et jeta un coup d'œil.

– Tout va bien, capitaine ?

– Une seconde, commandant. Chix, bon Dieu, qu'est-ce qui se passe ?

Chix consulta l'écran de la cabine.

– Il bouge. Le bruit lui a fait peur. Il sort ses griffes. Hou, là, là, c'est vraiment une sacrée bestiole. Je n'aimerais pas être à la place de la poupée du service de Détection si jamais elle se trouve sur son chemin.

Cudgeon éprouva un vague sentiment de culpabilité qu'il dissipa en s'imaginant confortablement installé dans l'un des fauteuils de velours beige du Grand Conseil.

La cage fut violemment secouée, faisant presque tomber Chix de son siège.

– Ça y est, il est parti. Tenez-vous prêts, le doigt sur la détente, les gars. J'ai l'impression qu'on ne va pas tarder à entendre des appels au secours.

Cudgeon ne jugea pas utile de mettre lui-même le doigt sur la détente. Il préférait laisser ce soin à sa troupe. Le commandant temporaire s'estimait trop important pour prendre le risque de se placer dans une situation périlleuse. Pour le bien du petit Peuple dans son ensemble, il valait beaucoup mieux qu'il se tienne à l'écart du théâtre des opérations.

Butler descendit l'escalier quatre à quatre. C'était sans doute la première fois qu'il abandonnait son maître dans un moment de crise. Mais Juliet, c'était la famille, et de toute évidence sa petite sœur avait de sérieux ennuis. Cette fée lui avait dit quelque chose et, à présent, elle restait assise dans la cellule à glousser de rire.

Butler craignait le pire. Si quoi que ce soit arrivait à Juliet, il ne s'en remettrait probablement jamais.

Il sentit une goutte de sueur couler sur son crâne rasé. Cette histoire partait dans d'étranges directions. Les fées, la magie, et maintenant une prisonnière qui se promenait à sa guise dans le manoir. Comment pouvait-il contrôler les choses ? Il fallait au moins quatre gardes du corps pour protéger le moindre politicien, alors que lui était censé affronter tout seul cette situation impossible.

Butler courut le long du couloir en direction de ce qui était encore récemment la cellule du capitaine Short. Juliet était vautrée sur le lit, fascinée par le spectacle d'un mur de béton.

– Qu'est-ce que tu fais ? s'exclama-t-il en dégainant son Sig Sauer neuf millimètres avec une aisance due à une longue pratique.

Sa sœur lui accorda à peine un regard.

– Silence, espèce de gros singe. Louie-le-Bourreau-d'Amour est en pleine action. En fait, il n'est pas si fort que ça. Je pourrais le battre facilement.

Butler eut un sursaut. Elle racontait des sottises. De toute évidence, on l'avait droguée.

– Viens. Artemis veut que nous allions le rejoindre dans la salle de contrôle.

Juliet pointa vers le mur un index manucuré.

– Artemis attendra. C'est le titre intercontinental qui est en jeu. En plus, ils ont un vieux compte à régler. Louie a mangé le cochon préféré de Porcher-la-Terreur.

Le serviteur examina le mur. Il était entièrement vierge. Ce n'était pas le moment de perdre du temps avec des absurdités.

– Bon, on y va, grogna-t-il, et il souleva sa sœur qu'il jeta sur ses larges épaules.

– Nooon ! Espèce de grosse brute ! s'indigna-t-elle en lui martelant le dos de ses poings minuscules. Pas maintenant ! Porcher ! Pooorcher !

Butler resta indifférent à ses protestations et repartit au pas de course. Qui pouvait bien être ce Porcher ? Un de ses soupirants, sans doute. A l'avenir, il ferait un peu plus attention aux visiteurs qui passaient la voir dans la maison des gardiens.

– Butler ? Répondez.

C'était Artemis qui l'appelait sur le talkie-walkie. Butler remonta sa sœur de quelques centimètres sur son épaule pour pouvoir atteindre l'appareil accroché à sa ceinture.

– Sucettes ! aboya son employeur.

– Pouvez-vous répéter, s'il vous plaît ? J'ai cru comprendre...

– Heu... Je veux dire, ne restez pas là. Mettez-vous à couvert ! A couvert !

A couvert ? Le terme militaire semblait déplacé dans la bouche de son maître. Comme une bague en diamant dans une pochette-surprise.

– Me mettre à couvert ?

– Oui, Butler. A couvert. J'ai pensé que l'emploi de termes primaires serait le plus court chemin pour atteindre vos fonctions cognitives. De toute évidence, je me suis trompé.

Voilà qui lui ressemblait davantage. Butler scruta le hall à la recherche d'un endroit où se cacher. Il n'y avait guère de choix. Seules les armures médiévales alignées le long des murs pouvaient fournir un abri. Le serviteur se glissa dans une niche, derrière un chevalier du XIVe siècle au complet, avec lance et masse d'armes.

Juliet tapota le plastron de l'armure.

– Tu te crois très fort ? Je te prends quand tu veux et d'une seule main.

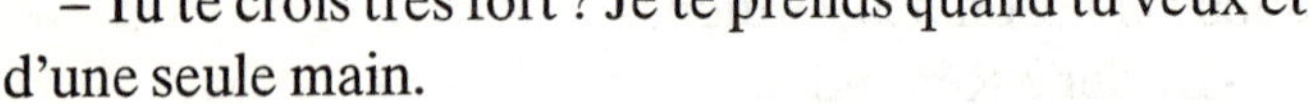

– Silence, siffla Butler.

Il retint son souffle et tendit l'oreille. Quelque chose approchait de la porte d'entrée. Quelque chose de très gros. Butler se pencha pour jeter un coup d'œil dans le vestibule...

Au même moment, la porte explosa. Ce n'est cependant pas le terme qui convient pour décrire exactement le phénomène. En fait, la porte se désintégra en une multitude de particules infinitésimales. Butler avait déjà vu quelque chose de semblable le jour où un séisme de force 7 avait ravagé le domaine d'un parrain de la drogue colombien quelques secondes avant le moment où il avait prévu de le faire sauter. Dans le cas présent, c'était un peu différent. Plus localisé. Très professionnel. Une tactique antiterroriste classique. Frapper un grand coup avec une bonne quantité de fumée et de décibels puis faire irruption en profitant du désarroi de l'adversaire. Butler ne savait pas ce qui allait venir maintenant, mais ce serait redoutable. Il en était certain. Et il avait parfaitement raison.

Le nuage de poussière se dissipa avec lenteur, déposant une mince pellicule grise sur le tapis d'Orient. Mrs. Fowl aurait été furieuse si elle avait seulement mis un orteil hors de sa chambre. L'instinct de Butler lui dicta de quitter son abri. De zigzaguer jusqu'à l'escalier, de monter dans les étages. De se baisser pour réduire la surface de la cible. C'était le moment idéal, avant que la visibilité se dégage. A tout instant, maintenant, une grêle de coups de feu allait s'abattre sur le hall et il n'avait pas du tout envie de rester coincé au rez-de-chaussée.

En temps normal, Butler aurait aussitôt réagi. Il aurait déjà monté la moitié des marches avant même que son cerveau ait eu le temps d'envisager une autre possibilité. Mais aujourd'hui, il portait sur son épaule sa petite sœur qui ne cessait de débiter des sornettes et il ne voulait à aucun prix l'exposer à une fusillade meurtrière. Dans l'état où elle était, elle allait sans doute mettre au défi le commando des fées de l'affronter dans un match de lutte. Et sa sœur avait beau parler fort, elle n'était encore qu'une enfant. Pas de taille à affronter un personnel militaire entraîné. Butler s'accroupit, adossa Juliet contre une tapisserie, derrière une armure, et vérifia le cran de sûreté de son pistolet. Relevé. Très bien. « Et maintenant, venez donc me chercher, mes petites fées. »

Quelque chose bougea dans le nuage de poussière. Il fut très vite évident aux yeux de Butler que ce *quelque chose* n'avait rien d'humain. Le serviteur avait trop souvent participé à des safaris pour ne pas reconnaître un animal lorsqu'il en voyait un. Il observa la démarche de la créature. Elle avait quelque chose de simiesque. La partie supérieure du corps était semblable au torse d'un grand singe, mais beaucoup plus massive que tout ce que Butler avait jamais vu parmi les primates. Si c'était un singe, son pistolet ne lui serait pas d'un grand secours. Même si on parvenait à lui loger cinq balles dans la tête, un grand mâle aurait toujours le temps de vous dévorer avant que son cerveau ne réalise qu'il est mort.

Mais ce n'était pas un singe. Les yeux des singes ne sont pas adaptés à la vision nocturne. Cette créature, au contraire, était dotée de pupilles écarlates et flamboyantes, à demi cachées derrière des poils hirsutes. Elle avait également des défenses, mais pas d'une taille éléphantine. Elles étaient courbes avec des bords dentelés. Des armes faites pour étriper. Butler sentit un picotement au creux de l'estomac. Il avait déjà éprouvé cette sensation. Lors de son premier jour à l'académie suisse. C'était de la peur.

La créature sortit du nuage de poussière. Butler eut un haut-le-corps. Là encore, c'était le premier depuis le temps de l'académie. Jamais il ne s'était trouvé face à un tel adversaire. Le serviteur comprit aussitôt : les fées avaient envoyé un chasseur primitif. Un être totalement indifférent a la magie ou aux règles, quelles qu'elles soient. Une chose qui se contenterait de tuer quiconque se trouverait sur son chemin, sans distinction de taille ou d'espèce. Le prédateur parfait. C'était évident quand on observait ses dents pointues, parfaites pour lacérer les chairs, le sang séché qui incrustait ses griffes et la haine que ses yeux distillaient.

Le troll s'avança d'un pas traînant, les yeux plissés dans la lumière du lustre. Les griffes jaunâtres de ses pieds raclaient les dalles de marbre en projetant des étincelles dans leur sillage. Il reniflait à présent, lançant d'étranges grognements par ses naseaux, la tête penchée de côté. Butler avait déjà vu semblable comportement : chez des pitbulls affamés, quelques instants avant que leurs maîtres russes les lancent à la poursuite de l'ours qu'ils chassaient.

La tête hirsute s'immobilisa et le museau de la créature pointa droit sur la cachette de Butler. Ce n'était pas une coïncidence. Le serviteur jeta un coup d'œil entre deux doigts d'un gantelet. La traque commençait. Maintenant qu'il avait senti une piste, le prédateur allait tenter une lente et silencieuse approche avant l'attaque foudroyante sur sa proie.

Mais apparemment, le troll n'avait pas lu le manuel du parfait prédateur car il ne s'encombra pas d'approche silencieuse et passa directement à l'attaque éclair. Avec une rapidité que Butler n'aurait jamais crue possible, le troll bondit à travers le hall et repoussa l'armure d'une pichenette comme s'il s'était agi d'un simple mannequin dans la vitrine d'une boutique.

Juliet sursauta.

– Oh ! s'exclama-t-elle. C'est Bob-les-Grands-Pieds, le champion 1999 du Canada. Je croyais que vous étiez parti dans les Andes à la recherche de votre famille.

Butler ne prit pas la peine de la détromper. Sa sœur avait perdu toute lucidité. Au moins mourrait-elle heureuse. Tandis que son cerveau se faisait cette macabre réflexion, la main dans laquelle il tenait son pistolet s'éleva machinalement.

Il pressa la détente à plusieurs reprises, aussi vite que le permettait le mécanisme du Sig Sauer. Deux balles dans la poitrine, deux autres entre les yeux. C'était tout au moins le plan prévu. Il logea les deux balles dans la poitrine, mais le troll passa à l'action avant qu'il ait eu le temps d'achever son programme. L'action prit la forme de deux défenses recourbées comme des faux qui frappèrent Butler sous sa garde et s'enroulèrent autour de son corps en lacérant son blouson renforcé de Kevlar avec la facilité d'un rasoir coupant une feuille de papier de riz.

Butler ressentit une douleur glacée lorsque l'ivoire dentelé lui transperça la poitrine. Il sut aussitôt que la blessure était fatale. Son souffle devint rauque. Un de ses poumons était touché et des taches de sang constellaient la fourrure du troll. Son sang à lui. Personne ne pouvait espérer survivre après en avoir perdu une telle quantité. La douleur laissa cependant place à une étrange euphorie. Les défenses de la créature devaient sans doute injecter un anesthésique naturel dans l'organisme de ses victimes. Plus dangereux encore que le plus mortel des venins. Quelques minutes plus tard, non seulement Butler avait cessé de lutter mais il pouffait de rire en allant vers la tombe.

Le serviteur s'efforça de combattre les effets du narcotique, se débattant furieusement dans l'étreinte du troll. Mais c'était inutile. Son combat cessa presque avant d'avoir commencé.

Le troll grogna, jetant le corps flasque de l'homme par-dessus sa tête. La charpente massive de Butler heurta le mur de plein fouet, à une vitesse que le squelette humain n'a jamais été conçu pour supporter. Les briques se fissurèrent du sol au plafond. La colonne vertébrale de Butler céda également. A présent, même si ce n'était pas la perte de sang qui avait raison de lui, ce serait la paralysie.

Juliet était toujours ensorcelée par le mesmer.

– Allez, grand frère, debout, tout le monde sait bien que c'est du chiqué.

Le troll s'interrompit, comme saisi d'une curiosité rudimentaire devant cette absence totale de peur. Il aurait soupçonné une ruse s'il avait été capable d'élaborer une pensée aussi complexe. Mais ce fut finalement l'appétit qui l'emporta. Cette créature sentait la chair fraîche. Fraîche et tendre. La chair qu'on trouvait en surface était différente. Imprégnée des arômes de l'atmosphère. Une fois qu'on a goûté de la viande élevée en plein air, il est difficile de revenir à autre chose. Le troll passa la langue sur ses incisives et tendit une patte velue...

Holly serra les ailes du Colibri contre ses flancs et se lança dans une descente en piqué. Elle frôla la rampe de l'escalier et émergea dans le hall, sous un dôme décoré de vitraux. La lueur surnaturelle de la suspension temporelle filtrait au travers, éclatée en d'épais rayons d'azur.

« La lumière », songea Holly. Elle avait déjà réussi à éblouir le troll avec les projecteurs d'un casque, il n'y avait aucune raison pour qu'elle n'y parvienne pas une deuxième fois. Il était trop tard pour le mâle, ce n'était plus qu'un sac d'os brisés. Mais il restait encore quelques secondes à la fille avant que le troll ne la déchire en deux.

Holly tournoya dans la fausse lumière, cherchant sur le tableau de commande de son casque la touche du Sonix. Le Sonix était généralement utilisé contre les chiens mais, dans le cas présent, il pourrait peut-être créer une brève diversion. Suffisante pour lui donner le temps de descendre au niveau du sol.

Le troll s'approchait de Juliet mains baissées, paumes en l'air. C'était un mouvement généralement réservé aux créatures sans défense. Ainsi, les griffes s'insinuaient sous les côtes, transperçant le cœur. La chair subissait un minimum de dommage et aucune tension de dernière minute ne risquait de faire durcir la viande.

Holly activa son Sonix... et rien ne se produisit. Raté. Généralement, le troll moyen était à tout le moins irrité par les sons à haute fréquence. Mais celui-ci ne remua même pas sa tête ébouriffée. Il y avait deux explications possibles : *primo*, le casque ne fonctionnait pas ; *secundo*, ce troll était sourd comme un pot.

Malheureusement, il était impossible à Holly de savoir la vérité puisque les ultrasons étaient inaudibles pour des oreilles de fées.

Quelle que fût la cause, Holly se trouvait désormais contrainte d'adopter une stratégie à laquelle elle aurait préféré ne pas recourir : le contact direct. Tout pour sauver une vie humaine. A croire qu'elle était devenue complètement timbrée. Aucun doute là-dessus.

Holly actionna brutalement la manette des gaz, passant directement de la quatrième vitesse à la marche arrière. Pas très bon pour les pignons. Elle allait s'attirer les foudres des mécaniciens, si jamais elle survivait à cet interminable cauchemar. Sa manœuvre, destructrice pour les engrenages, lui fit faire une cabriole dans les airs : à présent, les talons de ses bottes étaient poin-

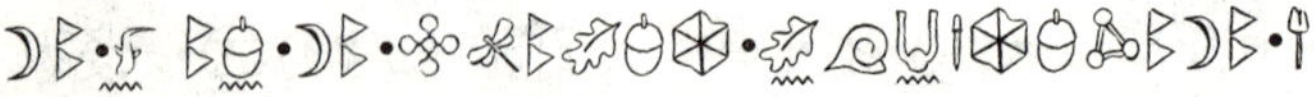

tés droit sur la tête de la créature. Holly grimaça. C'était la deuxième fois qu'elle se colletait avec le même troll. Incroyable.

Ses talons frappèrent le monstre en plein milieu du crâne. A cette vitesse, elle devait avoir une puissance d'impact d'au moins une demi-tonne. Seuls les anneaux qui renforçaient sa combinaison empêchèrent les os de la fée de se fracasser. Mais elle entendit quand même son genou craquer. La douleur remonta jusqu'à son front. Et lui fit rater sa manœuvre de dégagement. Au lieu de remonter à une altitude où elle aurait été en sécurité, Holly s'écrasa sur le dos du troll, s'empêtrant dans sa fourrure rêche.

Cette fois, la créature se montra passablement irritée. Non seulement quelque chose l'avait détournée de son dîner mais, en plus, la chose en question s'était prise dans sa fourrure, parmi les limaces antiparasites qui se chargeaient de lui nettoyer la peau. La bête se redressa, tendant une main griffue par-dessus son épaule. Ses ongles recourbés raclèrent le casque de Holly, traçant dans l'alliage des sillons parallèles. Juliet était en sécurité pour le moment, mais c'était Holly qui avait pris sa place sur la liste des individus menacés de disparition.

Le troll resserra les doigts, assurant sa prise sur le casque en dépit du revêtement antifriction qui, d'après Foaly, devait précisément empêcher qu'on s'en saisisse.

Il faudrait qu'elle ait une sérieuse conversation avec lui. Si c'était impossible dans ce monde, elle s'arrangerait pour que ce soit dans l'autre.

Le capitaine Short se sentit hissée par le bras du troll et se retrouva bientôt face à son vieil ennemi. Elle essaya de se concentrer en dépit de la douleur et de la confusion où elle était plongée. Sa jambe oscillait comme un pendule et le troll lui soufflait au visage son haleine fétide.

Elle avait dû avoir un plan, non ? Elle n'avait quand même pas fondu en piqué simplement pour venir mourir, ratatinée, entre les mains du troll. Elle avait sûrement pensé à une stratégie. Toutes ces années passées à l'académie avaient dû lui apprendre quelque chose. Quel qu'ait été son plan, il lui échappait à présent, flottant quelque part entre choc et douleur. Hors d'atteinte.

– Les lumières, Holly...

Une voix dans sa tête. Elle se parlait sans doute à elle-même. Peut-être son corps astral l'avait-il déjà quittée... Ha, ha ! Il faudrait qu'elle en parle à Foaly... Foaly ?

– Allumez les projecteurs, Holly. Si ses défenses entrent en action, vous serez morte avant que la magie puisse opérer.

– Foaly ? C'est vous ?

Elle avait peut-être prononcé ces paroles à haute

voix ou peut-être les avait-elle simplement pensées. Elle ne savait plus très bien.

– Les feux de tunnel, capitaine !

C'était une autre voix. Beaucoup moins tendre.

– Appuyez immédiatement sur le bouton ! C'est un ordre !

Aïe. C'était Root. Elle était en train d'échouer dans sa mission, une fois de plus. D'abord, Hambourg, puis Martina Franca et maintenant ici.

– Oui, commandant, marmonna-t-elle, essayant d'adopter un ton professionnel.

– Appuyez ! Vite, capitaine Short !

Holly regarda le troll droit dans ses yeux impitoyables et appuya sur le bouton. Moment très théâtral. Ou plutôt qui aurait dû l'être si les lumières avaient fonctionné. Malheureusement pour elle, dans sa hâte, elle s'était emparée de l'un des casques bricolés par Artemis Fowl. Et donc, pas de Sonix, pas de filtres et pas de feux de tunnel. Les ampoules halogènes étaient toujours en place mais les fils s'étaient débranchés au cours des investigations d'Artemis.

– Oh, là, là ! dit Holly dans un souffle.

– Qu'est-ce que ça veut dire, oh, là, là ? aboya Root.

– Les projecteurs sont débranchés, expliqua Foaly.

– Oh...

La voix de Root s'évanouit. Qu'y avait-il à ajouter ?

Holly fixa le troll. Si elle n'avait pas su que ces créatures étaient stupides, elle aurait juré que celui-ci souriait. Il restait là, immobile, du sang coulant de diverses blessures qu'il avait à la poitrine, et arborait un sourire carnassier. Or, le capitaine Short n'aimait pas qu'on lui adresse des sourires carnassiers.

– Toi, tu vas arrêter de sourire comme ça, dit-elle, et elle frappa le troll avec la seule arme dont elle disposait : sa tête casquée.

Courageux, sans aucun doute, mais à peu près aussi efficace que d'essayer d'abattre un arbre avec une plume. Par chance, ce geste peu réfléchi eut un effet secondaire.

Pendant une fraction de seconde, deux fils conducteurs entrèrent en contact, envoyant un courant électrique dans l'un des deux feux de tunnel. Quatre cents watts de lumière blanche transpercèrent alors les yeux écarlates du troll, projetant des flèches de douleur dans son cerveau.

– Hé, hé, marmonna Holly, un instant avant que le troll ne soit saisi de convulsions.

Ses spasmes la précipitèrent à terre où elle tournoya d'un bout à l'autre du parquet, ses jambes ballottant derrière elle.

Le mur se rapprochait à une vitesse inquiétante. « Peut-être, songea Holly avec espoir, que le choc sera de ceux dont on ne ressent la douleur que plus tard.

Non, répliqua son côté pessimiste, j'ai bien peur que ce ne soit pas le cas. » Elle heurta de plein fouet une tapisserie normande qui se décrocha sous l'impact et tomba sur elle. La douleur fut immédiate et débordante.

– Ouille, grogna Foaly. J'ai senti le choc. Ça a fait sauter les cadrans dans tous les sens. Les capteurs de douleur ont dépassé le degré maximal. Vos poumons ont pris un sale coup, capitaine. Vous allez perdre le contact avec nous pendant un moment. Mais ne vous inquiétez pas, Holly, vos pouvoirs magiques doivent déjà être à l'œuvre.

La fée sentit le fourmillement électrique de la magie se répandre dans ses multiples blessures. Bénis soient les dieux d'avoir créé les glands. Mais c'était insuffisant et un peu trop tard. La douleur dépassait son seuil de tolérance. Avant que l'inconscience ne l'engloutisse, Holly remua faiblement une main qui glissa sous la tapisserie et atterrit sur le bras de Butler, touchant sa peau nue. Incroyable : l'humain n'était pas mort. Des battements opiniâtres continuaient d'envoyer du sang dans ses membres fracassés.

« Guéris », pensa Holly. Et la magie ruissela dans ses doigts.

Le troll devait affronter un dilemme – quelle proie manger d'abord. Des choix, toujours des choix. Sa décision n'était guère facilitée par la douleur lancinante qui continuait de bourdonner autour de sa tête hirsute, ni par les projectiles logés dans les tissus adipeux de sa poitrine. Finalement, il opta pour la créature élevée à l'air libre. De la viande humaine bien tendre. Pas de muscle de fée trop coriace à mâcher.

L'animal s'accroupit puis, d'une griffe jaunâtre, inclina sur le côté le visage de la jeune fille. Une carotide palpitante s'étirait paresseusement le long de son cou. Le cou ou le cœur ? Le troll hésita. Le cou, il était plus près. Il tourna légèrement sa griffe, appuyant son bord tranchant contre la chair humaine. Un petit coup sec et ce seraient les propres battements de cœur de sa proie qui se chargeraient de faire jaillir le sang de son corps.

Butler se réveilla, ce qui constituait en soi une surprise. Il sut immédiatement qu'il était vivant en raison de la douleur aiguë qui pénétrait chaque centimètre cube de son corps. Il n'y avait pourtant pas de quoi se réjouir. Vivant, certes, mais son cou ayant fait un tour complet sur lui-même, il ne pourrait plus jamais ne serait-ce que promener le chien, encore moins venir en aide à sa sœur.

Le serviteur remua les doigts. La douleur était terrible mais, au moins, ils bougeaient. Il était stupéfiant qu'il pût encore avoir des fonctions motrices, compte tenu du traumatisme qu'avait subi sa colonne vertébrale. Ses orteils semblaient également normaux, mais il ne s'agissait peut-être que d'une illusion, étant donné qu'il lui était impossible de les voir.

Ses blessures à la poitrine avaient apparemment cessé de saigner et il avait les idées claires. Somme toute, il était dans une bien meilleure forme qu'il n'aurait dû l'être. Au nom du ciel, que se passait-il, ici ?

Butler remarqua quelque chose. Des étincelles bleues parcouraient son torse. Sans doute était-il victime d'une hallucination qui tentait de le distraire de l'inévitable. A dire vrai, l'hallucination était très réaliste.

Les étincelles se concentraient à l'endroit des blessures et s'enfonçaient dans sa peau. Butler fut parcouru d'un frisson. Finalement, ce n'était pas une hallucination. Un phénomène extraordinaire était en train de se produire. De la magie.

De la magie ? Voilà qui lui rappelait quelque chose dans son cerveau en voie de reconstitution. La magie des fées. Une force étrange guérissait ses blessures. Il tourna la tête avec une grimace de douleur lorsqu'il sentit ses vertèbres commencer à se remettre en place. Une main était posée sur son bras. Une main avec des doigts d'elfe d'où jaillissaient des étincelles qui se dirigeaient d'elles-mêmes vers ses contusions, ses fractures, ses plaies. Les blessures à soigner étaient nombreuses mais les minuscules étincelles s'en chargeaient avec rapidité et efficacité. On aurait dit une armée de castors immatériels réparant les dégâts d'une tempête.

Butler sentait ses os se réparer et le sang quitter ses plaies à demi coagulées. Sa tête tourna involontairement tandis que ses vertèbres retrouvaient définitivement leur place et un regain d'énergie parcourut son corps à mesure que se reconstituaient les trois litres de sang que ses blessures à la poitrine lui avaient fait perdre.

Butler se releva d'un bond – littéralement d'un bond. Il était redevenu lui-même. Non. Mieux encore. Sa force avait retrouvé son niveau maximal. Une force qui lui permettrait de s'attaquer à nouveau à la bête féroce accroupie devant sa petite sœur.

Il sentit s'accélérer le rythme de son cœur régénéré, telle la poussée d'un moteur de hors-bord. « Du calme, se conseilla-t-il à lui-même. La passion est l'ennemie de l'efficacité. » Mais calme ou pas, la situation était désespérée. Cette créature l'avait pratiquement tué une première fois et, maintenant, il n'avait même plus le Sig Sauer. Malgré toute son habileté en matière de combat rapproché, il aurait bien aimé disposer d'une arme. Quelque chose qui ait du poids. Sa botte heurta alors un objet métallique. Butler baissa les yeux vers les débris répandus dans le sillage du troll... Parfait.

Il n'y avait que de la neige sur l'écran.

– Allez, vite, dépêchez-vous, lança Root.

Foaly passa devant son supérieur en le repoussant du coude.

– Peut-être que si vous ne vous obstiniez pas à bloquer les panneaux de raccordement...

A contrecœur, Root s'écarta en traînant les pieds. De son point de vue, c'étaient les panneaux qui avaient le tort de se trouver derrière lui. La tête du centaure disparut dans un boîtier.

– Une panne ?

– Non. Une simple interférence.

Root tapa sur l'écran. Ce n'était pas une très bonne idée. D'abord, parce qu'il n'y avait pas une chance sur un million que les choses en soient améliorées, ensuite parce que les écrans à plasma deviennent brûlants après un usage prolongé.

– Nom de... !

– Ah oui, au fait, il vaut mieux ne pas toucher à cet écran.

– Ha, ha, très drôle. C'est le moment de plaisanter, bien sûr ?

– Non, pas vraiment. Vous voyez quelque chose ?

La neige laissa place à des formes reconnaissables.

– Ça y est, ça marche. On a une image.

– J'ai activé la caméra secondaire. C'est de la simple vidéo mais il faudra qu'on s'en contente.

Root ne fit pas de commentaire. Il avait les yeux fixés sur l'écran.

C'était sûrement un film. Il ne pouvait s'agir d'une scène de la vie réelle.

– Alors, qu'est-ce qui se passe ? C'est intéressant ?

Root essaya de répondre, mais son vocabulaire de soldat était dépourvu des superlatifs nécessaires.

– Qu'est-ce qu'on voit ?

Le commandant fit une tentative :

– C'est le... l'humain... Je n'ai jamais... Foaly, il faut que vous veniez voir ça vous-même.

Holly regarda la scène à travers une fente entre deux plis de la tapisserie. Si elle n'en avait pas été le témoin, elle n'y aurait jamais cru. En fait, ce fut seulement lorsqu'elle revit l'enregistrement vidéo pour faire son rapport qu'elle eut la certitude que tout cela n'était pas une hallucination due à un état comateux. En tout cas, la séquence vidéo devint une sorte de légende qui fut d'abord diffusée dans toutes les émissions câblées de films d'amateurs et que l'académie finit par intégrer à ses cours de combat rapproché.

L'humain, Butler, était en train de revêtir une armure médiévale. Aussi incroyable que cela puisse paraître, il avait apparemment l'intention de combattre le troll corps à corps. Holly essaya de l'avertir, d'émettre un son quelconque, mais la magie n'avait pas encore rendu leur souffle à ses poumons écrasés.

Butler abaissa la visière de son heaume et souleva une redoutable masse d'armes.

– Maintenant, grogna-t-il à travers le ventail, je vais te montrer ce qui se passe quand on s'en prend à ma sœur.

L'humain fit tournoyer la masse d'armes comme s'il s'était agi d'un bâton de majorette et l'abattit violemment entre les omoplates du troll. Sans être fatal, un tel coup était sans nul doute suffisant pour détourner la créature de sa victime.

Butler appuya le pied juste au-dessus des hanches du troll et dégagea son arme.

La bête relâcha sa prise en produisant un horrible bruit de succion. Butler recula et se mit en position de défense.

Le troll se retourna alors vers lui, les griffes de ses dix doigts s'étirant sur toute leur longueur. Des gouttes de venin scintillaient à l'extrémité de ses défenses. La récréation était terminée. Mais, cette fois, il n'y aurait pas d'attaque surprise.

La bête se méfiait, elle avait déjà été blessée. Ce nouvel adversaire allait bénéficier du même respect qu'elle aurait accordé à un autre mâle de son espèce. Aux yeux du troll, on était en train d'empiéter sur son territoire.

Et il n'existait qu'une seule manière de régler un conflit de cette nature. La manière des trolls, chaque fois qu'éclatait une dispute...

– Je te préviens, dit Butler, le visage impassible, je suis armé et, si c'est nécessaire, je n'hésiterai pas à tuer.

Holly aurait poussé un grognement si elle en avait été capable. Des fanfaronnades ! L'humain essayait d'entraîner le troll dans un échange de propos macho ! Le capitaine Short comprit alors son erreur. L'important, ce n'étaient pas les mots mais le ton sur lequel il les prononçait. Calme, apaisant. Comme un dresseur devant une licorne effrayée.

– Écarte-toi de la jeune fille. Bien gentiment.

Le troll gonfla ses joues et lança un long rugissement. Rituel d'intimidation. Histoire de tester l'adversaire. Butler resta de marbre.

– Oui, oui, très bien. C'est fou ce que ça fait peur. Maintenant, tu recules jusqu'à la porte et tu sors de cette maison si tu ne veux pas que je te découpe en petits morceaux.

Agacé par sa réaction, le troll s'ébroua. En général, ses rugissements provoquaient la panique chez les créatures qu'il avait en face de lui.

– Un pas après l'autre. Lentement, calmement. Vas-y, mon gros bonhomme.

On pouvait presque voir dans les yeux du troll une ombre d'incertitude. Peut-être que cet humain était...

Ce fut à ce moment précis que Butler frappa. Esquissant ce qui semblait un pas de danse, il se glissa sous les défenses de la bête et lui décocha un uppercut dévastateur à l'aide de son arme médiévale. Le troll recula, les jambes chancelantes, ses griffes battant l'air avec une frénésie sauvage. Mais il était trop tard : Butler s'était déjà mis hors d'atteinte en se précipitant de l'autre côté du hall.

D'un pas pesant, la créature se lança sur ses talons, crachant les dents arrachées à ses gencives en charpie. Butler tomba à genoux, glissant comme un patineur sur le sol bien ciré. Il se baissa et fit une pirouette pour se tourner face à son poursuivant.

– Devine ce que j'ai trouvé, dit-il en brandissant le Sig Sauer.

Pas de balles dans la poitrine, cette fois. L'homme vida le reste de son chargeur entre les deux yeux du troll, groupant ses projectiles sur une surface de dix centimètres de diamètre. Malheureusement pour lui, au cours de millénaires passés à s'affronter à coups de tête, les trolls avaient développé un os frontal d'une exceptionnelle épaisseur. Aussi magistral qu'il fût, son tir n'avait donc pas réussi à transpercer le crâne de la bête, malgré les balles recouvertes de Téflon.

Aucune créature au monde ne peut cependant résister sans dommage à dix projectiles aussi dévastateurs, et le troll ne fit pas exception à la règle. L'impact des balles dessina un tatouage en forme de coup de marteau sur son front et provoqua une commotion immédiate. L'animal recula d'un pas vacillant en se tenant le front. Butler bondit alors sur lui, plantant une pointe de sa masse d'armes dans l'un de ses pieds velus.

Le troll, à moitié assommé, aveuglé par le sang qui lui coulait dans les yeux, avait à présent du mal à marcher. Une personne normale aurait éprouvé une pointe de remords devant sa souffrance, mais pas Butler. Il avait connu trop d'exemples d'hommes qui s'étaient fait éventrer par un animal blessé. On entrait dans la phase dangereuse. Ce n'était pas le moment d'avoir pitié, il fallait mener le combat à son terme avec une opiniâtreté extrême.

Impuissante, Holly regarda l'humain assener en visant avec soin une série de coups ravageurs à la créature blessée. Il commença par lui sectionner les tendons, l'obligeant à tomber à genoux puis il abandonna la masse d'armes et continua à la frapper de ses mains protégées par des gantelets dont l'impact était peut-être encore plus destructeur. Le malheureux troll essaya de riposter tant bien que mal, réussissant même à porter quelques coups obliques. Mais ils ne parvinrent pas à pénétrer l'antique armure. Dans le même temps, Butler poursuivait sa besogne avec une méticulosité de chirurgien. Estimant que l'anatomie de l'homme et celle du troll devaient être fondamentalement semblables, il faisait pleuvoir les coups sur la stupide créature qu'il réduisit bientôt à un tas de fourrure tremblotante. C'était un spectacle pitoyable mais le serviteur n'en avait pas encore fini. Il ôta ses gantelets ruisselants de sang et glissa un nouveau chargeur dans son pistolet.

– Voyons si tu as autant d'os sous le menton que sur le front.

– Non, haleta Holly, qui venait de retrouver son premier souffle. Pas ça.

Sans lui prêter attention, Butler enfonça le canon de son pistolet sous le menton du troll.

– Ne tirez pas... Vous me devez quelque chose.

Butler s'interrompit. Il était vrai que Juliet était vivante. Les idées confuses sans aucun doute, mais vivante. Il releva le chien de son arme. Chaque cellule de son cerveau lui hurlait de presser la détente mais Juliet était vivante.

– Vous me devez quelque chose, l'humain.

Butler soupira. Il le regretterait plus tard.

– Très bien, capitaine. La bête survivra. Elle a de la chance, je suis de bonne humeur.

Holly émit un son. Quelque chose qui se situait entre le gémissement et le rire étranglé.

– Maintenant, débarrassons-nous de notre ami velu.

Butler fit rouler le troll inconscient sur un chariot qui servait à déplacer les armures et le traîna jusqu'à la porte d'entrée dévastée. D'un geste puissant, il jeta le tout dans la nuit suspendue.

– Et ne reviens jamais ici, cria-t-il.

– Stupéfiant, murmura Root.

– Je ne vous le fais pas dire, approuva Foaly.

CHAPITRE IX

UN ATOUT DANS LA MANCHE

Artemis essaya de tourner la poignée de la porte et se brûla la paume de la main. Bloquée. La fée avait dû faire fondre la serrure avec son arme. Très astucieux. Une variable de moins dans l'équation. C'était exactement ce que lui-même aurait fait.

Il ne perdit pas de temps à essayer de forcer la porte. Elle était en acier blindé et il n'avait que douze ans. Pas besoin d'être un génie pour en tirer la conclusion – bien qu'il en fût un. L'héritier présomptif des Fowl préféra retourner devant son mur d'écrans pour observer la suite des événements.

Il comprit aussitôt la tactique des FAR : envoyer le troll pour provoquer un appel au secours, l'interpréter comme une invitation à entrer et lâcher un commando de gobelins qui s'emparerait du manoir. Bien pensé. Et imprévu. C'était la deuxième fois qu'il sous-estimait ses adversaires.

Quoi qu'il arrive, il n'y en aurait pas de troisième.

A mesure que la scène du rez-de-chaussée se déroulait sur les écrans, les sentiments d'Artemis passèrent de la terreur à la fierté. Butler avait réussi. Il avait vaincu le troll sans que le moindre appel au secours franchisse ses lèvres. En regardant le spectacle, Artemis apprécia pleinement, et peut-être pour la première fois, les services fournis par la famille Butler.

Artemis brancha la radio à trois bandes, émettant sur toutes les fréquences.

– Commandant Root, j'imagine que vous êtes branché sur tous les canaux...

Pendant quelques instants, il n'y eut qu'un bruit de fond dans les haut-parleurs puis il entendit le déclic d'un micro qu'on branchait.

– Je vous entends, l'humain. Je peux faire quelque chose pour vous ?

– C'est le commandant ?

Un son filtra à travers la grille noire du haut-parleur. On aurait dit un hennissement.

– Non, ce n'est pas le commandant. C'est Foaly, le centaure. Et vous, vous êtes le résidu d'espèce humaine spécialisé dans le kidnapping ?

Il fallut un moment à Artemis pour comprendre qu'on venait de l'insulter.

– Monsieur... heu... Foaly, de toute évidence, vous n'avez pas consulté vos manuels de psychologie. Il n'est pas très prudent de contrarier un preneur d'otages. Je suis peut-être instable, qui sait ?

– *Peut-être* instable ? Le *peut-être* est de trop. Mais ça n'a aucune importance. Bientôt, vous ne serez plus qu'un nuage de molécules radioactives.

Artemis eut un petit rire.

– C'est là que vous vous trompez, mon cher quadrupède. Quand vous ferez exploser votre biobombe, il y a longtemps que j'aurai échappé à la suspension temporelle.

Ce fut au tour de Foaly de pouffer de rire.

– Vous bluffez, l'humain. S'il existait un moyen d'en sortir, je l'aurais découvert. Je ne sais pas pour qui vous vous...

Fort heureusement, Root prit alors le micro :

– Fowl ? Commandant Root, ici. Qu'est-ce que vous voulez ?

– Je voudrais simplement vous informer, commandant, qu'en dépit de votre tentative de trahison, je suis toujours disposé à négocier.

– Ce troll n'avait rien à voir avec moi, protesta Root. C'est une chose qui s'est faite contre ma volonté.

– En tout cas, cela a *été fait*, et ce sont les FAR qui l'ont fait. Toute confiance est donc désormais impossible entre nous. Alors, voici mon ultimatum. Je vous donne trente minutes pour envoyer l'or, sinon, je refuserai de relâcher le capitaine Short. Et, en plus, je ne l'emmènerai même pas avec moi quand je sortirai de la zone de suspension temporelle, si bien qu'elle sera désintégrée par votre propre biobombe.

– Ne soyez pas stupide, l'humain. Vous vous faites des illusions. La technologie des Êtres de la Boue a des siècles de retard sur la nôtre. Il n'existe aucun moyen d'échapper à la zone de suspension temporelle.

Artemis se pencha tout près du micro, souriant de son sourire de loup.

– Il n'y a qu'une seule façon de voir qui a raison, Root. Êtes-vous prêt à risquer la vie du capitaine Short en vous fiant uniquement à votre intuition ?

L'hésitation de Root fut soulignée par le sifflement d'une interférence.

Lorsque vint sa réponse, sa voix avait juste la petite note de défaite adaptée à la circonstance.

– Non, soupira-t-il, je n'y suis pas prêt. Vous aurez votre or, Fowl. Une tonne. Vingt-quatre carats.

Artemis eut un sourire narquois. Un sacré acteur, le commandant Root.

– Trente minutes, commandant. Comptez les secondes si votre montre est arrêtée. J'attendrai. Mais pas longtemps.

Artemis coupa la communication et se laissa aller contre le dossier de son fauteuil pivotant. Apparemment, ils avaient mordu à l'appât Aucun doute : les analystes des FAR avaient découvert son invitation « involontaire ». Les fées allaient payer parce qu'elles pensaient pouvoir récupérer l'or dès qu'il serait mort. Pulvérisé par la biobombe. Ce qui ne se produirait pas, bien sûr.

En théorie.

Butler tira trois balles dans l'encadrement de la porte. La porte elle-même était en acier et aurait fait ricocher vers lui les balles dévastatrices. L'encadrement, en revanche, était constitué de la pierre poreuse qui avait servi à construire le manoir à l'origine. Elle s'effritait comme de la craie. Un défaut fondamental dans le système de sécurité, auquel il faudrait remédier dès que cette affaire serait terminée.

Maître Artemis attendait, tranquillement assis dans son fauteuil, devant le mur d'écrans.

– Beau travail, Butler.

– Merci, Artemis. Nous avons eu quelques ennuis à un certain moment. Sans l'aide du capitaine...

Le garçon acquiesça d'un signe de tête.

– Oui. J'ai vu. Le pouvoir de guérison, un art majeur chez les fées. Je me demande pourquoi elle a fait ça.

– Moi aussi, dit doucement Butler. Il est certain que nous ne l'avons pas mérité.

Artemis leva vivement les yeux.

– Gardez confiance, mon vieux. On approche du dénouement.

Butler hocha la tête. Il s'efforça même de sourire. Mais il avait beau sourire de toutes ses dents, le cœur n'y était pas.

– Dans moins d'une heure, le capitaine Short aura retrouvé son peuple et nous aurons suffisamment de fonds pour relancer certaines de nos entreprises les plus raffinées.

– Je sais. Simplement...

Artemis n'eut pas besoin de poser la question. Il savait exactement ce que ressentait Butler. La fée leur avait sauvé la vie, à sa sœur et à lui, et pourtant, il persistait à exiger la rançon. Pour un homme d'honneur comme Butler, c'était plus qu'il n'en pouvait supporter, ou presque.

– Les négociations sont terminées. D'une manière ou d'une autre, elle sera rendue à ses semblables. Il ne sera fait aucun mal au capitaine Short. Vous avez ma parole.

– Et Juliet ?

– Oui ?

– Est-ce qu'il existe un danger pour ma sœur ?

– Non. Aucun danger.

– Les fées vont se contenter de nous donner cet or et s'en aller ?

Artemis eut un petit rire à peine perceptible.

– Non, pas exactement. Elles vont envoyer une biobombe sur le manoir dès que le capitaine Short aura été libéré.

Butler prit une inspiration pour dire quelque chose, mais il hésita.

De toute évidence, le plan ne se réduisait pas à cela. Maître Fowl lui donnerait les explications nécessaires lorsqu'il le jugerait utile. Aussi, plutôt que d'interroger son employeur, il se contenta de déclarer :

– J'ai confiance en vous, Artemis.

– Oui, répondit celui-ci, le front plissé sous le poids de cette confiance. Je sais.

Cudgeon faisait ce que les politiciens savent le mieux faire : essayer de fuir leurs responsabilités.

– Ton officier a apporté son aide aux humains, lança-t-il, en s'efforçant de se gonfler d'indignation. L'opération se déroulait comme prévu jusqu'à ce que ta femelle s'attaque à notre adjoint.

– Adjoint ? s'étrangla Foaly. Le troll est devenu un adjoint, maintenant ?

– Oui. En effet. Et cet humain en a fait du hachis. Toute l'affaire serait déjà terminée si votre département ne s'était pas montré aussi incompétent.

En temps normal, Root aurait eu une crise de fureur en entendant cela, mais il savait que Cudgeon se raccrochait au moindre fil pour tenter désespérément de sauver sa carrière. Le commandant se contenta donc de sourire.

– Hé, Foaly ?

– Oui, commandant ?

– Est-ce qu'on a enregistré sur disque l'assaut du troll ?

Le centaure poussa un soupir théâtral.

– Hélas, non, commandant, nous n'avions plus un seul disque en réserve lorsque le troll est entré dans la maison.

– Quel dommage.

– C'est vraiment triste.

– Ces disques auraient pu apporter une aide inestimable au commandant temporaire Cudgeon lors de son audition devant la commission de discipline.

Cudgeon perdit son sang-froid.

– Donne-moi ces disques, Julius ! Je sais qu'ils sont ici ! C'est de l'obstruction caractérisée.

– Celui qui fait de l'obstruction, c'est toi, Cudgeon. En te servant de cette affaire pour ton seul avancement.

Le teint de Cudgeon prit une couleur qui pouvait rivaliser avec celle de Root. La situation lui échappait et il le savait. Même Chix Verbil et les autres lutins se tenaient à distance de leur chef, à présent.

– C'est toujours moi qui commande, ici, Julius, alors donne-moi ces disques ou je te fais mettre aux arrêts.

– Vraiment ? Et qui va m'arrêter ?

Pendant un instant, le visage de Cudgeon retrouva sa gravité arrogante. Mais elle se dissipa aussitôt lorsqu'il remarqua que les officiers qui auraient dû se trouver à ses côtés brillaient par leur absence.

– Eh oui, dit Foaly dans un hennissement. Vous n'êtes plus commandant temporaire. L'appel est venu d'en dessous. Vous avez rendez-vous avec le Grand Conseil mais je ne pense pas que ce soit pour vous offrir un siège.

Ce fut sans doute le sourire de Foaly qui fit perdre la tête à Cudgeon.

– Donnez-moi ces disques ! rugit-il, en plaquant le centaure contre la navette.

Root fut tenté de les laisser aux prises pendant un certain temps mais le moment était mal choisi pour s'offrir ce petit plaisir.

– Oh, comme c'est vilain de se battre, dit-il en agitant l'index. Personne n'a le droit de taper sur Foaly à part moi.

Le centaure pâlit.

– Faites attention avec votre doigt. Vous avez toujours ce...

Accidentellement, Root effleura la jointure de son index, ouvrant une valve minuscule qui libéra un gaz. Sous sa poussée, une fléchette enduite de narcotique fut projetée à travers l'extrémité du faux doigt en latex et vint se planter dans le cou de Cudgeon. Le commandant temporaire, qui allait bientôt devenir simple soldat, tomba comme une pierre.

Foaly se massa la nuque.

– Bien visé, commandant.

– Je ne sais pas de quoi vous parlez. Il s'agit d'un simple accident. J'avais complètement oublié ce faux doigt. J'imagine qu'il doit y avoir des précédents.

– Oh, bien sûr. Malheureusement, Cudgeon va rester inconscient pendant plusieurs heures et, quand il se réveillera, il aura raté le spectacle.

– Dommage.

Root s'accorda un sourire fugitif puis il revint aux choses sérieuses.

– L'or est là ?

– Ouais, ils viennent de l'apporter.

– Très bien.

Root s'adressa aux lutins de Cudgeon qui attendaient, l'air penaud :

– Vous allez le charger sur un chariot à coussin d'air et l'envoyer dans la maison. A la moindre anicroche, je vous fais manger vos galons. Compris ?

Personne ne répondit mais il n'y avait aucun doute possible : tout le monde avait compris.

– Bon, alors, remuez-vous maintenant.

Root disparut à l'intérieur de la navette. Foaly le

suivit dans un bruit de sabots et le commandant referma soigneusement la porte.

– Elle est armée ?

Le centaure se tourna vers la console centrale et actionna quelques boutons à l'aspect impressionnant.

– Ça y est, c'est fait.

– Je veux qu'elle soit lancée aussi vite que possible.

Le commandant jeta un coup d'œil à travers le hublot réfringent à l'épreuve des rayons laser.

– C'est une question de minutes, maintenant. Je vois apparaître des rayons de soleil.

Foaly se pencha sur son clavier d'un air sérieux.

– La magie est en train de se dissiper, dit-il. Dans quinze minutes, nous allons nous trouver en pleine lumière terrestre. Les courants de neutrinos perdent de leur intégrité.

– Je vois, dit Root, ce qui constituait fondamentalement un nouveau mensonge. Enfin, bon, d'accord, je ne vois rien du tout. Mais j'ai compris l'histoire des quinze minutes. Ça vous laisse dix minutes pour sortir le capitaine Short de là. Sinon, nous allons devenir des cibles idéales pour toute l'espèce humaine.

Foaly activa une caméra supplémentaire. Celle-ci était reliée à un chariot qui se déplaçait sur coussin d'air. Il passa le doigt sur un pavé tactile pour faire un essai. Le chariot bondit en avant et faillit décapiter Chix Verbil.

– Pilotage impeccable, marmonna Root. Vous croyez que ce machin-là va monter les marches ?

Foaly ne leva même pas les yeux de ses ordinateurs.

– Compensateur automatique de niveau. Un mètre cinquante de hauteur minimum. Pas de problème.

Root le transperça du regard.

– Alors, vous faites ça simplement pour m'agacer ?

Foaly haussa les épaules.

– C'est bien possible.

– Vous pouvez vous estimer heureux que je n'aie pas d'autres fléchettes au bout du doigt. Vous voyez ce que je veux dire ?

– Oui, commandant.

– Très bien. Maintenant, on va ramener le capitaine Short à la maison.

Holly s'éleva sous le dôme du hall. Des traits de lumière orange rayaient le bleu azur. La suspension temporelle se dissipait. Il ne restait plus que quelques minutes avant que Root passe la maison au rinçage bleu.

La voix de Foaly bourdonna dans son écouteur.

– Ça y est, capitaine Short, l'or est en route. Tenez-vous prête à sortir.

– D'habitude, nous ne négocions jamais avec des ravisseurs, s'étonna-t-elle. Qu'est-ce qui se passe ?

– Rien, répondit Foaly d'un ton détaché. Il s'agit

d'un simple échange. L'or entre, vous sortez. Nous envoyons le missile. Il y aura une grosse explosion bleue et tout sera terminé.

– Fowl est au courant pour la biobombe ?

– Ouais. Il sait tout. Et il affirme qu'il pourra échapper à la suspension temporelle.

– C'est impossible.

– Exact.

– Donc ils vont tous se faire tuer !

– Et alors ? répliqua Foaly – Holly pouvait presque le voir hausser les épaules. Voilà ce qui arrive quand on embête le petit Peuple.

Holly se sentait déchirée. Il ne faisait aucun doute que Fowl représentait un danger pour la civilisation souterraine. On ne verserait pas beaucoup de larmes sur son cadavre. Mais la fille, Juliet, était innocente. Elle méritait qu'on lui donne une chance.

Holly descendit à une altitude de deux mètres. A hauteur d'œil pour Butler. Les humains s'étaient rassemblés dans les ruines de ce qui avait été un hall d'entréc. Ils n'avaient pas l'air d'accord entre eux.

Elle le sentait.

Holly lança un regard accusateur à Artemis.

– Vous les avez prévenus ?

Artemis soutint son regard.

– Prévenus de quoi ?

– Oui, prévenus de quoi, madame la fée ? répéta

Juliet d'un air belliqueux, toujours furieuse d'avoir subi le mesmer.

– Ne faites pas l'idiot, Fowl. Vous savez très bien de quoi je veux parler.

Artemis ne parvenait jamais à faire l'idiot bien longtemps.

– Oui, capitaine Short, je le sais. Vous voulez parler de la biobombe. Votre inquiétude serait émouvante si j'en étais moi aussi l'objet. Mais ne vous tracassez pas. Tout se déroule conformément au plan.

– Conformément au plan ? s'exclama Holly en montrant le hall dévasté. Et ça, c'est conforme au plan ? Et Butler qui a failli se faire tuer, c'était aussi prévu dans le plan ?

– Non, admit Artemis. La présence du troll a constitué un léger accident de parcours. Mais négligeable par rapport à l'ensemble du projet.

Holly résista à l'envie de donner un nouveau coup de poing à cet humain au teint pâle et se tourna vers Butler.

– Pour l'amour du ciel, écoutez la voix de la raison. Il est impossible d'échapper à la suspension temporelle. Personne n'y est jamais parvenu.

Les traits de Butler semblaient sculptés dans la pierre.

– Si Artemis dit que c'est possible, alors ça l'est.

– Et votre sœur ? Vous êtes prêt à risquer sa vie par loyauté envers un bandit ?

– Artemis n'est pas un bandit, c'est un génie. Et maintenant, s'il vous plaît, veuillez vous écarter de mon champ de vision, je surveille l'entrée.

Holly s'éleva à une hauteur de six mètres.

– Vous êtes fous. Tous autant que vous êtes ! Dans cinq minutes, vous ne serez plus qu'un petit tas de poussière. Vous vous en rendez compte ?

Artemis soupira.

– Vous avez eu votre réponse, capitaine. Alors, maintenant, s'il vous plaît, laissez-nous. C'est une phase délicate de la cérémonie.

– La cérémonie ? C'est un enlèvement ! Ayez au moins le cran d'appeler les choses par leur nom.

La patience d'Artemis commençait à se fatiguer.

– Butler, vous reste-t-il des fléchettes tranquillisantes ?

Le serviteur géant acquiesça d'un signe de tête mais ne répondit rien.

En cet instant précis, si l'ordre lui avait été donné d'endormir Holly, il n'aurait pas été sûr de pouvoir obéir. Heureusement, l'attention d'Artemis fut attirée par des signes d'activité dans l'allée centrale.

– Ah, il semble que les FAR se soient décidées à capituler. Butler, veillez au bon déroulement de la livraison. Mais restez sur vos gardes. Nos amies les fées ne répugnent pas à la fourberie.

– Vous êtes bien placé pour dire ça, marmonna Holly.

Butler se précipita vers l'entrée en ruine, vérifiant que son neuf millimètres Sig Sauer était chargé et armé. Il était presque reconnaissant qu'un peu d'action de type militaire vienne le distraire de son dilemme. Dans des situations comme celles-ci, son entraînement prenait le pas sur tout le reste. Il n'y avait plus de place pour les sentiments.

Un léger nuage de poussière flottait toujours dans l'air.

Butler plissa les yeux pour observer au travers ce qui se passait dans l'allée centrale. Les filtres qu'il avait devant les yeux lui indiquaient qu'aucune créature à sang chaud n'approchait. En revanche, une sorte de grand chariot avançait apparemment tout seul vers la porte d'entrée. Il reposait sur un coussin d'air qu'on voyait trembloter au-dessous.

Maître Artemis aurait sans nul doute compris le fonctionnement de cette machine ; Butler, lui, se souciait seulement de savoir s'il allait réussir à la neutraliser.

Le chariot heurta la première marche du perron.

– Bravo pour le compensateur de niveau ! lança Root avec dédain.

– C'est la rançon ! s'écria Butler.

Artemis essaya de contenir l'excitation qu'il sentait

monter dans sa poitrine. Le moment n'était pas venu de laisser les émotions se manifester.

– Vérifiez qu'il n'y ait pas de piège.

Butler s'avança prudemment sur le perron. Des débris de gargouilles désintégrées par l'explosion étaient répandus à ses pieds.

– Pas de présence hostile. Il semble que la chose se déplace toute seule.

Le chariot heurta les marches et fit une embardée.

– Je ne sais pas qui conduit cette machine mais il devrait prendre quelques leçons.

Butler se pencha tout près du sol pour regarder sous le chariot.

– Pas d'explosifs visibles.

Il sortit de sa poche un analyseur dont il déploya l'antenne télescopique.

– Pas de micros non plus. Rien qui soit détectable. Tiens, qu'est-ce que c'est que ça ?

– Aïe, aïe, aïe ! murmura Foaly.

– C'est une caméra.

Butler tendit la main et arracha l'objectif grand angle en tirant sur le câble.

– Bonne nuit, messieurs.

En dépit du poids qu'il portait, le chariot était très maniable et Butler le fit glisser sans difficulté jusqu'au vestibule. Le chariot s'immobilisa en ronronnant doucement, comme s'il attendait d'être vidé de son chargement.

A présent que le grand moment était arrivé, Artemis avait presque peur de s'emparer de l'or. Il avait du mal à croire que, après tout ce temps, son plan diabolique n'était plus qu'à quelques minutes de la réussite. Bien entendu, ces quelques minutes étaient vitales et représentaient le plus grand danger.

– Déballez-le, dit-il enfin, surpris d'entendre sa propre voix trembler.

Ce fut un instant saisissant. Juliet s'approcha timidement, écarquillant ses yeux étincelants. Même Holly réduisit les gaz et se laissa descendre, ses pieds effleurant les dalles de marbre. Butler ouvrit la fermeture à glissière de la grande bâche de toile noire qu'il écarta pour découvrir la cargaison.

Personne ne prononça un mot. Artemis se dit qu'un peu de musique symphonique serait la bienvenue, l'ouverture de 1812 de Tchaïkovski, par exemple. L'or était là, disposé en rangées scintillantes. Il s'en dégageait comme une sorte d'aura, de chaleur, mais aussi une impression de danger intrinsèque. Tant de gens étaient prêts à mourir ou à tuer pour l'inimaginable richesse que cet or pouvait apporter !

Holly était fascinée. D'une manière générale, les

fées ont une attirance pour les minéraux, elles appartiennent elles aussi à la terre. Mais l'or est leur métal préféré. Pour son éclat. Son envoûtement.

– Ils ont payé, dit-elle dans un souffle. Je n'arrive pas à y croire.

– Moi non plus, murmura Artemis. Butler, c'est du vrai ?

Le serviteur prit un lingot. Il y enfonça la pointe d'un couteau et en détacha une petite lamelle qu'il leva vers la lumière.

– Il est parfaitement authentique, dit-il. Ce lingot-ci en tout cas.

– Bien. Très bien. Commencez le déchargement, voulez-vous ? Nous renverrons le chariot avec le capitaine Short.

Entendre prononcer son nom la tira de sa fascination.

– Artemis, laissez tomber. Aucun humain n'a jamais réussi à garder de l'or des fées. Ils ont pourtant essayé pendant des siècles. Les FAR sont prêtes à tout pour conserver leur bien.

Artemis hocha la tête. Amusé.

– Je vous ai dit...

Holly le prit par les épaules.

– Vous ne pourrez pas vous échapper ! Vous ne comprenez donc pas ?

Il lui rendit froidement son regard.

– Je peux m'échapper, Holly. Regardez-moi dans les yeux et répétez-moi que ça m'est impossible.

Elle fit ce qu'il demandait. Elle fixa les yeux bleu-noir de son ravisseur et y vit la vérité. Pendant un instant, elle le crut.

– Il reste encore un peu de temps, dit-elle d'un ton désespéré. On doit pouvoir faire quelque chose. J'ai des pouvoirs magiques.

Une expression d'agacement dessina une ride sur le front du jeune garçon.

– Je suis navré de vous décevoir, capitaine, mais il n'y a absolument rien à faire.

Artemis s'interrompit, levant momentanément les yeux vers le grenier aménagé. « Après tout, peut-être, songea-t-il. Ai-je vraiment besoin de tout cet or ? » N'était-ce pas sa conscience qui le tourmentait, aspirant comme une sangsue la douceur de sa victoire ?

Il se reprit. S'en tenir au plan. Rien qu'au plan. Pas d'émotion.

Artemis sentit sur son épaule une main familière.

– Tout va bien ?

– Oui, Butler. Continuez à décharger. Demandez à Juliet de vous aider. Je dois m'entretenir avec le capitaine Short.

– Vous êtes sûr qu'il n'y a pas de problème ?

– Non, mon très cher ami, je n'en suis pas sûr. Mais c'est trop tard, à présent

Butler hocha la tête et retourna à sa tâche. Juliet le suivit comme un terrier.

– Maintenant, capitaine. En ce qui concerne votre magie.

– Oui, et alors ?

Il y avait une ombre de méfiance dans les yeux de Holly.

– Que devrais-je faire pour avoir droit à la réalisation d'un souhait ?

Holly jeta un coup d'œil au chariot.

– Ça dépend. Qu'est-ce que vous avez à proposer en échange ?

On ne pouvait pas dire que Root était vraiment détendu.

Des rayons de lumière jaune de plus en plus larges perçaient l'azur. Il ne restait plus que quelques minutes. De toutes petites minutes. Le cigare âcre qui répandait des toxines dans son organisme n'arrangeait pas sa migraine.

– Est-ce que le personnel non indispensable a été évacué ?

– Oui, à moins qu'ils soient revenus en douce depuis la dernière fois que vous m'avez posé la question.

– Je vous en prie, Foaly, pas maintenant. Croyez-moi, ce n'est vraiment pas le moment. Vous avez des nouvelles du capitaine Short ?

– Non. Nous avons perdu le contact vidéo après l'histoire du troll. J'imagine que la batterie est cassée. Nous ferions bien de lui ôter son casque dès que possible sinon les radiations risquent de lui passer le cerveau à la friture. Ce serait dommage, après tout le travail que nous avons fait.

Foaly retourna devant sa console. Une lumière rouge commença à clignoter doucement.

– Attention. Détecteur de mouvement. Quelque chose bouge du côté de l'entrée principale.

Root se précipita vers les écrans.

– Vous pouvez agrandir l'image ?

– Pas de problème.

Foaly appuya sur un bouton, agrandissant l'image de quatre cents pour cent.

Root s'assit dans le fauteuil le plus proche.

– J'ai une hallucination, ou quoi ?

– Pas du tout, commandant.

Foaly pouffa de rire.

– C'est encore mieux que le coup de l'armure.

Holly sortait de la maison. Avec l'or.

Une demi-seconde plus tard, elle était entourée par le commando de Récupération.

– On va vous emmener hors de la zone dangereuse, capitaine, dit aussitôt un lutin en attrapant Holly par le bras.

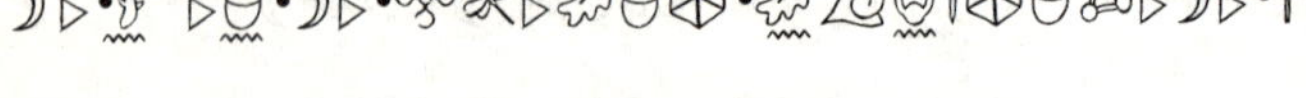

Un autre passa son casque au détecteur de rads.

– Il y a une fuite d'énergie radioactive, capitaine. Nous devons vous asperger la tête immédiatement.

La fée ouvrit la bouche pour protester mais les lutins en profitèrent pour la lui remplir de mousse anti-radiations.

– Ça ne peut pas attendre ? balbutia-t-elle en crachotant.

– Désolé, capitaine. Il est essentiel d'agir vite. Le commandant veut un rapport avant la mise à feu.

Holly fut précipitamment emmenée au centre d'opérations mobile, ses pieds touchant à peine le sol.

Autour d'elle, l'équipe de nettoyage du commando de Récupération passait le sol au peigne fin pour le débarrasser de toute trace du siège. Les techniciens démontaient les antennes paraboliques pour qu'on puisse débrancher le système. Des soldats rapportèrent le chariot vers le portail. Il était indispensable que tout soit déménagé à bonne distance avant le lancement de la biobombe.

Root attendait sur la passerelle d'accès à la navette.

– Holly ! lança-t-il. Je veux dire, capitaine. Vous avez réussi !

– Oui, commandant. Merci, commandant.

– Vous avez même rapporté l'or. C'est un véritable exploit.

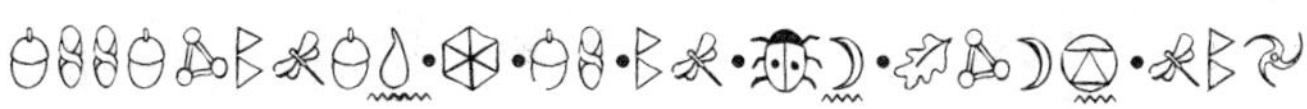

– Tout n'y est pas, commandant. Il doit en manquer la moitié.

Root hocha la tête.

– Ce n'est pas grave, nous aurons bientôt le reste.

Holly essuya la mousse antiradiations qui lui couvrait le front.

– J'y ai pensé, commandant. Fowl a commis une autre erreur. Il ne m'a jamais donné l'ordre de ne pas revenir dans sa maison et, comme c'est lui qui m'y a amenée la première fois, son invitation reste valable. Je vous propose de retourner là-bas pour effacer la mémoire de tous les occupants. Ensuite, nous pourrions cacher l'or dans les murs et procéder à une autre suspension temporelle demain soir...

– Non, capitaine.

– Mais, commandant...

Les traits de Root retrouvèrent la tension qu'ils avaient perdue.

– Non, capitaine. Le Grand Conseil n'est pas disposé à accorder des délais de grâce à un Être de Boue qui s'amuse à enlever nos officiers. Il n'en est pas question. J'ai reçu des ordres et, croyez-moi, ils sont gravés dans le marbre.

Holly suivit Root à l'intérieur de la navette.

– Mais la fille, commandant. Elle est innocente !

– Victime de guerre. Elle s'est mise du mauvais côté. On ne peut plus rien faire pour elle, maintenant.

Holly était incrédule.

– Une victime de guerre ? Comment pouvez-vous dire une chose pareille ? Une vie est une vie.

Root fit brusquement volte-face et la saisit par les épaules.

– Vous avez fait ce que vous pouviez, Holly, dit-il. Personne n'aurait pu en faire davantage. Vous avez même réussi à récupérer la plus grande partie de la rançon. Vous êtes atteinte de ce que les humains appellent le syndrome de Stockholm : vous avez pris fait et cause pour vos ravisseurs. Ne vous inquiétez pas, ça va passer. Mais les gens qui sont dans cette maison savent, désormais. Ils connaissent notre existence. Plus rien ne peut les sauver.

Foaly leva les yeux de ses manipulations.

– Pas vrai. Théoriquement, en tout cas. Au fait, content de vous revoir, capitaine. Bienvenue parmi nous.

Holly ne perdit pas de temps en politesses.

– Qu'est-ce que vous entendez par « pas vrai » ?

– Oh, moi, ça va très bien, puisque vous mc posez la question.

– Foaly ! s'écrièrent Root et Holly d'une même voix.

– Eh bien le Livre dit :

Si un Homme de Boue a recueilli de l'or,
Se jouant de la magie des fées et de leurs sorts,
Le trésor restera aux mains de ce mortel,
Jusqu'à ce qu'il repose en sommeil éternel.

Donc s'il survit, il a gagné. C'est tout simple. Même le Grand Conseil ne peut s'opposer au Livre.

Root se gratta le menton.

– Est-ce que je dois m'inquiéter ?

Foaly eut un rire sans joie.

– Non, c'est comme s'ils étaient morts, là-dedans.

– Comme si, ce n'est pas suffisant.

– S'agit-il d'un ordre ?

– Affirmatif, soldat.

– Je ne suis pas un soldat, répliqua Foaly.

Et il appuya sur le bouton.

Butler était plus que surpris

– Vous avez rendu l'or ?

Artemis approuva d'un signe de tête.

– Environ la moitié. Il nous reste une jolie cagnotte. Quinze millions de dollars, au prix du marché.

Habituellement, Butler ne posait pas de questions. Mais cette fois, il ne put s'en empêcher :

– Pourquoi, Artemis ? Vous pouvez m'expliquer ?

– Sans doute.

Le jeune homme sourit.

– J'ai pensé que nous devions quelque chose au capitaine. Pour services rendus.

– C'est tout ?

Artemis aquiesça. Inutile de parler du souhait. Cela aurait pu passer pour une faiblesse.

– Mmm, dit Butler, plus perspicace qu'il ne le paraissait.

– Et maintenant, nous devrions fêter ça, proposa Artemis d'un ton enthousiaste, se hâtant de changer de sujet. Un peu de champagne nous ferait du bien, je crois.

Le jeune homme se dirigea vivement vers la cuisine avant que le regard de Butler ait eu le temps de le disséquer.

Lorsque les deux autres l'eurent rejoint, Artemis avait déjà rempli trois verres de Dom Pérignon.

– Je n'ai pas l'âge de boire de l'alcool, je sais, mais je suis sûr que ma mère n'y verrait pas d'inconvénient. Juste pour cette fois.

Butler sentit qu'il se mijotait quelque chose. Il prit cependant la flûte de cristal que lui tendait Artemis.

Juliet regarda son grand frère.

– J'ai le droit d'en boire ?

– Je pense que oui.

Butler prit une profonde inspiration.

– Tu sais que je t'aime beaucoup, petite sœur ?

Juliet fronça les sourcils – encore quelque chose que les voyous des environs trouvaient très séduisant chez elle.

Elle donna une grande tape sur l'épaule de son frère.

– Tu es bien sentimental pour un garde du corps.

Butler regarda son employeur droit dans les yeux.

– Vous voulez que nous buvions ceci, n'est-ce pas. Artemis ?

Le garçon lui rendit son regard sans ciller.

– Oui, Butler, je le veux.

Sans ajouter un mot, l'homme vida son verre et Juliet l'imita. Le serviteur reconnut aussitôt le goût du narcotique. Il aurait eu largement le temps de tordre le cou d'Artemis mais il s'en abstint. Inutile d'affoler Juliet dans ses derniers moments.

Artemis regarda ses amis s'effondrer sur le sol. C'était bien triste de devoir les tromper ainsi. Mais s'ils avaient été au courant du plan, leur anxiété aurait pu neutraliser les effets du sédatif. Il regarda les bulles tourbillonner dans sa propre flûte. Le moment était venu de franchir l'étape la plus audacieuse de son plan. Après un soupçon d'hésitation, il avala son champagne aux tranquillisants.

Artemis attendit patiemment que le produit fasse son effet. Il n'eut pas à attendre longtemps : les doses avaient été calculées en fonction du poids de chacun. Tandis que ses pensées commençaient à tournoyer dans sa tête, il songea qu'il ne se réveillerait peut-être jamais. « Il est un peu tard pour avoir des doutes », se reprocha-t-il avant de sombrer dans l'inconscience.

– C’est parti, dit Foaly en s’écartant de la console. Je ne peux plus rien faire, maintenant.

Ils suivirent la progression du missile à travers les hublots à vitres polarisées. C’était vraiment un engin remarquable. L’arme elle-même étant très légère, les retombées pouvaient être ciblées dans un rayon très précis. L’élément radioactif utilisé dans le cœur de la bombe était du solinium 2 qui avait une vie de quatorze secondes. Ce qui signifiait que Foaly pouvait régler la biobombe pour passer le manoir au rinçage bleu sans que le moindre brin d’herbe extérieur soit atteint. En plus, moins d’une minute plus tard, la maison serait débarrassée de toutes ses radiations. Et s’il arrivait que des retombées de solinium s’écartent de la cible, elles resteraient prisonnières de la zone de suspension temporelle. Un moyen simple et efficace de tuer.

– La trajectoire est préprogrammée, expliqua Foaly, bien que personne ne lui accordât la moindre attention. Elle va pénétrer dans le hall et exploser. Le corps de la bombe et son mécanisme de mise à feu sont constitués d’un alliage de plastique et se désintègrent entièrement. Une propreté parfaite.

Root et Holly suivirent des yeux l’arc décrit par le missile. Comme prévu, il s’engouffra par la porte d’entrée dévastée sans arracher ne serait-ce qu’un fragment de pierre aux murs médiévaux. Holly reporta son attention sur les images transmises par la caméra installée dans le nez de la fusée. Pendant un instant, elle revit le grand hall où, récemment encore, elle avait été prisonnière. Il était vide. Pas un seul humain en vue. « Peut-être que..., pensa-t-elle. Peut-être... » Puis elle regarda Foaly et toute la technologie dont il disposait au bout de ses doigts. Elle comprit alors que c'était comme si les humains étaient déjà morts.

La biobombe explosa. Une sphère bleue de lumière condensée se craquela en se répandant alentour, remplissant le moindre recoin du manoir de ses rayons mortels. Les fleurs se fanaient, les insectes se ratatinaient et les poissons mouraient dans leurs aquariums. Pas un seul millimètre cube ne fut épargné. Artemis Fowl et ses acolytes ne pouvaient pas s'être échappés. C'était impossible.

Holly soupira, détournant les yeux de l'image du rinçage bleu qui commençait déjà à se dissiper. Malgré tous ses grands projets, Artemis n'avait été en définitive qu'un simple mortel. Et, pour une raison inconnue, sa mort l'attristait.

Root se montra plus pragmatique.

– O.K. Habillons-nous. L'équipement antiradiations complet.

– Il n'y a aucun danger, répliqua Foaly. Vous n'avez pas écouté ce qu'on vous a dit à l'école ?

Le commandant eut une exclamation de dédain :

– La confiance que j'ai dans la science ne va pas plus loin que le bout de votre nez, Foaly. Les radiations ont tendance à s'attarder au moment même où certains savants nous assurent qu'elles se sont dissipées. Personne ne sort d'ici sans l'équipement adéquat. Ce qui vous met en dehors du coup, Foaly. Les combinaisons sont prévues pour les bipèdes uniquement. De toute façon, je veux que vous restiez devant vos écrans, au cas où...

« Au cas où quoi ? » se demanda le centaure, mais il s'abstint de tout commentaire. Mieux valait se préparer à un « Je vous l'avais bien dit » un peu plus tard.

Root se tourna vers Holly.

– Vous êtes prête, capitaine ?

Retourner là-bas... L'idée d'avoir à identifier trois cadavres ne lui disait rien du tout. Mais elle savait que c'était son devoir. Elle était la seule à bien connaître les lieux.

– Oui, commandant. J'y vais.

Holly choisit une combinaison antiradiations sur l'étagère et la revêtit. Conformément à ce qu'on lui avait appris lors de son entraînement, elle vérifia l'indicateur de pression avant de fermer le capuchon vulcanisé.

Si la pression baissait, c'était l'indication qu'il y avait une déchirure, ce qui pouvait se révéler fatal à long terme.

Root disposa l'équipe d'intervention à la limite du périmètre. Les membres rescapés du commando de Récupération étaient à peu près aussi impatients de pénétrer dans le manoir que de jongler avec des boules puantes grand format.

– Vous êtes sûr que le gros type n'est plus là ?

- Oui, capitaine Kelp. Il est forcément parti, d'une manière ou d'une autre.

Baroud n'était pas convaincu.

– Cet humain est vraiment malfaisant. Il a sa propre forme de magie.

Le caporal Grub ricana et reçut aussitôt une claque sur l'oreille. Il marmonna quelque chose au sujet de ce qu'il allait dire à maman et se hâta de boucler son casque.

Root sentit son teint devenir de plus en plus rouge.

– Allons-y. Vous avez pour mission de récupérer l'or. Attention aux pièges. Je n'avais aucune confiance en Fowl de son vivant, je n'ai pas plus confiance en lui maintenant qu'il est mort.

Le mot « piège » éveilla l'attention de tous. L'éventualité de sauter sur une mine antipersonnel explosant à hauteur d'œil suffit à dissiper toute nonchalance chez les soldats. Les Êtres de la Boue n'avaient pas leur pareil pour inventer les armes les plus cruelles.

En tant qu'officier le plus jeune du service de Détection, Holly marchait en tête. Et bien qu'il n'y eût en principe aucune force hostile dans le manoir, elle s'aperçut que sa main s'était automatiquement posée sur la crosse du Neutrino 2000.

Il régnait autour de la maison un calme à faire froid dans le dos ; seul le craquement de quelques ultimes étincelles de solinium troublait l'immobilité des lieux. La mort était également présente, dans le silence. Le manoir tout entier était devenu un berceau de mort. Holly le sentait.

Derrière ces murs du Moyen Age, des millions d'insectes avaient cessé de vivre et sous les lames du parquet reposaient les cadavres de centaines d'araignées et de souris.

Ils s'approchèrent avec précaution de la porte d'entrée. Holly passa les environs immédiats au scanner à rayons X. Sous les dalles, il n'y avait que de la terre et un nid d'araignées mortes.

– La voie est libre, dit-elle dans son micro. J'entre. Foaly, vous avez mis vos écouteurs ?

– Je suis tout près de vous, ma chérie, répondit le centaure. Sauf si vous sautez sur une mine, auquel cas je serai très loin, dans le centre d'opérations.

– Vous recevez des signaux thermiques ?

– Jamais après un rinçage bleu. Nous avons des traces résiduelles un peu partout. Surtout des étincelles de solinium. Ça va durer pendant encore deux jours.

– Mais pas de radiations, c'est ça ?

– Exactement.

Root eut un ricanement incrédule. Transmis par les écouteurs, on aurait dit un éléphant qui éternuait.

– Je crois que nous allons devoir fouiller la maison de manière traditionnelle, grogna-t-il.

– Dépêchez-vous quand même, conseilla Foaly. Dans cinq minutes maximum, le manoir des Fowl aura rejoint le temps extérieur.

Holly franchit ce qui avait été la porte d'entrée. Le lustre se balançait encore lentement sous l'effet de l'explosion, sinon, tout le reste était dans le même état que lorsqu'elle avait quitté les lieux.

– L'or est en bas, dans ma cellule.

Personne ne répondit. En paroles tout au moins. Quelqu'un eut un haut-le-cœur. En plein dans le micro. Holly fit volte-face. Baroud, plié en deux, se tenait le ventre.

– Je ne me sens pas bien, gémit-il.

Une précision qui n'était pas vraiment nécessaire quand on voyait la flaque de vomissures qui s'étalait à ses pieds.

Le caporal Grub prit une inspiration, sans doute pour dire quelque chose au sujet de maman. Mais il ne parvint qu'à émettre un jet de bile. Malheureusement, il n'eut pas le temps d'ouvrir la visière de son casque avant que la nausée le frappe. Le spectacle n'était guère attrayant.

– Eûrk ! dit Holly, en appuyant sur le bouton qui permettait de relever la visière du caporal.

Un flot de rations réglementaires régurgitées se déversa sur la combinaison antiradiations de Grub.

– Qu'est-ce que c'est que ça ? marmonna Root en écartant les deux frères d'un coup de coude.

Il n'alla pas très loin. A peine avait-il franchi le seuil qu'il se mit à vomir à son tour.

Holly dirigea la caméra de son casque vers les officiers malades.

– Vous pouvez m'expliquer ce qui se passe, Foaly ?

– Je cherche. Un instant.

Holly l'entendit pianoter furieusement sur son clavier.

– Voyons. Vomissements soudains. Mal de l'espace... Oh, non !

– Quoi ? demanda Holly.

Mais elle savait déjà. Peut-être l'avait-elle toujours su.

– C'est la magie, s'exclama le centaure, dans un tel état d'excitation que ses paroles étaient à peine compréhensibles. Il leur est impossible d'entrer dans la maison tant que Fowl n'est pas mort. C'est comme une réaction allergique aiguë. Ça signifie, c'est incroyable, ça signifie...

– Qu'ils ont réussi, acheva Holly. Il est vivant. Artemis Fowl est vivant.

– Nom de... grogna Root avant de vomir à nouveau sur les dalles de terre cuite.

Holly poursuivit son chemin seule. Elle voulait en avoir le cœur net. Si Fowl était là, mort ou vivant, il serait auprès de l'or ; de cela, au moins, elle était sûre.

Les mêmes portraits de famille la regardaient d'un œil noir mais, à présent, leur expression était plus arrogante qu'austère. Holly fut tentée de tirer dessus à coups de Neutrino 2000. Mais c'était contraire aux règles. Si Artemis Fowl s'était montré plus fort qu'eux, il fallait l'accepter. Il n'y aurait pas de récriminations.

Elle descendit l'escalier jusqu'à sa cellule. La porte se balançait encore légèrement sous l'effet de l'onde de choc. Une étincelle de solinium rebondit sur les murs de la pièce, comme un éclair prisonnier. Holly entra avec une vague appréhension à l'idée de ce qu'elle allait découvrir.

Il n'y avait rien. Rien qui ressemblât à un cadavre, en tout cas. Simplement de l'or. Environ deux cents lingots. Empilés sur son lit de camp. En rangées bien nettes, dans un ordre militaire. Ce bon vieux Butler, le seul humain qui eût jamais affronté un troll et remporté la victoire.

– Commandant ? Vous me recevez ? A vous.

– Affirmatif, capitaine. Combien de cadavres ?

– Pas de cadavres, commandant. J'ai trouvé le reste de la rançon.

Il y eut un long silence.

– Laissez-le là, Holly. Vous connaissez les règles. On s'en va.

– Mais, commandant, il doit y avoir moyen de...

Foaly intervint :

- Il n'y a pas de mais, capitaine. La lumière du jour va arriver dans quelques secondes et nos chances de rentrer sans dommage seront très minces si nous devons sortir en plein midi.

Holly soupira. C'était la voix de la raison. Il leur fallait partir avant la fin de la suspension temporelle, ils n'avaient pas le choix. Elle était simplement exaspérée à l'idée qu'un humain ait pu se montrer plus fort qu'eux.

Et un adolescent, de surcroît.

Elle jeta un dernier regard autour d'elle. Elle se rendit compte alors qu'une haine tenace, semblable à une grosse boule au creux de l'estomac, était née dans cette cellule et qu'il faudrait bien, tôt ou tard, en affronter les conséquences. Holly remit son pistolet dans son holster. Tôt ou tard ? Il valait mieux que ce soit le plus tôt possible.

Fowl avait gagné cette fois-ci, mais quelqu'un comme lui ne se reposerait pas sur ses lauriers. Il reviendrait un jour avec un nouveau plan pour ramasser beaucoup d'argent. Et lorsqu'il reviendrait, Holly Short serait là pour l'attendre. Avec un sourire et un gros pistolet.

Le sol était mou près du périmètre de suspension temporelle. Un demi-millénaire de mauvais écoulement des eaux dû aux murailles médiévales avait transformé les fondations en un quasi-marécage. Ce fut donc là que Mulch refit surface.

La souplesse du terrain n'était pas la seule raison pour laquelle il avait choisi de sortir à cet endroit précis. L'autre raison, c'était l'odeur. Un bon nain de tunnel peut sentir le parfum de l'or à travers une couche d'un demi-kilomètre de granite.

Et Mulch Diggums possédait l'un des meilleurs nez de la profession.

Le chariot sur coussin d'air flottait quasiment sans surveillance. Deux des meilleurs membres du commando de Récupération se trouvaient à proximité de la rançon récupérée mais, pour le moment, ils étaient occupés à pouffer de rire en voyant leur commandant pris de nausées.

– Non mais, tu l'as vu, Chix ? Il n'y va pas à moitié !

Chix approuva et imita Root en train de vomir.

La pantomime burlesque de Chix Verbil offrait une occasion parfaite de se livrer à un petit larcin. Mulch prit soin de dégager ses entrailles avant de sortir du tunnel. Ce n'était pas le moment d'alerter les FAR par un bruit incongru. Mais il n'avait pas à s'inquiéter. Il aurait pu jeter un ver gluant au visage de Chix Verbil sans que le lutin remarque quoi que ce soit.

En quelques secondes, il avait transféré deux douzaines de lingots dans le tunnel. C'était le travail le plus facile qu'il eût jamais fait. Mulch étouffa un rire lorsqu'il laissa tomber les deux derniers lingots au fond du trou. Julius lui avait vraiment rendu un grand service en le mêlant à toute cette affaire. Les choses auraient difficilement pu se passer mieux. Il était libre comme l'oiseau, riche et, mieux encore, considéré comme mort. Lorsque les FAR s'apercevraient de la disparition de cet or, Mulch Diggums aurait déjà mis la moitié d'un continent entre eux et lui. En admettant qu'ils s'en aperçoivent.

Le nain se glissa sous terre. Plusieurs voyages seraient nécessaires pour transporter son trésor mais cela valait la peine de s'attarder un peu. Avec cet argent, il allait pouvoir prendre une retraite anticipée. Bien entendu, il lui faudrait disparaître complètement mais un plan s'ébauchait déjà dans son esprit tortueux.

Il vivrait en surface pendant un certain temps. Il se ferait passer pour un nain humain, allergique à la lumière. Il achèterait peut-être un bel appartement avec d'épais volets. A Manhattan ou à Monte-Carlo.

Bien sûr, un nain qui refuse catégoriquement de voir la lumière du jour paraîtrait étrange.

Mais, encore une fois, il serait un nain d'une richesse obscène.

Et les humains sont prêts à accepter n'importe quelle bizarrerie, du moment qu'ils peuvent en retirer quelque chose. De préférence, des rectangles de papier vert faciles à glisser dans la poche.

Artemis entendait une voix appeler son nom. Cette voix évoquait un visage, mais un visage flou, difficile à distinguer. Son père, peut-être ?

– Père ?

Le mot paraissait étrange dans sa bouche. Jamais utilisé. Comme rouillé. Artemis ouvrit les yeux.

Butler était penché sur lui.

– Artemis. Vous êtes réveillé.

– Ah, Butler. C'est vous.

Il se leva et l'effort lui fit tourner la tête. Il attendit que son majordome lui prenne le coude pour le soutenir. En vain. Juliet était étendue sur un sofa, toujours endormie. Chez elle, de toute évidence, les effets du somnifère ne s'étaient pas dissipés.

– C'étaient de simples pilules pour dormir, Butler. Inoffensives.

Il y avait une lueur menaçante dans le regard du serviteur.

– Expliquez-vous.

Artemis se frotta les yeux.

– Plus tard, Butler. Pour l'instant, je me sens un peu...

Butler lui barra le chemin.

– Artemis, ma sœur dort sur ce canapé, assommée par une drogue. Elle a failli se faire tuer. Alors expliquez-vous tout de suite !

Le garçon se rendit compte qu'on venait de lui donner un ordre. Il se demanda s'il devait se montrer offensé, puis estima que Butler avait peut-être raison. Il était allé trop loin.

– Je ne vous ai rien dit au sujet des somnifères de peur que vous ne cherchiez à combattre leurs effets. C'est un réflexe naturel. Et il était impératif pour la réalisation du plan que nous nous endormions immédiatement.

– Le plan ?

Artemis s'assit dans un fauteuil confortable.

– La suspension temporelle était la clé de toute cette affaire. Pour les FAR, c'est l'atout dans la manche. Grâce à elle, il a été impossible de les vaincre pendant des années. La suspension temporelle confine n'importe quelle situation de conflit dans un espace limité, coupé de l'extérieur. Ajoutez à cela la biobombe et vous obtenez une formidable combinaison qui leur garantit la victoire.

– Et pourquoi fallait-il que nous soyons drogués ?

Artemis sourit.

– Regardez par la fenêtre. Vous voyez ? Ils sont partis. Tout est fini.

Butler jeta un coup d'œil à travers les rideaux. La lumière du jour était claire et brillante. Plus la moindre trace d'azur surnaturel. Mais le serviteur n'en était pas plus impressionné pour autant.

– Ils sont partis pour l'instant. Ce soir, ils seront de retour, je peux vous le garantir.

– Non. C'est contre les règles. Nous avons été plus forts qu'eux. C'est tout. Le jeu est terminé.

Butler haussa un sourcil.

– Et les pilules pour dormir ?

– Je vois qu'il n'y a pas moyen de vous ôter une idée de la tête...

Butler répondit par un implacable silence.

– Les pilules. Très bien. Je devais réfléchir à un moyen d'échapper à la suspension temporelle. J'ai examiné le Livre en détail mais je n'ai rien trouvé. Pas le moindre indice. Le Peuple lui-même n'a pas découvert de solution. Je suis donc revenu à leur Ancien Testament, à l'époque où leur vie et la nôtre étaient mêlées. Vous connaissez toutes ces histoires : les elfes qui fabriquaient les chaussures du cordonnier pendant la nuit, les lutins qui faisaient le ménage dans les maisons. Au temps où nous coexistions, dans une certaine mesure. Ils échangeaient des services magiques contre leurs forts de fée. Le personnage le plus connu, bien sûr, c'était saint Nicolas. Qui devint plus tard le père Noël.

On aurait dit que les sourcils de Butler allaient bondir plus haut que son front

– Le père Noël ?

Artemis leva les mains comme pour le calmer.

– Je sais, je sais, j'ai été moi-même un peu sceptique. Mais apparemment, notre bon petit père Noël et son image de patron de multinationale n'a rien à voir avec un saint turc. C'est l'ombre de San N'Klass, le troisième roi de la dynastie des Frondelfe. Il est connu sous le nom de San le Naïf.

– Pas très glorieux, comme surnom.

– C'est vrai. N'Klass pensait qu'il serait possible d'apaiser la cupidité des Êtres de la Boue qui habitaient son royaume en leur distribuant généreusement des cadeaux. Ainsi, une fois par an, il faisait appel aux plus grands sorciers pour qu'ils déclenchent une suspension temporelle dans de vastes régions. Des troupes de lutins apportaient alors des cadeaux chez les humains pendant leur sommeil. Bien sûr, ce ne fut pas suffisant. La cupidité humaine ne peut jamais être apaisée, surtout pas par de simples cadeaux.

Butler fronça les sourcils.

– Et si les humains... c'est-à-dire, nous... si quelqu'un se réveillait pendant la distribution ?

– Ah oui, excellente question. Le cœur de toute l'affaire. Il était impossible que quelqu'un se réveille. C'est la nature même de la suspension temporelle. On reste jusqu'au bout dans le même état de conscience, quel qu'il soit. On ne peut ni se réveiller, ni tomber endormi. Vous avez dû constater la fatigue de votre corps au cours de ces dernières heures et, pourtant, votre esprit refusait de vous laisser dormir.

Butler approuva d'un hochement de tête. Les choses devenaient plus claires, d'une manière un peu détournée.

– Ainsi donc, ma théorie était que le seul moyen d'échapper à la suspension temporelle consistait tout simplement à tomber endormi. Ce qui nous retenait prisonniers, c'était notre propre conscience.

– Vous avez pris de terribles risques sur une simple théorie, Artemis.

– Pas une simple théorie. Nous avions quelqu'un qui servait de test.

– Qui ? Ah, Angeline.

– Oui. Ma mère. Son sommeil provoqué par des narcoleptiques lui permettait de suivre l'ordre naturel des heures, sans être affectée par la suspension temporelle. Dans le cas contraire, je me serais simplement rendu aux FAR pour me soumettre à leur effacement de mémoire.

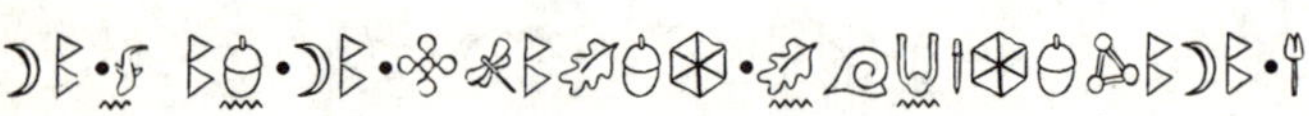

Butler eut une petite exclamation ironique. Il en doutait.

– Et donc, puisque nous ne pouvions pas nous endormir naturellement, j'ai simplement distribué à chacun une dose des pilules de ma mère. Très simple.

– Vous vous y êtes pris au dernier moment. Une minute de plus et...

– C'est vrai, approuva le jeune garçon. Les choses ont été tendues vers la fin. C'était nécessaire pour bluffer les FAR.

Il s'interrompit pour laisser le temps à Butler d'assimiler ses explications.

– Alors, je suis pardonné ?

Butler soupira.

Sur le sofa, Juliet ronflait comme un marin ivre. Soudain, il sourit.

– Oui, Artemis. Tout est pardonné. Une chose, cependant..

– Oui ?

– Plus jamais de fantaisies de ce genre. Les fées sont trop... humaines.

– Vous avez raison, dit-il.

Les pattes-d'oie, au coin de ses yeux, se creusèrent.

– Plus jamais. A l'avenir, nous nous en tiendrons à des aventures d'un meilleur goût. Mais je ne peux pas vous promettre qu'elles seront conformes aux lois.

Butler hocha la tête. C'était déjà bien comme ça.

– Et maintenant, mon jeune maître, ne pensez-vous pas que nous devrions aller voir comment va votre mère ?

Artemis devint un peu plus pâle, si c'était possible. Le capitaine Short aurait-elle manqué à sa promesse ? Elle en aurait certes eu le droit.

– Oui, je crois que c'est une bonne idée. Laissons Juliet se reposer, elle l'a bien mérité.

Il leva les yeux vers l'escalier. C'était une illusion de penser qu'il pouvait faire confiance à la fée. Après tout, il l'avait retenue prisonnière contre sa volonté. Il se réprimanda en silence. Se séparer de tous ces millions pour la simple promesse d'exaucer un vœu. Quelle naïveté !

A cet instant, la porte du grenier s'ouvrit.

Butler sortit aussitôt son arme.

– Artemis, cachez-vous derrière moi. Des intrus.

Le jeune garçon l'apaisa d'un geste de la main.

– Non, Butler. Je ne crois pas.

Il sentait le sang battre à ses oreilles, et jusqu'au bout de ses doigts. Était-ce vraiment possible ? Une silhouette se dessina alors en haut de l'escalier. On aurait dit une apparition emmitouflée dans un peignoir, les cheveux mouillés par la douche.

– Arty ? Arty, tu es là ?

Artemis aurait voulu répondre. Il aurait voulu se

précipiter dans l'escalier, les bras tendus. Mais il en fut incapable. Ses fonctions cérébrales étaient paralysées.

Angeline Fowl descendit, une main sur la rampe. Artemis avait oublié à quel point sa mère était gracieuse. Ses pieds nus se posaient avec légèreté sur le tapis qui recouvrait les marches et, bientôt, elle se retrouva devant lui.

– Bonjour, mon chéri, dit-elle d'une voix claire comme s'il s'agissait d'un jour comme un autre.

– M... mère, balbutia Artemis. Maman.

– Eh bien, embrasse-moi.

Il fit un pas vers sa mère qui lui tendait les bras. Ce fut une étreinte forte et chaleureuse. Elle avait mis du parfum. Tout à coup, il se sentait redevenir le jeune garçon qu'il était toujours.

– Je suis désolée, Arty, lui murmura-t-elle à l'oreille.

– Désolée pour quoi ?

– Pour tout. Ces derniers mois, je n'étais plus moi-même. Mais les choses vont changer. Il est temps de cesser de vivre dans le passé.

Artemis sentit une larme sur sa joue. Il ne savait pas très bien qui l'avait versée.

– Je n'ai même pas de cadeau pour toi.

– De cadeau ? s'étonna-t-il.

– Bien sûr, répondit sa mère d'un ton chantant en le faisant tourner dans ses bras. Tu ne sais donc pas quel jour nous sommes ?

– Quel jour ?

– C’est Noël, petit sot. Noël ! C’est la tradition de se faire des cadeaux ce jour-là, non ?

« Oui, pensa Artemis. C’est la tradition. San N’Klass. »

– Et regarde-moi cette maison. Elle est sinistre, on dirait un mausolée. Butler ?

Le serviteur se hâta de ranger son Sig Sauer.

– Oui, madame ?

– Téléphonez chez Brown Thomas. Le numéro de la carte platinum. Faites rouvrir mon compte. Dites à Hélène que je veux une grande fête de Noël. Avec toute la panoplie.

– Oui, madame, toute la panoplie.

– Ah oui, et réveillez donc Juliet. Je veux qu’elle transporte mes affaires dans la grande chambre. Le grenier est beaucoup trop poussiéreux.

– Oui, madame, tout de suite, madame.

Angeline Fowl prit son fils par le bras.

– Maintenant, Arty, je veux tout savoir. D’abord, qu’est-ce qui s’est passé, ici ?

– On a fait des travaux, répondit-il. L’ancienne porte était rongée par l’humidité.

Angeline fronça les sourcils, pas du tout convaincue.

– Je vois. Et l’école ? Tu as décidé de ce que tu voulais faire plus tard ?

Tandis qu’il répondait machinalement à ces questions, l'esprit d'Artemis bouillonnait. Il était redevenu un jeune garçon et sa vie allait changer du tout au tout. Ses plans devraient être beaucoup plus tortueux qu'à l'ordinaire s'il voulait échapper à l'attention de sa mère. Mais cela en vaudrait la peine.

Angeline Fowl se trompait. Finalement, elle lui avait fait un très beau cadeau de Noël.

ÉPILOGUE

A présent que vous avez pris connaissance du dossier, vous avez pu mesurer à quel point Fowl est un personnage dangereux.

Certains ont tendance à entourer Artemis d'une aura romanesque. A lui attribuer des qualités qu'il ne possède pas. Le fait que son vœu le plus cher ait été de voir sa mère guérie ne doit pas être interprété comme un signe d'affection. Il savait simplement que les services sociaux enquêtaient déjà sur son cas et que son placement dans un centre d'éducation n'était plus qu'une question de temps.

S'il a gardé le silence sur l'existence du Peuple, c'est pour pouvoir continuer à l'exploiter, ce qu'il fit à plusieurs reprises au cours des années qui suivirent.

Sa plus grosse erreur fut de laisser le capitaine Short en vie.

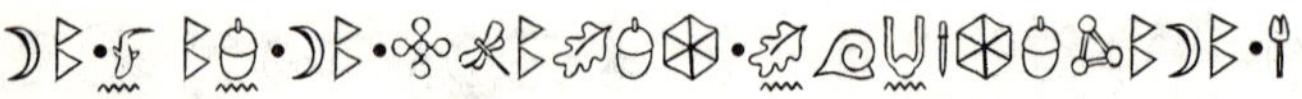

Holly devint le meilleur expert des FAR dans les divers dossiers concernant Artemis Fowl et fournit une aide inestimable à la lutte du Peuple contre son ennemi le plus redouté.

Le combat qui les opposa devait durer plusieurs décennies.

Ironie du sort, les deux protagonistes remportèrent leur plus grand triomphe lorsqu'ils furent contraints de coopérer à la suite de l'insurrection des gobelins. Mais il s'agit d'une tout autre histoire.

Rapport établi par : docteur J. Argon, psychologue diplômé, pour le compte des FAR.

Les détails sont exacts à quatre-vingt-quatorze pour cent, les six pour cent restants étant dus à d'inévitables extrapolations.

FIN

TABLE DES MATIÈRES

EOIN COLFER

L'AUTEUR

Eoin (prononcer Owen) Colfer est né en 1965 à Wexford, en Irlande. Enseignant, comme l'étaient ses parents, il vit avec sa femme Jackie et son jeune fils dans sa ville natale, où sont également installés son père, sa mère et ses quatre frères. Tout jeune, il s'essaie à l'écriture et compose une pièce de théâtre pour sa classe, une histoire dans laquelle, comme il l'explique, « tout le monde mourait à la fin, sauf moi ». Grand voyageur, il a travaillé en Arabie Saoudite, en Tunisie et en Italie avant de revenir en Irlande. Eoin Colfer avait déjà publié plusieurs livres pour les moins de 10 ans et il était, même avant la publication d'*Artemis Fowl*, un auteur pour la jeunesse reconnu dans son pays.

Artemis Fowl a été un livre événement que se sont arraché les éditeurs du monde entier et qui a propulsé son auteur au rang d'écrivain vedette de la littérature pour la jeunesse. Les aventures d'Artemis Fowl forment une trilogie, dont les deux volumes suivants (*Mission Polaire* et *Code éternité*) sont disponibles en format hors-série chez Gallimard Jeunesse.

Loi n° 49-956
du 16 juillet 1949
sur les publications
destinées à la jeunesse

ISBN : 2-07-055250-0
Numéro d'édition : 134028
N° d'impression : 70877
Imprimé en France
sur les presses de la Société
Nouvelle Firmin-Didot
Dépôt légal : novembre 2004
1er dépôt légal dans la même collection : juin 2004